Effective Personal Tutoring

IN HIGHER EDUCATION

This book will be an important resource for all those who advise students, whether they are new to the role or more experienced. The approach is inclusive; the authors are careful to stress that the traditional separation between academic personal tutors and professional advisors is changing, and the publication will be of use to all those engaged in supporting students' learning. The book is innovative; although firmly based on relevant research and with wide reference to literature on the subject, the approach is essentially practical. Theoretical discussions of aspects of personal tutoring are followed by case studies, critical thinking activities and critical reflections, with learning checklists enabling the reader to assess his or her understanding of the chapter. I found the encouragement to engage in critical thinking and reflective practice the most original, valuable and stimulating aspect of the book; the personal tutor or other advisor is urged to reflect not only on her or his own practice, but on that of the institution as a whole, and to engage in conversations with leadership, to see how it may be improved. The structure will enable the reader to return to individual chapters as the need arises; this is not a book to be read once and put to one side, but one to be used as an ongoing resource and toolkit, by the experienced tutor or advisor as well as the beginner. The former will find ideas for refreshing his or her approach, while the latter will be helped to gain confidence at an early career stage. The authors are to be congratulated on this excellent contribution to an area of vital and growing importance in higher education.

Penny Robinson,
Chair of the UK Advising and Tutoring (UKAT) Executive Committee

This book is an important addition to the field of personal tutoring and academic advising. The structure of the chapters in this text makes it the perfect training tool for new advisors and a great reference for experienced advisors. The case studies, critical thinking activities, and discussions make the content come alive. Every personal tutor, advisor and support services or advising administrator needs this book in their toolkit.

Amy Sannes,
President of NACADA, the Global Community for Academic Advising

Effective Personal Tutoring

IN HIGHER EDUCATION

*Dave Lochtie, Emily McIntosh,
Andrew Stork & Ben W Walker*

Foreword by Professor Liz Thomas

First published in 2018 by Critical Publishing Ltd

British Library Cataloguing in Publication Data
A CIP record for this book is available from the British Library

ISBN: 978-1-910391-98-3

This book is also available in the following e-book formats:

MOBI ISBN: 978-1-910391-99-0
EPUB ISBN: 978-1-911106-00-5
Adobe e-book: 978-1-911106-01-2

Text design by Greensplash
Cover design by Out of House Ltd
Project Management by Out of House Publishing
Printed and bound in Great Britain by Bell & Bain, Glasgow

Critical Publishing
3 Connaught Road
St Albans
AL3 5RX
www.criticalpublishing.com

Our titles are also available in a range of electronic formats. To order please go to our website www.criticalpublishing.com or contact our distributor, NBN International, 10 Thornbury Road, Plymouth PL6 7PP, telephone 01752 202301 or email orders@nbninternational.com.

Contents

Meet the authors

Dave Lochtie

I am Chair of the Professional Development Committee for UK Advising and Tutoring (UKAT). I am also the Student Voice & Development Manager at the University of Derby Union of Students, having previously worked at the Universities of New Orleans and Roehampton in the management of personal tutoring, success coaching, administration and admissions. At the University of Roehampton and Bournemouth University Students' Union I served as an elected Director, Trustee and Governor and have published research on international comparative education, retention and personal tutoring. Prior to this I worked as a qualified primary school teacher.

Emily McIntosh

I am Director of Student Life at the University of Bolton, Principal Fellow of the Higher Education Academy and Chair of the UKAT (UK Advising and Tutoring) Research Committee. I lead on a number of cross-institutional student experience initiatives, as well as various aspects of teaching and learning activity. My research interests include student retention, transition, personal tutoring, student resilience, student learning development and peer learning. I have been a keynote and invited speaker at several national and international conferences and have authored a number of research articles and reports related to my research interests. I am a member of the executive committee of UKAT and an editorial board member of NACADA, the Global Community for Academic Advising. I previously held positions at the University of Manchester, the University of Liverpool and Keele University, working in a variety of roles in teaching, learning, researcher development and the broader student experience.

Andrew Stork

I am a lecturer in marketing, Senior Fellow of the Higher Education Academy and co-author of the highly regarded book *Becoming an Outstanding Personal Tutor: Supporting Learners through Personal Tutoring and Coaching.* As well as presenting at national and international conferences I have published research in personal tutoring and coaching. I have held the roles of cross-institutional quality lead for personal tutoring and student experience, course leader of the post-graduate certificate of education course, and a variety of curriculum leadership, quality and staff development positions. I am a chartered marketer and, prior to working in education, I worked in marketing management and consultancy roles.

Ben W Walker

I am a senior lecturer and doctoral researcher at the University of Lincoln. My research is focused on academic and pastoral support of students informed by critical pedagogy. I am the co-author of the highly regarded book *Becoming an Outstanding Personal Tutor: Supporting Learners through Personal Tutoring and Coaching.* I have authored research articles on personal tutoring, am a member of the UKAT (UK Advising and Tutoring) Professional Development Committee and am a Senior Fellow of the Higher Education Academy. I have presented at national and international conferences. Previously, I was a manager of personal tutoring and student experience, course leader for teacher training, head of English and a full-time English teacher for several years.

Authors' websites

To find out more about the authors' work, visit their websites. The self-assessment systems can also be downloaded in full from these sites and from the publisher's website: www.criticalpublishing.com.

Dave Lochtie: www.davelochtie.com

Emily McIntosh: www.eamcintosh.co.uk

Andrew Stork: www.andrewstork.co.uk

Ben W Walker: www.benwwalker.co.uk

Acknowledgements

We would like to thank:

- our families, for getting us through when it was difficult, being patient in our absence and for their unwavering support;

- Liz Thomas for providing the foreword, for the body of work we have referenced throughout, and for permission to use Figure 1.6 *Features of effective practice*;

- David Grey for ongoing advice, support and published works;

- Michelle Morgan for her support and steadfast dedication to supporting and raising awareness of student transitions, and for use of Figure 5.1 *The Student Experience Practitioner Model*;

- Shaun Lincoln for demonstrating how to always 'walk the talk', and for Figure 6.1 *The OSKAR framework*;

- Penny Robinson and UK Advising and Tutoring (UKAT);

- Amy Sannes and NACADA, the Global Community for Academic Advising;

- Becca Ward for assisting with technical changes;

- Susan Wallace for permission to use Figure 1.2 *Ways in which mentors give support* and Figure 1.4 *Four basic styles of helping*;

- Julia Morris for her continuing advice and support.

- Gerard Egan and Robert J Reese for their permission to use Figure 3.1 *Skilled Helper Model*;

- Jean Mutton for her permission to use Figure 4.2 *Engagement Analytics Diagram*.

Dedication

To Hannah, William, Violet and May for their inspiration.
DL

To Klo – thanks for teaching me so much.
EM

To Lorna, Josh, Jake, Mum, Dad, Kay and Keith. Always.
AS

To Jenn and Arthur. Much missed.
BW

A note on terminology

In the world of higher education (HE), the terms 'learner' and 'student' are often used interchangeably. We have used 'student' because this is the term used by the Office for Students (OfS) but 'learner' could just as easily be used for the situations covered by this book. 'Teacher', 'lecturer' and 'academic' can be similarly interchangeable. We have used these different terms, as appropriate, to contextualise the examples we discuss since they have slightly different meanings. The naming conventions used to describe the role of personal tutor differ too, so we use the term 'personal tutor' to capture the range of tutoring roles that typically exist within universities, which can include academic tutor, progress tutor, student support officer, academic advisor, student advisor and student liaison officer. On occasion, 'tutor' is used as an abbreviation of 'personal tutor'. We also acknowledge that HE institutions differ significantly in their structures and systems. We have therefore referred to 'Dean' and 'Head of School' when referring to anyone who holds an academic management position and to highlight the role of those who carry overall responsibility for tutoring within their remit. Finally, we have referred to 'faculty' and 'school' given this is the most common structure within HE institutions, although often organisations have 'departments' and 'units' too.

This book draws on the transferable structure and principles of *Becoming an Outstanding Personal Tutor: Supporting Learners through Personal Tutoring and Coaching* (2015), a current Critical Publishing book by Andrew Stork and Ben W Walker which was written for the further education market.

Foreword

Personal tutoring was identified as an effective way to improve student success in higher education and beyond through the *What Works? Student Retention and Success* programme. Personal tutoring can provide a way to help ensure that all students have the opportunity to develop relationships with academic staff within their institution, and potentially with other students through group tutoring. These relations are central to students' ability to develop a sense of belonging within their higher education institution, and their course of study. Personal tutoring also offers opportunities to increase belonging by developing personal, academic and professional capacities, and by assisting students to make connections between their current interests and future goals, and their curriculum. A sense of belonging alone does not guarantee success, but it can be a vital element to achieving it, especially in the early stages of the higher education experience. For this and related reasons many higher education providers in England are either reintroducing or revamping their tutoring systems to ensure they are fit for purpose in the twenty-first century, where mass higher education and tuition fees are the norm.

The field of personal tutoring in higher education however is something of an academic research desert. Very little scholarly research has been undertaken about personal tutoring. A group of staff set out to remedy this in 2005/6, when the first national conference on personal tutoring was organised in the UK, and subsequently published a book drawing together research, evaluation and reflective practice on tutoring and academic support. Since then, the field of personal tutoring has waxed and waned; annual conferences were organised for a number of years, including international collaboration with NACADA, the global community for academic advising. After a substantial gap UKAT was formed in 2015, which is a UK membership organisation for personal tutors and advisors. This book is therefore a much-needed resource to develop understanding of the role, and the values and skills required to be an effective personal tutor in the higher education in contemporary times.

Effective Personal Tutoring in Higher Education is a practical handbook for staff – and managers – with a personal tutoring remit. The book sets out the different models of personal tutoring and positions itself within the curriculum model. Crucially, the authors draw attention to the similarities between good tutoring and good teaching. The text takes you on a journey to better understand what it is to be a personal tutor, the skills required, and how you will know if you are successful. There is an interesting chapter on solution-focused coaching, which offers tools to use with students in the co-creation of solutions to everyday dilemmas and more serious problems. The final chapter also prompts you to continue developing as personal tutor, and work towards or contribute to wider change within your institution and beyond. Overall, the book offers an impressive blend of scholarly thinking about personal tutoring and related issues, drawing on leading research and models in the field, and practical guidance.

The authors have taken a very 'hands on' approach, using a range of ways to engage the reader – indeed it is very good distance-learning material. The text is illustrated with real-life scenarios, designed to prompt you to engage with the realities and challenges of undertaking a personal tutoring role. These draw on the authors' experiences, and give insight into the everyday experiences and dilemmas of personal tutors. 'Critical thinking activities' are provided throughout the book; these are designed to encourage you to engage with the text, relate it to your own experience, and develop your own understanding. These are supported with the authors' ideas about how you might have reacted to particular scenarios. At the end of each chapter there is a summary, a learning checklist and your critical reflections are encouraged. The personal tutor self-assessment system, introduced at the end of Chapter 2, is a comprehensive approach to helping you to engage with the material in the book, and assess your individual and institutional current level of adoption of the core values and core skills developed, discussed and exemplified in the text.

Effective Personal Tutoring in Higher Education is likely to be an essential companion for all new personal tutors, and a helpful reference guide for those who have been in the role for longer, those who are managing tutors, and those developing training. Underpinning the book is the authors' whole-hearted commitment to the importance of personal tutoring as a teaching role to enable students to maximise their success in higher education and beyond, identifying the best routes they could take at all stages of their journey.

Professor Liz Thomas,
Independent higher education researcher and consultant
and Professor of Higher Education at Edge Hill University,
September 2018

Introduction

Personal tutoring in higher education

Personal tutoring is becoming increasingly important to the effective delivery of higher education (HE) programmes in the United Kingdom (UK) and is fundamental to realising student-centred strategy. The 2012 increase in tuition fees to over £9,000 a year unsettled the sector; it prompted a fundamental change and re-evaluation of the relationship between universities and students. Debates still continue about whether or not to regard students as customers, consumers or partners in their learning journey (McIntosh and Cross, 2017). As a consequence, universities have placed greater emphasis on personalising the learning experience, with many institutions reviewing their tutorial arrangements to ensure they are robust and fit for purpose (McIntosh and Grey, 2017). At the same time, the *Higher Education and Research Act* (2017) has introduced a regulatory framework for the sector, establishing the Office for Students (OfS) and launching the Teaching Excellence Framework (TEF) with a firm focus on metrics to assess student retention, student satisfaction and employability.

The volatile external policymaking landscape, together with the disruption caused by this metrics-based approach, means that it is now more important than ever to preserve the quality of the day-to-day interactions that universities have with their students. The way in which academic and professional support staff work in partnership with students, in a variety of curricular, co-curricular and extra-curricular contexts, is vital to managing student expectations and nurturing independent learning. Human interactions are fundamental to the core values of UK HE, that is, to champion lifelong learning, to advocate learning for learning's sake and to support students, from a variety of backgrounds, to achieve autonomy, to pursue their dreams and to realise their potential. This book is written in the spirit of staff–student partnership; it is intended for a broad audience and introduces practical strategies for working with students, and with other colleagues, to improve the quality of these interactions and to encourage students to think critically, to solve problems and to try out new things.

A brief history of personal tutoring

Personal tutoring in UK HE is certainly not a new phenomenon. Rather, in the HE sector's quest to restore its value base and improve the personalisation of student learning, tutoring is experiencing a renewed focus, even renewed vigour. The models to articulate this delivery can differ quite substantially, as can the definitions and naming conventions associated with tutoring (Walker, 2018) and this is covered in significant detail in Chapters 1 and 2. For the purposes of this book, the term 'personal tutoring', discussed in more detail in Chapter 1, encompasses all activities where academic or professional staff work in partnership with students to provide one-to-one support, advice and guidance, of either an academic or pastoral nature. The broad definition of the term, as adopted here, is designed to ensure that the guidance provided in this book is applied widely and flexibly.

Tutoring, in one form or another, has always been present in the delivery of HE. In 1852, Cardinal Henry Newman, a clergyman and Oxford academic, gave a series of lectures reflecting on the purpose of the university, which was later published in his book *The Idea of the University*. For Newman, the university's 'soul' can be best measured in the mark it leaves on its students, with his notion of the 'ideal university' described as a place which is residential, where teaching is prized above research, where a community of students, as learners, engage in the pursuit of a broad, liberal education and where students simply 'flourish' (Newman, 2014, p 68). While Newman brought personalised, even individualised, learning to the forefront of university consciousness in the mid-1800s, models of tutoring in fact go back further than this.

The tutorial method of teaching, that is, one where students learn in small groups of two or three, can be traced back to the eleventh century when the universities of Oxford and Cambridge established their collegiate systems. In the fifteenth century the role of the tutor was described in more detail; it was made clear that older academics were given responsibility for the conduct and instruction of their younger colleagues (Moore, 1968; Palfreyman, 2008). In this regard, early models of tutoring were clearly pastoral as well as academic. The University of Oxford's highly regarded tutorial system, as it is conceived of today, with its significant emphasis on the dialectic of the individual, was established by Professor Benjamin Jowett several decades after the time when Newman was writing, in 1882 (Markham, 1967). These tutorials embraced the Socratic Method, where students were engaged in discussion and supported to learn and to think for themselves. Thus, the earliest models of tutoring were designed to foster independence of thought, harnessing the key skills of critical thinking and problem-solving. These student-centred pedagogies, with tutorials at the heart of the system, are still highly valued today. Nevertheless, just over a century later in the 1960s when universities were expanding considerably, the tutorial method was once again under the spotlight with critics arguing that it was outdated, inefficient and unfit for purpose. While the tutorial method, as originally conceived, is still a hallmark of an Oxbridge education today, it has evolved considerably and been adapted significantly in other universities, both modern and old, in order to suit different institutional missions, curricula and values. The concept of tutoring, as originally conceived, is therefore less coherent today. As universities are expanding, fewer resources have been dedicated to personal tutoring, it has become less structured and, in many institutions, has become somewhat separated from the mainstream delivery of the curriculum. In the quest for efficiency, and with increasing massification and diversification of the student body, the models and fundamental practices of tutoring require further examination.

Who this book is for

You may have picked up this book because you are a new academic within HE or delivering higher education in a further education setting. It could be that you are an experienced academic or specialised personal tutor within one of these sectors. Or, you may work within HE but be employed purely within student support or student services. Equally, you could be a manager within HE who oversees student support, the student experience or curriculum delivery. More widely, you may be employed in one of the many different student-facing roles such as Graduate Teaching Assistant (GTA) or within a student support co-ordinator or liaison role. It is important to state that whichever one of these describes you best – and there will be other related roles that come under a slightly different description to those mentioned – this book is relevant to you. As you will see from the next section, the book has been written with the new academic foremost in our minds; however, it is not exclusive to this audience. Student support, which is at the core of the book, is delivered in many ways and through a variety of roles so, indeed, anyone who works with students in any capacity will find this book useful in the day-to-day context of carrying out their role.

Your first activity

» *In terms of your personal tutor or support role, think about your level of knowledge and how effective you feel you are. On a scale of one to ten, with one being very little knowledge and very limited effectiveness and ten being extensive knowledge with highly effective practice, where are you on the scale? Keep this number in mind because we will be revisiting it at the end of the book.*

Why this book is useful

The life of an academic – and particularly a new academic – can seem like a whirlwind. The pace of life in HE is fast and roles in teaching and learning change rapidly. Academic staff are increasingly asked to perform more duties and carry out additional responsibilities. Typical activities include teaching, creating resources, student support, marking assessments, working with colleagues, designing the curriculum and attending meetings as well as undertaking research and, often, additional qualifications and continuing professional development (CPD) opportunities. Working with students directly remains one of the most rewarding, and challenging, parts of the role.

Most academics working in HE are mindful of students' welfare and support needs. However, these needs are difficult to balance given the other demands on academics' time. As mentioned previously, tutoring in the UK has been chronically under-resourced and, until now, neglected. There is a lack of evidence-informed practice on which to draw and the importance of tutoring has not been well articulated (McIntosh and Grey, 2017). Providing support for students in a consistent and well-structured way can be a particular challenge for individual tutors. While personal tutoring is often discussed as part of Postgraduate Certificate (PG Cert) programmes, it is often not covered comprehensively and, therefore, most experience gained by tutors is acquired while performing the role itself, thinking on one's feet and very much in practice. Tutoring is often undefined and unstructured in many institutional contexts and, as previously mentioned, it is therefore difficult to determine which model(s) of tutoring your institution embraces and even more tricky to understand how to perform the role effectively. Even less has been said about the importance of coaching skills to personal tutoring and how they can be employed to support learner autonomy. This book aims to address both of these issues.

Of course, your first experiences of personal tutoring may be more positive in terms of clarity of expectation and content. However, to ensure that personal tutoring practice is covered in sufficient depth, the focus of this book is to unearth good practice in tutoring and to help you to develop your own approach to tutoring by linking it with coaching and the delivery of the curriculum.

Furthermore, the purpose of this book is to provide a highly effective approach for delivering personal tutoring and coaching, which, given this is an underdeveloped area in HE, is increasingly important for new and experienced academic tutors.

The book will also act as a 'toolkit' for you by providing the tools to achieve effectiveness in personal tutoring and coaching to meet student needs. In turn, these key elements will have a positive impact on key performance indicators, the strategic ambitions of your university and the measurement of core metrics such as student retention, success, engagement, learning gain (a term described in Chapter 4, p 75) and employability. These will inform the ongoing development of your academic role, whether you are a new or an experienced member of staff.

It is also important to emphasise that the book should not only be viewed as relevant to your personal tutor role. Since personal tutoring values and skills are fundamental to student-centred pedagogy, the book is intended to inform your whole practice and locate tutoring as central to, rather than separate from, the mainstream delivery of the curriculum regardless of academic discipline. The book covers these aspects comprehensively and provides an invaluable resource in what is currently an under-researched and under-resourced area of practice.

Why is personal tutoring so important?

The challenges presented by the ever-changing and diverse backgrounds of students means that understanding and supporting students individually is key to supporting their success. As explained by Harriet Swain in her article 'The Personal Tutor':

> *The diverse backgrounds of today's students mean that the role of the personal tutor is more important than ever. As the student population expands and changes, traditional expectations of the tutor's role may no longer be accurate.*
>
> (Swain, 2008, online)

Swain doesn't discuss what these traditional expectations are, but they are likely to be similar to the expectations held by many academics at the beginning of their careers. Although, as we have seen, institutional expectations of tutoring are not well articulated, this must be addressed if we are to attend to the challenging and complex individual issues that students present. For example, some institutions are supporting an extremely diverse profile of students from different backgrounds and with varying degrees of disadvantage. Although it is not just these students that experience difficulties, the make-up of the student profile in every institution should drive the interventions designed to provide relevant and timely support. Whatever the make-up of your student population, you will be faced with particularly complex issues.

In the face of these, a new set of expectations for the personal tutor role is needed for the HE sector. Moreover, new expectations are required of tutors to stretch and challenge more able students. Whether this is through individualised tracking and monitoring (Chapter 4), identifying and supporting 'at risk' and 'vulnerable' students (Chapter 4) or effectively supporting students through all stages of the student lifecycle (Chapter 5), the new expectations of the personal tutor will be set out clearly for you.

By drawing on our experience of working with varied cohorts of students and staff, the book will cover, in a comprehensive way, the tools and skills you will need in order to become an effective personal tutor.

Why is personal tutoring so crucial in the higher education context?

The current HE context is one where the increasing diversity of students' needs demand that our professional skills be multi-faceted; this is reinforced by the expectations set out in the aforementioned *Higher Education and Research Act* (2017) and the TEF, in particular. There is significant overlap between the themes discussed in this book and the objectives set out in the regulatory framework for HE in England, governed by the OfS. These objectives ensure that all students, from all backgrounds, and with the ability and desire to undertake HE:

- are supported to access, succeed in, and progress from, HE;

- receive a high-quality academic experience, and their interests are protected while they study or in the event of provider, campus or course closure;

- are able to progress into employment or further study, and their qualifications hold their value over time;

- receive value for money.

(The Office for Students, 2018, p 14)

These objectives are multi-faceted and, when combined with the metrics assessed by the TEF, namely student retention, progression, satisfaction and employability, they will be used to judge an institution's ability and capacity to support its students. The emphasis on a *'high quality academic experience'* means that, in order to meet these objectives, it is even more critical to develop the whole student, not just their academic capabilities, and to support them to develop the critical skills required for lifelong learning. Holistic academic and pastoral student support, advice and guidance are fundamental to the personal tutoring approach and, crucially, to students' perception of value for money. This is further brought into focus by the requirement that HE providers will support students to progress into employment or further study and respond to demand from employers for good employability and transferable skills. Moreover, the objectives and criteria previously mentioned (alongside high-level metrics) arguably place implied obligations and new expectations on you and your colleagues as personal tutors. They have long-term implications both for you as an individual performing this role as well as for how the institution organises and indeed recognises the tutor role within its overall structures.

The profile and importance of personal tutoring has been further enhanced by the National Occupational Standards for Personal Tutoring, which are explored further in Chapter 5 (key activities) and Chapter 8 (measuring impact).

The change in language, as shown by the objectives just outlined and the evident shift in the student experience to incorporate the *social* as well as the *academic*, shows the many and varied roles and functions performed by the modern academic. Indeed, it is not uncommon to hear comments from academics such as 'I feel more like a therapist or counsellor some days'. We could add to this list of roles by including personal organiser, referee, mediator, advocate and careers advisor. Depending on the stage of your career, you have either not had a chance to understand the breadth of skills you are required to demonstrate or know very well the number of hats that a modern academic and personal tutor is expected to wear.

The current HE context, then, is one where the increasing diversity of students' needs demands that personal tutors develop a large range of professional skills. This has to be done in the face of a very volatile external, metrics-driven HE landscape. Personal tutors also face a significant challenge, not only to develop the skills required to perform the role itself but to keep these skills and experiences current. This pressure is intensified by the fact that, until now, tutoring has been chronically under-resourced in HE meaning that the purpose of tutoring, and its associated models and structures, are, largely, not well articulated and supported. This has separated tutoring from other teaching and learning activities such as the delivery of lectures and seminars. As a consequence, training opportunities for personal tutors can be superficial, lacking in sufficient depth and unfit for purpose. These all affect the impact of tutoring on student success. Despite this lack of coherence and clarity, you, as a personal tutor, can play a key role in helping a student to develop their learner identity, and to stretch and challenge any student to achieve more. So, in terms of both enabling higher achievement as well as providing essential support, this book will provide you with the knowledge and skills needed to deliver this support.

How does this book link to your role?

If you are a new academic, the link between the book's content and your PG Cert qualification is clear when you consider that personal tutoring, coaching and student-centred pedagogy are areas that are implicit within your qualification. Moreover, it will contextualise this content into real-world educational situations that you will come across in various teaching and learning contexts or in your day-to-day encounters with students. If you are a new or experienced academic, it will provide an in-depth overview of the role of personal tutoring, coaching and supporting students.

Of course, hopefully you can see that principles to be covered are not restricted to academics but also are invaluable to those in other student-facing roles, for example dedicated support staff (such as student support advisors) and, as such, are transferable. As we mentioned at the outset, the skills are delivered in many ways and sometimes through different roles – indeed, by anyone who works with students in any capacity.

Chapter summaries

Chapter 1 sets the scene for the whole book by answering the question 'what is a personal tutor?' It does this, firstly, by exploring the natural overlap between effective teaching and personal tutor practice, along with defining the term and looking at the relationship between personal tutoring and coaching. Some different theoretical models are used to further understand the role, as well as how it fits into organisational structures.

In the first part of Chapter 2 we outline and explore the core values of the personal tutor through examples of these in action. We discuss the core skills in the second part of the chapter, differentiating these from the core values by clarifying that values are able to be seen through actions, whereas core skills are the actions themselves. The necessary boundaries between you and students, and between students themselves, are explored in Chapter 3.

Chapters 4 and 5 are lengthier chapters which comprehensively cover the toolkit you need to provide effective support to students. We have named these 'key activities' since, by putting these tools into action, you will be covering all aspects of a student's experience. Firstly, we define the overall aims of using these tools: student retention and standards of attendance, student success, engagement, progression and learning gain. We have divided the key activities into identifying and supporting student populations (Chapter 4) and effectively supporting all stages of the student lifecycle (Chapter 5). Here the topics include: the tracking and monitoring of students; one-to-one tutorials (we refer to these as 'one-to-ones' throughout); group tutorial planning and teaching; transition and progression; working with students who have additional support needs; and safeguarding.

In Chapters 6 to 8 we build on the toolkit to develop your higher-level support skills through exploring solution-focused coaching (Chapter 6), reflective practice and professional development (Chapter 7) and measuring impact (Chapter 8).

Finally, in Chapter 9 we look at the 'bigger picture'. This allows you to explore and prioritise your own professional development activities as well as to consider the development activities of the institution you work within and how you could influence positive change within your organisation.

About the book and how to use it

We hope the experience of reading the book will be engaging and rewarding, with the additional opportunity to dip in and out of content to suit your needs since each chapter can be read and used in isolation. Therefore, it can be used as a reference book or read in sequence as a whole.

Chapter content includes aims, case studies and examples which are linked to critical thinking activities. All examples are rooted in experience. However, names of people and departments have been changed to protect confidentiality. Examples are transferable to different institutions, making this book vital for anyone working with students in a learning capacity.

At the end of each chapter there is a chapter summary, a learning checklist to check your understanding of key points, and critical reflections which pose some key questions for you to answer in note or essay form and prompt you to critically analyse your practice.

In addition, at the end of each chapter (from Chapter 2 onwards), there is an individual and institutional self-assessment system which allows you to score your own performance and that of your educational institution on the key theme of each chapter. The rating will be measured against minimum standard, beginner, intermediate, advanced and expert levels, all accompanied with a star rating, enabling you to reach a cumulative score and level at the end of the book.

References

Higher Education and Research Act 2017 (c.25). London: TSO. [online] Available at: www.legislation. gov.uk/ukpga/2017/29/pdfs/ukpga_20170029_en.pdf (accessed 30 June 2018).

Markham, F (1967) *Oxford.* London: Weidenfeld and Nicolson.

McIntosh, E and Cross, D (2017) Who Sets the Agenda in Student Engagement? *Journal of Educational Innovation, Partnership and Change*, 3: 1–3.

McIntosh, E and Grey, D (2017) How to be an Effective Personal Tutor. *Times Higher Education.* [online] Available at: www.timeshighereducation.com/news/career-advice-how-to-be-an-effective-personal-tutor (accessed 30 June 2018).

Moore, W G (1968) *The Tutorial System and its Future.* Oxford: Pergammon Press.

Newman, J H (2014) *The Idea of a University.* London: Assumption Press.

The Office for Students (2018) *Securing Student Success: Regulatory Framework for Higher Education in England*. Bristol: The Office for Students. [online] Available at: www.officeforstudents.org.uk/media/1406/ofs2018_01.pdf (accessed 30 June 2018).

Palfreyman, D (ed) (2008) *The Oxford Tutorial.* Oxford: OxCHEPS.

Swain, H (2008) *The Personal Tutor.* [online] Available at: www.timeshighereducation.co.uk/news/the-personal-tutor/210049.article (accessed 30 June 2018).

Walker, B W (2018) A Defining Moment in Personal Tutoring: Reflections on Personal Tutoring Definitions and Their Implications. *IMPact: The University of Lincoln Journal of Higher Education*, 1(1): 104–18. [online] Available at: http://lncn.eu/IMPact9 (accessed 30 June 2018).

1 What is a personal tutor?

Chapter aims

This chapter helps you to:

- understand the role of personal tutoring within the modern academic profession;
- explore the natural overlap between effective teaching and personal tutoring practice;
- define the personal tutor;
- explore the useful relationship between personal tutoring and coaching;
- consider different coaching and support models and how to apply these to different situations;
- understand how personal tutoring can form an important part of a holistic model of student support;
- understand and evaluate different organisational and structural models of student support;
- explore how organisational and structural models of student support are applied at institutional level and reflect upon personal tutoring at your own institution.

The role of personal tutoring within the modern academic profession

The academic profession is complex. In recent years, more students are entering HE and many of these students are from increasingly diverse backgrounds. The role of the academic is therefore constantly evolving in response to the massification and diversification of

HE. At the same time, the culture of HE is changing, most especially amid concerns about tuition fees and the impact that this has had not only on student engagement but also on the relationship between the university and its students, and the language and terminology used to describe that relationship (McIntosh and Cross, 2017). As a result of this there have been some inevitable and fundamental changes in the student–tutor relationship (Thomas, 2006; Enders, 2007; Morgan, 2012; Thomas et al, 2015). It has been suggested that the expansion and diversification of HE may render the informal relationships between staff and students as less reliable and potentially inequitable (Myers, 2008). Many modern academics are asked to juggle *'lecturing, assessing, researching and administrative commitments'* (Ghenghesh, 2017, pp 1–2) while assisting a more diverse population of students (identified in Chapters 4 and 5) who require further and more structured support. As more traditional forms of engagement may have become *'inappropriate for a new generation of diverse student experiences'* (Thomas and Jones, 2017, p 3), navigating the *'web of events that shape student leaving and persistence'* (Tinto, 2006–7, p 1) may be more complex than ever.

Many of these changes have had a direct impact on student expectations of university and their programme of study. Student transition into and across HE, involving the management of expectations and the overcoming of certain challenges, has therefore become central to student success. Kift (2009) has called for a holistic transition pedagogy which transcends the silos of individual university department support (as discussed in Chapter 5). The recently created OfS promises a fresh look at approaches to managing these important transitions throughout the student journey (Department for Education, 2017). In this book, we argue that personal tutors are key to managing these transitions. Often they provide the 'face' of the university; an important first point of contact who can help 'buffer' against some of the challenges that first-year students typically face, as well as contribute towards a sense of belonging (Zepke and Leach, 2010; Thomas et al, 2017; Yale, 2017). If the time spent on these vital activities is not, or at least not sufficiently, recorded within staff workloads, they may neglect to carry out this duty, be forced to work additional hours beyond their contract or perform the duties at the expense of their research and well-being (Hart, 1996; Owen, 2002; Dobinson-Harrington, 2006; Havergal, 2015). This delicate balance of academic activities is covered in more detail in Chapter 3.

At the same time, tutors require accurate and timely information about their students in order to understand how to support them. In recent years, dashboard systems (Chapter 4) have been developed across the sector to gather learner and engagement analytics. These dashboards present engagement data to tutors, often in a visual format, and offer insights into how a student is engaging with the university. They often gather data from other university systems and hold it in one place. It must be noted that different dashboards report on different types of engagement data, for example attendance, library engagement and activity on the virtual learning environment (VLE). Learner analytics have the potential to assist tutors by identifying disengaged students as well as students with significant potential. Analytics can help tutors to recommend activities to students but this may add to tutors' workloads (at least in the short term), which carry implications in terms of training and follow-up activities (Sclater et al, 2017). While dashboards are useful, the data provided offers 'flags' and snapshots for tutors which must be explored with the student in person. This is covered in greater detail in Chapter 4.

How effective personal tutoring principles link to effective teaching

The principles of being an effective academic teacher, such as listening and relating to people, as well as sound pedagogical skill and subject expertise, are closely aligned with the principles of being an effective personal tutor (Owen, 2002; Braine and Parnell, 2011). For example, both the lecturer and personal tutor demonstrate a commitment to students through respecting their uniqueness and individuality and therefore provide appropriate learning experiences as well as aiming to motivate and inspire students to achieve their potential. Personal tutoring principles are ones that most new and experienced tutors use many times throughout their working day. Even though these are principles that students find particularly helpful, they tend to be the least written about and are not always covered in staff induction.

As access and participation in HE have widened over recent years, the need for a more holistic approach to student support has become greater, with a particular focus on student success, including, but not limited to, student engagement, transition, advice and student learning development (Whittaker, 2008; National Union of Students, 2015; Department for Education, 2017; Thomas et al, 2017; Webb et al, 2017). A holistic approach to personal tutoring is at the heart of student guidance and support and this is highlighted as a key benchmark in the literature (Watts, 1999; Grant, 2006; Stephen et al, 2008; Thomas et al, 2017). It is the holistic and supportive model of personal tutoring that we advocate here (see Figure 1.1).

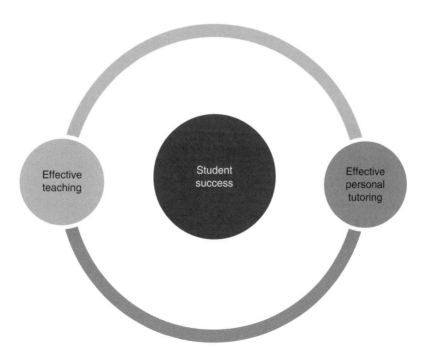

Figure 1.1 *Student success: effective teaching and personal tutoring*

So, what are these principles? We refer to *effective personal tutoring principles* as the umbrella term which includes the numerous aspects covered within this book, from values and skills through to key activities, measuring impact and everything in between. Your induction programme or PG Cert in Teaching and Learning in Higher Education may have shown you how to plan a curriculum of highly effective lectures and seminars, which is of course important. However, it is also important to explore how other complementary approaches, which help students succeed, can be learned and mastered.

Good academics and good teaching aim to put each student at the centre of everything, whether that is when planning a lesson, marking an assignment or even having a departmental meeting with colleagues. In today's modern, fast-paced, target-driven and ever-changing educational landscape, tutors, whether you agree with it or not, are expected to offer more to a student's success than just traditional classroom delivery. Whatever your methods, you are trying to help students to get from point A to point B more quickly than they could do by themselves. Point B is student success, although 'success' for each student looks very different and, if we are honest, probably *should* look very different. This is where the effective personal tutoring principles will enable you to help your students achieve more, not only in terms of passing an exam or achieving a good mark on a piece of coursework, but also in terms of developing the *whole* student, one who can confidently overcome all of the many and varied challenges they encounter.

It is important to understand that the line between effective teaching and personal tutoring principles overlap and naturally become blurred as you face different situations and challenges both within and outside of the classroom. The likelihood is that the personal tutoring principles will be performed alongside curriculum teaching and vice versa.

When working with students for the first time as new academics, we have a tendency to be overly analytical and critical of our teaching practice. This is natural and also positive in moderation because it shows that you are keen to get it right and to improve. The fundamental principles of becoming an effective personal tutor are built upon training, practical experience and reflection on that experience. If you continue to apply the personal tutoring principles in different situations and with different types of students and reflect on the impact, then you will quickly move from being a keen beginner to becoming an effective personal tutor.

Definitions of the personal tutor

As the role has evolved over time, the number of descriptions, and uses of, the term 'personal tutor' has increased. These descriptions also consider the role as it relates to, and interfaces with, other mainstream teaching and learning activities. Despite this, there has been little written on the characteristics of the role itself (particularly in HE) and even less research has been undertaken on how to be an effective personal tutor (Grant, 2006; Walker, 2018). While a single, succinct, one-sentence definition may be too *'reductionary'* (Wootton, 2007, p 157) and inflexible, the lack of an agreed definition of personal tutoring and a shared understanding of the role and responsibilities of the personal tutor is problematic, creating some indistinguishable boundaries which must be acknowledged and examined (Wootton, 2006; Mynott, 2016; Yale, 2017), as they are in Chapter 3.

The summaries of personal tutoring provided in Thomas (2006) and Walker (2018) are the closest to single definitions of personal tutoring in HE in the existing literature. Written in the context of further education, but of use to HE is the following one-sentence definition of the personal tutor in terms of good practice: *'one who improves the intellectual and academic ability, and nurtures the emotional well-being of learners through individualised, holistic support'* (Stork and Walker, 2015, p 3).

These working definitions are used as the starting point here, cross-referenced and combined with a range of other complementary literature on broader student support, advice and guidance. In short, a personal tutor is typically, though not always, an academic member of staff who supports a number of students (often referred to as tutees) on a range of academic and pastoral issues. They usually draw on a variety of insights and expertise, signposting and referring to other academic and professional colleagues, where appropriate, to provide consistent and robust advice and guidance.

As mentioned later on in this chapter, the tutoring model in which academics are working can have a significant impact on how this works in practice. This description therefore represents an ideal which may or may not be reflected in the reality of your institution. There are also a wide variety of advisor and counsellor roles who may perform aspects of the tutor role and for whom this book is also intended. We have grouped the following working definitions of a personal tutor in the existing literature into a list of activities which relate closely to the general roles and responsibilities of personal tutors in UK HE. It is recommended you consider these in relation to your own role and organisation.

- **Academic feedback and development** with support for study skills and other learning development activities to maximise learning (Myers, 2008; Stephen et al, 2008; Smith, 2008; Robinson, 2012; Small, 2013; Yale, 2017).

- **Personal welfare support** by advising, informing, suggesting and providing insight to meet students' pastoral needs (Kuhn, 2008; Smith, 2008; Robinson, 2012; Small, 2013; Gubby and McNab, 2013).

- **Referral to further information and support** with a broad knowledge of university professional services and the support that they provide (Myers, 2008; Smith, 2008; Stephen et al, 2008; Small, 2013; Gubby and McNab, 2013; Yale, 2017). This is covered in Chapter 3.

- **Embodiment and representative of the university** assisting students to navigate systems/processes and normalise features of the learning experience (Neville, 2007; Small, 2013; Yale, 2017).

- **Information about HE processes, procedures and expectations** – explained during induction to support effective transition (Stephen et al, 2008; Luck, 2010; Braine and Parnell, 2011; Calcagno et al, 2017).

- **Engendering a sense of belonging** – provided as part of a transition and induction experience, with personal tutors as the key first points of contact (Swain, 2008; Zepke and Leach, 2010; Lindsay, 2011; Small, 2013; Yale, 2017).

- **Goal/target setting and monitoring of achievements** evidenced by data and conversations with students (Wootton, 2007; Braine and Parnell, 2011; Ross et al, 2014; Department of Business, Innovation and Skills, 2011; Ghenghesh, 2017; Calcagno et al, 2017).

- **Solution-focused coaching** to unlock a student's potential and support their academic success as an independent learner (Whitmore, 2002; Kuhn, 2008; Palmer and Szymanska, 2008; Gurbutt and Gurbutt, 2015; Thomas et al, 2015; Ralston and Hoffshire, 2017).

Personal tutoring and coaching: definitions and history of the terms

Viewing the 'stock' dictionary definitions of the terms and their derivation (source and original meanings) aids understanding. *The Concise Oxford English Dictionary* and the online etymology dictionary give us the following definitions and derivations.

Table 1.1 Personal and tutor: dictionary definition and history

Term	Definition	History
Personal	Adjective 1. one's own; individual; private	Late fourteenth century Middle English via Old French (twelfth century) from Latin *personalis* – 'as person'
Tutor	*Noun* a private teacher, esp. one in general charge of a person's education *Verb* 1. act as a tutor to 2. work as a tutor 3. restrain, discipline (*The Concise Oxford Dictionary*, 1995)	Late fourteenth century From Latin *tutor*– 'Guardian, Watcher' (noun) or *tutor* (verb) – 'to watch over'

As you can see, the modern word 'tutor' is rooted within the academy. However, the original Latin meaning of 'guardian, watcher' and its verb form 'watch over' is certainly relevant to personal tutoring principles. Also, by putting the two together, with the adjective 'personal' modifying the noun 'tutor', we have a sense of a practice tailored to the individual.

Table 1.2 *Coach: dictionary definition and history*

Term	Definition	History
Coach	*Noun* 1. an instructor or trainer in sport 2. a private tutor *Verb* 1. train or teach (a pupil, sports team etc) as a coach 2. give hints to; prime with facts (*The Concise Oxford Dictionary*, 1995)	From the French *coche* (sixteenth century) as in *stagecoach*. Used in the athletic sense from 1861. Used as *instructor/trainer* from circa 1830 as a result of Oxford University slang for a tutor as one who 'carries a student through an exam'. (Online Etymology Dictionary, nd, online)

Although there is an association with a particular field (sport), the term coach, both as a noun and a verb, contains meanings with immediate relevance: instructor, trainer, train, teach, give hints to. Its history gives us the highly relatable sense of 'carrying through'. A very pertinent image is provided with the meaning broadening from the literal physical carrying of 'stagecoach' to the metaphorical sense of carrying a student through an exam. In our context, the 'carrying through' is widened to include many aspects of the learning process such as the programme of study and barriers to learning, to name but two.

The relationship between personal tutoring and coaching

It is possible to see the common ground and also the subtle distinctions between these two terms. More often than not, definitions try to harness all of the component parts into what is usually quite a clunky and awkward sentence or series of sentences. With this in mind, Table 1.3 provides our interpretation of the two elements divided into approach, core focus and context, along with how it helps students. The jagged line illustrates the close relationship between the two.

Table 1.3 Relationship between personal tutoring and coaching

	Personal tutoring	**Coaching**
Approach	Can be prescriptive/directive (you take more of a lead and offer advice and guidance) or non-directive/developmental (encouraging the student to take more of the lead and reflect back the content they bring), focusing on stretching (intellectual/academic need) or nurturing (emotional need).	Can be directive or non-directive. Generally focuses on stretching (usually intellectual/academic need, but can be related to an emotional need if required).
Core focus	Following an educational/learning agenda. Develop longer-term trusting relationship.	Affect an immediate improvement in skills, approach or knowledge. Usually within short time frames.
Context	More relationship-based between the personal tutor and student than a functional process.	More of a functional process, in other words designed to be immediately practical and useful.
How it helps students	Helps students acquire new skills and knowledge, nurturing emotional well-being through regular communication, either through group tutorials and/or one-to-ones.	Helps to improve student performance and skills through one-to-one coaching conversations.

Personal tutoring focuses on developing a trusting longer-term relationship with a student through listening and regular communication. It can take the form of being prescriptive or developmental, focusing on working with individual students over a significant period of time to help them acquire new skills and improve their confidence and approach to learning. It can assist in developing their focus, motivation and skills in independent learning and reflection – as well as in co-ordination with central support services.

Coaching skills and actions lend themselves more towards regular one-to-one conversations with students either within a class, in the corridor or while having an arranged one-to-one meeting, in order to influence a more immediate improvement in performance and the development of skills.

To avoid confusing personal tutoring and coaching, we need to view them as related to each other but not the same. A coach is not a personal tutor. However, tutoring may include elements of coaching when formulating personal learning goals or personal development planning with students (Gurbutt and Gurbutt, 2015). Personal tutoring is relationship-based while coaching is a development activity that can be used as part of that relationship to develop specific personal or professional competencies (Thomas, 2012; Gurbutt and Gurbutt, 2015).

Critical thinking activity 1

1.   How well do the definitions of personal tutoring and coaching fit with your own experience, whether that is through 'doing', being on the receiving end or from observing these activities in practice?

2. From your own experience, how would you define personal tutoring and coaching? Make a note of your definitions so that you can see whether your definitions change as you read though the rest of the book.

As a new academic, an awareness of these definitions is a good starting point in terms of understanding personal tutoring. However, it is important to explore the tutoring and coaching roles further and situate them, as defined, into relatable contexts.

CASE STUDY

Sarah's story

Sarah is a new academic working in her first role at a post-1992 institution.

Week 1

Sarah has been allocated a large number of level six business students as tutees and weekly group tutorials as part of an academic and career development module. This is to be completed in addition to her teaching commitments. She has been charged with delivering engaging group sessions focusing on employability skills and CV/application writing as well as researching employers or routes to further study. She must also work with each student individually to review their personal development plans (particularly focusing on assessing how each student is progressing against their target marks) and to regularly review and set new SMART (specific, measurable, achievable, realistic and time-related) targets. Sarah is expected to track and monitor the students' progress via the university's dashboard system and give feedback on their progress to the rest of the programme team at a Student Progress and Review meeting at the end of each semester. Sarah has had to discuss punctuality, attendance or attainment issues with several of her students, which she has found challenging but rewarding.

Week 2

In her second week, while delivering a group tutorial Sarah finds that she has time to work with students individually to discuss their learning and progress. Paul, a student in the class, confides in her that he is finding he cannot keep up with all of the expectations of the course and he feels he is falling behind. It is obvious that he feels anxious. Sarah allows Paul to express his concerns and uses exploratory questions to find out whether he is actually behind with his work and the reasons behind this. As the conversation develops, it becomes clear to Sarah that Paul isn't actually too far behind but that his recent unexpected poor assessment results have knocked his confidence. Sarah steers the conversation towards Paul's strengths and enables him to explore the potential actions he could take to regain his confidence and get back on track. They agree some small next steps for Paul to take and decide to review the outcomes of Paul's actions in the class the following week.

Week 3

During her third week, Sarah arranges to meet her tutees for one-to-ones. She explores with each student how they are feeling and encourages them to discuss the issues they are facing both inside and outside of their course. Sarah asks questions and challenges the students to think about and express their issues more deeply than they might normally do, providing encouragement and guidance if needed. Her main aim is to give the students a chance to look at themselves more closely, reflecting on their progress and exploring new ideas to help build their confidence. She encourages the students to take the initiative – any actions resulting from the meeting that contribute to their learning and progress remain their responsibility. She helps them to think about potential outcomes in more detail and how long they think it would take for them to make progress. Sarah has discovered that tutees tend to behave differently in a one-to-one setting than they do in a lecture theatre or seminar. She has found working with her tutees on this basis a rewarding and welcome change from normal lecture delivery.

Critical thinking activity 2

» *Having read through this case study of interactions between a tutor and tutee, and drawing on your own knowledge and experience, decide which aspect of the role is being described in each instance – personal tutoring or coaching. Then compare your answers with those offered in the discussion below.*

Discussion

Week 1: more personal tutoring than coaching; Sarah worked on monitoring and developing the tutees' academic performance and their employability skills.

Week 2: more coaching than personal tutoring; through questioning and discussion Sarah helps Paul to explore the reasons behind his drop in academic performance and helps him to set his own actions and the dates to review.

Week 3: personal tutoring (however, there are strong elements of a coaching approach); Sarah starts to develop a long-term trusting relationship with the students individually through regular communication to develop their emotional well-being as well as develop new knowledge and skills.

Models to further understand the personal tutor role

It is important to unpick the role of the personal tutor and recognise the different types of help and support you can give to your students. To do this, it is useful to look at the diagram developed by Clutterbuck (1985, cited in Gravells and Wallace, 2007) which should start to provide greater clarity. The diagram was designed to explore the role of the mentor in education, but it is also a useful one to apply to the role and functions of the personal tutor.

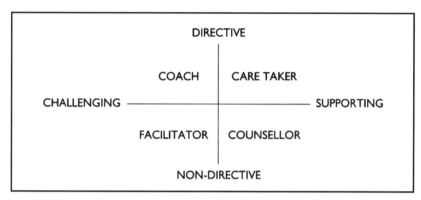

Figure 1.2 *Some ways in which mentors give support*
(Gravells and Wallace, 2007, 2nd edition)

As a lecturer, the majority of your time is devoted to helping students but the help you provide can take many guises. Figure 1.3 gives an overview of typical personal tutoring examples related to Clutterbuck's 1985 model.

COACH (directive and challenging)	CARE TAKER (directive and supporting)
The directive actions you take with students are where you actively attempt to help your students to achieve a desired outcome and the challenging aspect is where you develop an intellectual need, for example to develop an improvement in a skill or in the student's approach to a problem. For example, the coaching role could be where Sarah is observing a student's presentation, providing feedback and advice as to how they may improve it and setting targets for the next time they present. It is worth nothing at this point that teaching, training and assessment (assessment for learning and assessment of learning) also appear within this section.	The supporting aspect of the model relates to helping a student address an emotional need. Therefore, the care taking part of Sarah's role might be where she takes a student to student support services to make a referral such as for a meeting with a trained counsellor or an assessment for additional support. Best practice and the boundaries in doing so are explored in Chapter 3.
FACILITATOR (non-directive and challenging)	**COUNSELLOR (non-directive and supporting)**
The non-directive approach is helping a student in response to a need that has arisen through a discussion or observation of a student's circumstances. The facilitator role could be where Sarah passes on names of colleagues within the institution who can offer possible career pathway advice or passing on contacts within local businesses who might be able to provide the student with work experience opportunities.	The counsellor aspect of helping students usually relates to actively listening to them. An example of this is where a student may approach Sarah to discuss that they are suffering from course-related stress. They may want to tell her how this is making them feel and discuss whether what they are doing about it is the right course of action. Sarah may ask questions to help the student understand the situation more fully. More directive actions may happen at the end of this conversation to seek further support for stress management.

Figure 1.3 *Personal tutoring examples related to Clutterbuck's 'Some ways in which mentors give support' model (1985)*

As you can see, as a personal tutor you may be called upon to show an abundance of skills and perform a variety of roles within one lecture or seminar, group tutorial or one-to-one conversation.

It is important to give more focused consideration to the model and look in more detail at styles of helping students. In 2002, Klasen and Clutterbuck developed a more detailed model (see Figure 1.4) which helps us consider this further (Klasen and Clutterbuck, 2002, cited in Gravells and Wallace, 2007). Like Figure 1.2, this diagram was designed to explore the role of the mentor in further education, but we also find it useful to apply to the role and functions of the personal tutor in HE.

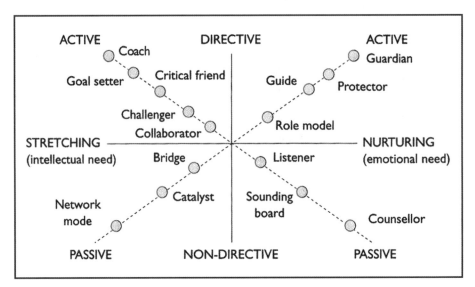

Figure 1.4 *Four basic styles of helping (Gravells and Wallace, 2007, 2nd edition)*

Critical thinking activity 3

Take a detailed look at Figure 1.4: Klasen and Clutterbuck's (2002) model as adapted by Gravells and Wallace (2007).

1. Pick the two styles you feel you relate to the most in your current position (if you are yet to start lecturing or your personal tutor role, from your own knowledge, choose which two you think you would relate to the most) and note down specific examples of when you have had to, or might have to, exhibit these styles of helping.

2. Using the examples you provided for question 1, list the qualities and attributes you:

    a. feel you displayed well which benefitted the student and the situation;

    b. feel you did less well and you would like more opportunity to develop.

3. Note down specific next steps that you will take to start to improve the qualities and attributes you identified as requiring further development. Ensure you make your next steps specific, measurable, actionable, relevant and time-bound (SMART). They may be simple, small actions, for example talking to someone experienced who you have seen do these things well, practising them again with the same or a different set of students, or asking someone to observe you and provide feedback.

Through varying degrees it is likely that you will exhibit all of the different styles of helping contained in Klasen and Clutterbuck's model and probably more within your teaching and personal tutoring career. As a lecturer and personal tutor, both within and outside of class, you will switch between being directive and challenging (stretching) in one situation to being non-directive and supportive (nurturing) in the next. As your skills, knowledge and experience develop through constant practice and reflection, your ability to judge and even predict what approach you may take with students will start to become less planned and more intuitive, making the transition from being 'consciously incompetent' to 'unconsciously competent'. However, you will not always get it right. The unpredictability of students' needs will always present new challenges. Nevertheless, this is part of the enjoyment of teaching and personal tutoring.

Student support: organisational models

Why is it important to know about models?

As will be demonstrated in the upcoming chapters, becoming effective means thinking critically about your role and its relationship to other roles in the institution as well as the HE sector. This affects the level of influence you may have. In order to do this, you will need clarity over your place in the institution along with knowledge of the organisational structure and the model of tutoring that it employs. This knowledge will help you to see how your activities and objectives link to other roles within the institution, which will help you with personal development and promotional opportunities. As shown in the final chapter, thinking about how you 'integrate vertically' – in other words how your objectives meet the objectives of different layers ascending through your organisation – means employing critical thinking skills to be most effective in your role and to see beyond this immediate role. This is central to your career development.

How were the models established and how have they evolved?

In 1992, Earwaker proposed three broad approaches to student support. These models, the pastoral, professional and curricular, have become the baseline of much of the subsequent literature on personal tutoring (Walker, 2018). Clearly, the HE landscape has evolved significantly since then and these models require review and updating so that they reflect our current ways of working, as well as capture a vast range of institutional best practice in tutoring approaches. Table 1.4 outlines the dimensions of all three models.

Table 1.4 *Established student support models*

	Pastoral	Professional	Curriculum
Description	Long established in practice and research as the default model of support. Rooted in Oxbridge sixteenth-century practices of being *in loco parentis*.	All students referred immediately to centralised, trained specialists. Established as the primary alternative to pastoral model in the US and UK.	Recommended by Earwaker (1992) and others as embedded into the academic experience, mainstream and potentially credit-bearing to maximise impact.
Rationale	Aims to support beyond academic issues, a need well established in the literature.	Can reduce academic workload and allow greater research focus.	Developmental not remedial and linked to learning outcomes as part of an effective transition.
Challenges	Reactionary, deficit model which can be insufficient for current students' needs and difficult to monitor.	Distinction between academic/pastoral may be unclear and referrals may be problematic.	Student populations are not settled and progress at their own pace, which may differ from planned curriculum support.
References	Malik (2000); Grant (2006); Dobinson-Harrington (2006); Stephen et al (2008); Gubby and McNab (2013); Small (2013); Grey and Lochtie (2016).	Owen (2002); Thomas (2006); Stevenson (2009); Lochtie (2016); McFarlane (2016); Laycock (2017); Stenton (2017); Yale (2017).	Owen (2002); Kift (2009); Laycock (2009, 2017); Stevenson (2009); Thomas (2012); Mynott (2016).

(Building upon Earwaker, 1992)

How might the models be applied?

For institutions, as for new tutors, there is no single or correct approach when it comes to building a robust personal tutoring infrastructure. Considerable diversity in the sector, and within each model, may affect their application and effectiveness (Ridley, 2006; Grey and Lochtie, 2016). For example, in recent years, several institutions have implemented a senior or enhanced personal tutor role whose responsibilities are multi-faceted. In some institutions, senior tutors provide more co-ordinated or whole cohort support and lead teams of personal tutors by scheduling tutorials, overseeing tracking systems, liaising with central services and providing advice or support materials for their colleagues and for students (Bath University, nd, online; Newcastle University, nd, online; Plymouth University, nd, online). In other universities, senior or enhanced personal tutors have been trained to work specifically with students who are 'at risk', either academically or pastorally. We address the limitations of using terms such as 'at risk' or 'vulnerable' to label students in Chapter 4 and advocate that the context in which we use these is paramount. It is clear that the personal tutoring infrastructure must reflect the structure and culture of the institution and evolve alongside it. It must be noted that if the work of personal and senior tutors is not fully integrated with that of academic colleges, departments or schools (with effective referral arrangements and useful data available to tutors) there is a danger that students who need support may get lost in the system.

Learner analytics and dashboard systems (explored further in Chapter 4) can help to inform planning and decision-making as well as identify students who need, or are predicted to need, assistance. They can also identify students who would benefit from participating in specific interventions. These systems are useful in that they offer a series of flags to enable tutors to explore student support needs. That said, the data that these systems provide should not stand alone – it must be contextualised. Dashboard systems should not drive the tutorial process itself; rather, they add value when they are part of a much broader and robust decision-making approach, one in which tutors use the data to support their students and assist them in having exploratory conversations. This approach ensures that human and social interaction prevails in the personal tutoring process (Grey and McIntosh, 2017).

As mentioned previously, little research has been conducted in the UK since Earwaker's work was completed. In the time between then and now, structures and approaches to teaching, learning and personal tutoring in HE have evolved considerably. Models of tutoring must therefore evolve to reflect these changes and adequately fit today's rapidly changing HE context. It is our view that the future of tutoring lies in articulating an integrated model of tutoring as part of a wider, holistic approach to student academic and well-being support. Figure 1.5 outlines the blended model of tutoring which combines the proactive elements of all three models explored by Earwaker and, at the same time, celebrates the partnership working that should take place between tutors, students and professional services, while being aware of the boundaries discussed in Chapter 3. You may find that your institution has moved, or is moving towards, a variation of the blended model so it may be useful to reflect upon how this might be applied.

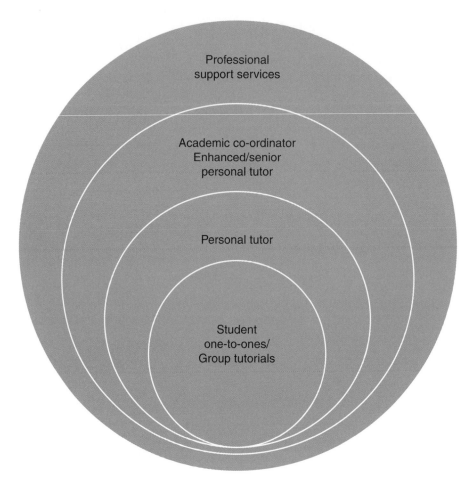

Figure 1.5 *An integrated model of personal tutoring*
Reproduced with permission (McIntosh, 2018)

It is recommended that in effective integrated or blended models of personal tutoring:

• academic tutoring is supported by professional services including, but not limited to, the library, student services, academic registry and the students' union;

• tutoring is co-ordinated in each school or department and senior tutors may be appointed to support students who are deemed to be 'at risk' and may also champion tutoring;

• academic tutoring is integrated within programme structures, underpinned by a robust tutoring curriculum which reflects the demands of the programme and is aligned with the student lifecycle. Tutoring spans all year groups, is structured and provided in both a group and one-to-one setting, facilitating student transition and helping students to connect with their programme and with each other.

Critical thinking activity 4

1. Thinking about the institution you work in, how does it compare to the blended approach suggested in Figure 1.5?

2. How do your student support interventions match up with Figure 1.5?

3. What changes, if any, would you consider in light of this?

Whatever the model of tutoring in your own organisation, it is clear that students crave structured and consistent support (Small, 2013). This can only come from understanding the model you are operating within and maximising its potential benefits. Ensuring you, and your institution, fulfil the features of effective practice listed in Figure 1.6 may be as important as the model in which you operate. This broad, holistic model of student retention and success highlights the key principles and processes involved in the design and delivery of impactful interventions to support students and enable their learning.

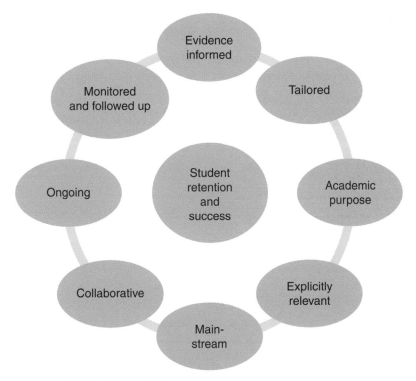

Figure 1.6 *Features of effective practice*
Reproduced with permission (Thomas et al, 2017)

Summary

This chapter has focused on the definition of personal tutoring. It has explored the similarities and differences between personal tutoring and coaching and how effective personal tutoring encompasses these complementary principles. Whether you are an experienced lecturer or a new academic, you will usually be expected to support student success beyond the context of the classroom and this is where personal tutoring can make a huge impact on a student's progression. Through examples and the two theoretical models in Figures 1.2 and 1.4 we have looked at the different types of support a personal tutor can offer to students.

Remember that developing the personal tutoring principles alongside your lecturing skills will make you a more effective practitioner overall, which will positively impact upon your students' progress and success.

We have also considered the rationale for, and challenges of, various institutional personal tutoring models. In the following chapter we will consider the core values and skills that make an effective personal tutor.

Learning checklist

Tick off each point when you feel confident you understand it.

☐   *I recognise that the principles of being an effective personal tutor are very similar, if not the same in most instances, as the principles of being an effective lecturer.*

☐   *I appreciate that what 'success' ultimately looks like for each student is very different because they all come from different backgrounds, have varying levels of skills and abilities, and each face different challenges throughout their learning both within and outside the classroom.*

☐   *I understand that as a lecturer I am increasingly expected to support student success beyond the classroom.*

☐   *I recognise that there is a natural overlap between personal tutoring and coaching.*

☐   *I recognise that the key to becoming an effective personal tutor is regularly practising, and reflecting on the impact of, the personal tutoring principles.*

☐   *I understand Earwaker's three models of student support and understand which model (or blend of models) my institution adopts and can evaluate them by considering their relative advantages and disadvantages.*

Critical reflections

1.   To what extent do you believe your PG Cert, induction, training and development have focused on improving your personal tutoring practice?

2.   Analyse the focus that your current institution places on personal tutoring and explain how you have arrived at that judgement. If you have experience of more than one institution then, using examples, compare and contrast the two institutions' approaches to this.

3. Discuss what impact you feel a significant improvement in personal tutoring practice could have on:

   a. students' progress;

   b. a department's performance;

   c. an educational institution's performance.

4. From your experience, compare and contrast the benefits and importance of traditional classroom teaching and personal tutoring.

References

Bath University (nd) *Senior Tutor Profile*. [online] Available at: www.bath.ac.uk/learningandteaching/pdf/courses/seniortutorprofile.pdf (accessed 30 June 2018).

Braine, M E and Parnell, J (2011) Exploring Students' Perceptions and Experience of Personal Tutors. *Nurse Education Today*, 31: 904–10.

Calcagno, L, Walker, D and Grey, D J (2017) Building Relationships: A Personal Tutoring Framework to Enhance Student Transition and Attainment. *Student Engagement in Higher Education Journal*, 1(2): 88–99.

Department for Business, Innovation and Skills (2011) *Higher Education: Students at the Heart of the System*. London: Department of Business, Innovation and Skills.

Department for Education (2017) *Securing Student Success: Risk-Based Regulation for Teaching Excellence, Social Mobility and Informed Choice in Higher Education*. London: Department for Education.

Dobinson-Harrington, A (2006) Personal Tutor Encounters: Understanding the Experience. *Nursing Standard*, 20(50): 35–42.

Earwaker, J (1992) *Helping and Supporting Students*. Buckingham: Open University Press.

Enders, J (2007) The Academic Profession. In Forest, J J F and Altbach, P G (eds) *International Handbook of Higher Education. Springer International Handbooks of Education* (vol 18; pp 5–21). Dordrecht: Springer.

Ghenghesh, P (2017) Personal Tutoring from the Perspective of Tutors and Tutees. *Journal of Further and Higher Education*, 42(4): 570–84.

Grant, A (2006) Personal Tutoring: A System in Crisis? In Thomas, L and Hixenbaugh, P (eds) *Personal Tutoring in Higher Education* (pp 11–20). Stoke-on-Trent: Trentham Books.

Gravells, J and Wallace, S (2007) *Mentoring in the Lifelong Learning Sector* (2nd ed). Exeter: Learning Matters.

Grey, D and Lochtie, D (2016) Comparing Personal Tutoring in the UK and Academic Advising in the US. *Academic Advising Today*, 39(3). [online] Available at: www.nacada.ksu.edu/Resources/Academic-Advising-Today/View-Articles/Comparing-Personal-Tutoring-in-the-UK-and-Academic-Advising-in-the-US.aspx (accessed 30 June 2018).

Grey, D and McIntosh, E (2017) Student Dashboards: The Case for Building Communities of Practice. Presentation at *UK Advising and Tutoring Conference*, Leeds, 12 April 2017.

Gubby, L and McNab, L (2013) Personal Tutoring from the Perspective of the Tutor. *Capture*, 4(1): 7–18.

Gurbutt, D J and Gurbutt, R (2015) Empowering Students to Promote Independent Learning: A Project Utilising Coaching Approaches to Support Learning and Personal Development. *Journal of Learning Development in Higher Education*, 8: 1–17.

Hart, N (1996) The Role of the Personal Tutor in a College of Further Education: A Comparison of Skills Used by Personal Tutors and by Student Counsellors When Working with Students in Distress. *British Journal of Guidance and Counselling*, 24(1): 83–96.

Havergal, C (2015) Is 'Academic Citizenship' Under Strain? [online] Available at: www.timeshigher education.com/features/is-academic-citizenship-under-strain/2018134.article (accessed 30 June 2018).

Kift, S (2009) *Articulating a Transition Pedagogy to Scaffold and to Enhance the First Year Student Learning Experience in Australian Higher Education.* [online] Available at: www.olt.gov.au/resource-first-year-learning-experience-kift-2009 (accessed 30 June 2018).

Kuhn, T (2008) Historical Foundations of Academic Advising. In Gordon, V N, Habley, W R and Grites, T J (eds) *Academic Advising: A Comprehensive Handbook* (2nd ed). San Francisco: Jossey-Bass.

Laycock, M (2009) Personal Tutoring in Higher Education – Where Now and Where Next? Literature Review and Recommendations. *SEDA Specials*, 25. London: Staff and Educational Development Association.

Laycock, M (2017) Personal Tutoring in HE: Where Now and Where Next? Presentation at *Personal Tutoring and Academic Advising: Contemporary Narratives and Developing Practice. The Fourth National Seminar. Centre for Recording Achievement.* Sheffield, 11 October 2017.

Lindsay, S (2011) Do Students in UK Higher Education Institutions Need Personal Tutors? *Learning at City Journal*, 1(1): 40–5.

Lochtie, D (2015) A 'Special Relationship' in Higher Education? What Influence Might the US Higher Education Sector Have in Terms of Support for International Students in the UK? *Perspectives: Policy and Practice in Higher Education*, 20:(2–3): 67–74.

Luck, C (2010) Challenges Faced by Tutors in Higher Education. *Psychodynamic Practice,* 16(3): 273–87.

Malik, S (2000) Students, Tutors and Relationships: The Ingredients of a Successful Student Support Scheme. *Medical Education*, 34: 635–41.

McFarlane, K J (2016) Tutoring the Tutors: Supporting Effective Personal Tutoring. *Active Learning in Higher Education*, 17(1): 77–88.

McIntosh, E and Cross, D (2017) Who Sets the Agenda on Student Engagement? Opinions. *Journal of Educational Innovation, Partnership and Change*, 3: 2. [online] Available at: https://journals. gre.ac.uk/index.php/studentchangeagents/article/view/540 (accessed 30 June 2018).

McIntosh, E (2018) The 4 Step Tutorial Pathway – A Model of Early Intervention & Transitional Support (EI) to Facilitate Resilience and Partnership Working in Personal Tutoring. Presentation at *UK Advising and Tutoring (UKAT) Conference*, Derby, 27 March 2018.

McIntosh, E and Lochtie, D (2018) Embracing Partnership Working in Personal Tutoring – Exploring a Blended Model of Personal Tutoring for UK HE. Presentation at *UK Advising and Tutoring (UKAT) Conference*, Derby, 27 March 2018.

Morgan, M (2012) *Improving the Student Experience: A Practical Guide for Universities and Colleges*. London: Routledge.

Myers, J (2008) Is Personal Tutoring Sustainable? Comparing the Trajectory of the Personal Tutor with that of the Residential Warden. *Teaching in Higher Education*, 13(5): 607–11.

Mynott, G (2016) Personal Tutoring: Positioning Practice in Relation to Policy. *Innovations in Practice*, 10(2): 103–12.

Neville, L (2007) *The Personal Tutor's Handbook*. Basingstoke: Palgrave Macmillan.

Newcastle University (nd) *Senior Tutor Role Description*. [online] Available at: www.ncl.ac.uk/ltds/assets/documents/qsh-personaltutoring-st-role.pdf (accessed 30 June 2018).

National Union of Students (NUS) (2015) *Academic Support Benchmarking Tool*. [online] Available at: www.nusconnect.org.uk/resources/academic-support-benchmarking-tool (accessed 30 June 2018).

Online Etymology Dictionary (nd) Terms searched for: personal, tutor, coach. [online] Available at: www.etymonline.com (accessed 30 June 2018).

Owen, M (2002) 'Sometimes You Feel You're in Niche Time': The Personal Tutor System, a Case Study. *Active Learning in Higher Education*, 3(1): 7–23.

Palmer, S and Szymanska, K (2008) *Cognitive Behavioural Coaching: An Integrative Approach Handbook of Coaching Psychology: A Guide for Practitioners*. New York: Routledge/Taylor and Francis Group.

Plymouth University (nd) *Role Description for Senior Tutors*. [online] Available at: www.plymouth.ac.uk/uploads/production/document/path/2/2456/Role_description_for_Senior_Tutors.pdf (accessed 30 June 2018).

Ralston, N C and Hoffshire, M (2017) An Individualized Approach to Student Transition: Developing a Success Coaching Model. In Cintron, R, Samuel, J and Hinson, J (eds) *Accelerated Opportunity Education Models and Practices* (pp 34–50). Hershey, PA: IGI Global.

Ridley, P (2006) 'Who's Looking After Me?' – Supporting New Personal Tutors. In Thomas, L and Hixenbaugh, P (eds) *Personal Tutoring in Higher Education* (pp 127–36). Stoke-on-Trent: Trentham Books.

Robinson, P (2012) Leeds for Life, Preparing our Students for their Future. *Academic Advising Today*, 35(2). [online] Available at: www.nacada.ksu.edu/Resources/Academic-Advising-Today/View-Articles/Leeds-for-Life-Preparing-Our-Students-for-Their-Future.aspx (accessed 30 June 2018).

Ross, J, Head, K, King, L, Perry, P M and Smith, S (2014) The Personal Development Tutor Role: An Exploration of Student and Lecturer Experiences and Perceptions of That Relationship. *Nurse Education* Today, 34(9): 1207–13.

Sclater, N, Webb, M and Danson, M (2017) *The Future of Data-Driven Decision-Making*. [online] Available at: www.jisc.ac.uk/reports/the-future-of-data-driven-decision-making (accessed 30 June 2018).

Small, F (2013) Enhancing the Role of Personal Tutor in Professional Undergraduate Education. *Inspiring Academic Practice*, 1(1): 1–11.

Smith, E (2008) *Personal Tutoring: An Engineering Subject Centre Guide*. Leicester: Higher Education Academy.

Stenton, A (2017) *Why Personal Tutoring is Essential for Student Success.* [online] Available at: www.heacademy.ac.uk/blog/why-personal-tutoring-essential-student-success (accessed 30 June 2018).

Stephen, D E, O'Connell, P and Hall, M (2008) 'Going the Extra Mile', 'Fire-fighting', or Laissez-faire? Re-evaluating Personal Tutoring Relationships within Mass Higher Education. *Teaching in Higher Education*, 13(4): 449–60.

Stevenson, N (2009) Enhancing the Student Experience by Embedding Personal Tutoring in the Curriculum. *Journal of Hospitality, Leisure, Sport and Tourism Education*, 8(2): 117–22.

Stork, A and Walker, B (2015) *Becoming an Outstanding Personal Tutor: Supporting Learners through Personal Tutoring and Coaching.* Northwich: Critical Publishing.

Swain, H (2008) *The Personal Tutor.* [online] Available at: www.timeshighereducation.co.uk/news/the-personal-tutor/210049.article (accessed 30 June 2018).

The Concise Oxford English Dictionary (1995) Oxford: Clarendon Press.

Thomas, L (2006) Widening Participation and the Increased Need for Personal Tutoring. In Thomas, L and Hixenbaugh, P (eds) *Personal Tutoring in Higher Education* (pp 21–31). Stoke-on-Trent: Trentham Books.

Thomas, L (2012) *Building Student Engagement and Belonging in Higher Education at a Time of Change: Final Report from the What Works? Student Retention and Success Programme.* London: Paul Hamlyn Foundation.

Thomas, L and Jones, R (2017) Student Engagement in the Context of Commuter Students. [online] Available at: http://tsep.org.uk/student-engagement-in-the-context-of-commuter-students (accessed 30 June 2018).

Thomas, L, Hill, M, O'Mahony, J and Yorke, M (2017) *Supporting Student Success: Strategies for Institutional Change. What Works? Student Retention and Success Programme.* Final Report. London: Paul Hamlyn Foundation.

Thomas, L, Hockings, C, Ottaway, J and Jones, R (2015) *Independent Learning: Student Perceptions and Experiences.* York: Higher Education Academy.

Tinto, V (2006–7) Research and Practice of Student Retention: What Next? *Journal of College Student Retention*, 8(1): 1–19.

Walker, B W (2018) A Defining Moment in Personal Tutoring: Reflections on Personal Tutoring Definitions and Their Implications. *IMPact: The University of Lincoln Journal of Higher Education*, 1(1): 104–18. [online] Available at: http://lncn.eu/IMPact9 (accessed 30 June 2018).

Watts, A G (1999) The Role of the Personal Adviser: Concepts and Issues. *Centre for Guidance Studies Occasional Paper.* Derby: Centre for Guidance Studies.

Webb, O, Wyness, L and Cotton, D (2017). Enhancing Access, Retention, Attainment and Progression in Higher Education. [online] Available at: www.heacademy.ac.uk/system/files/resources/enhancing_access_retention_attainment_and_progression_in_higher_education_1.pdf (accessed 30 June 2018).

Whitmore, J (2002) *Coaching for Performance: GROWing People, Performance and Purpose* (3rd ed). London: Nicholas Brealey Publishing.

Whittaker, R (2008) *Quality Enhancement Themes: The First Year Experience – Transition to and During the First Year.* Glasgow: Quality Assurance Agency Scotland.

Wootton, S (2006) Changing Practice in Tutorial Provision Within Post-Compulsory Education. In Thomas, L and Hixenbaugh, P (eds) *Personal Tutoring in Higher Education* (pp 115–25). Stoke-on-Trent: Trentham Books.

Wootton, S (2007) An Inductive Enquiry into Managing Tutorial Provision in Post-Compulsory Education. PhD. Sheffield Hallam University. [online] Available at: https://search-proquest-com.proxy.library.lincoln.ac.uk/pqdtglobal/docview/1913902798/fulltextPDF/5B739D42 F2A846B6PQ/1?accountid=16461 (accessed 30 June 2018).

Yale, A (2017) The Personal Tutor–Student Relationship: Student Expectations and Experiences of Personal Tutoring in Higher Education. *Journal of Further and Higher Education.* doi:10.1080/ 0309877X.2017.1377164

Zepke, N and Leach, L (2010) Beyond Hard Outcomes: 'Soft' Outcomes and Engagement as Student Success. *Teaching in Higher Education*, 15(6): 661–73.

2 Core values and skills of the personal tutor

Chapter aims

This chapter helps you to:

- understand the core values and skills of the effective personal tutor and be able to distinguish between them;

- consider approaches to embedding the core values within your teaching and personal tutoring practice and apply them to different situations;

- develop techniques to improve your personal tutoring core skills and apply them to different situations.

Introduction

This chapter explores the core values and skills of the effective personal tutor in two separate sections. It does so by exploring typical scenarios that you are likely to face.

Section 1: What are the core values of the effective personal tutor?

We have already explored the ways in which students can be supported. Here, we look at the core values which should become increasingly evident in your day-to-day actions, behaviour and approach. This section does not aim to explore extensively professional values in academia or in HE more generally as they are detailed elsewhere (for example, Higher Education Academy, 2011; Quality Assurance Agency, 2018; Department for Education, 2017). Instead it aims to build upon the context they provide in order to focus specifically on the values of an effective personal tutor. The core values of the effective personal tutor are:

- high expectations;

- approachability;

- diplomacy;

- being non-judgemental;

- compassion;

- the 'equal partner, not superior' approach;

- authenticity;

- valuing students as individuals.

What is a core value and how do I know what mine are?

Embodying the core values of the personal tutor, when compared with other positive values, is fundamental to providing effective student support. Furthermore, when values underpin core skills (section 2 of this chapter, beginning on page 39) and key activities (Chapters 4 and 5), they can have a significant impact on student outcomes.

So, what is a value and how does it relate to your personal tutor role? Values are things that you believe are important to the way that you live and work; and core values are those which hold the greatest amount of meaning to you. They are central to the decisions you make in the lecture theatre, seminar room and while working one-to-one with your students. Another way to look at it is that your values are your guiding principles which shape your priorities and in many cases dictate your day-to-day behaviours and approach to people and work. Your values can be seen in the actions you take and in the way you respond to dilemmas, challenges and adversity. These should be in line with the *'underlying values of higher education... the joy and value of knowledge pursued for its own sake; the pursuit of the good... the fundamental importance of freedom of speech and vigorous disagreement based on mutual respect'* (Department for Education, 2017, p 8).

A core value is only truly a core value if you *live* by it and it can be seen in your actions (at least the majority of the time). When the things that you do and the way you behave match your core values, then you are likely to feel satisfied and content. For example, if you value working with people and you sit in front of a computer screen from 9am to 5pm every day you are less likely to be satisfied with your profession. This is because it is important for your core values and actions to align in order for you to feel that you are doing valuable work. At this point, it is useful to consider the reasons why you chose to pursue a career in higher education and academia.

Usually, values are perceived as quite abstract as well as difficult to identify and explain to others. When you discover your own core values, you discover what is truly important to you. A good way for you to try to understand your values is to think deeply about the following questions from a work-life and personal perspective.

Critical thinking activity 1

Identify examples of when you were the most happy, proud, fulfilled and satisfied at work.

1. Why did you feel that way?

2. What factors contributed to you feeling like that?

3. Now, try to encapsulate each of those examples into a descriptive word or words. For example, achievement, balance, generosity, happiness, mastery, self-reliance, teamwork.

4. Write these down in no particular order. Compare them as pairs and ask yourself: 'If I could satisfy only one of these regularly, which one would I choose?' Keep doing this until they are in order.

The words that you have listed could be seen as your individual core values. Identifying your core values isn't an easy task. When working with students there can be many conflicting pressures and choices to make, and when many of the options seem reasonable it is reassuring to rely on your core values, as well as the values of the institution you work for, to guide you in the right direction.

How to develop the personal tutor core values

The values of an academic department or programme rarely, if ever, appears on a meeting agenda. For you to understand the core values of the personal tutor, you need to see the values in action and the following case study and related activity allows you to do this.

CASE STUDY

Mansoor's story

Mansoor is in his second year of teaching sport and exercise science at a high-ranking university.

1. During a seminar on the exercise, fitness and health module with a group of level 4 students studying sport and exercise science, Mansoor leads a discussion around the emotive subjects of health, cancer and bereavement. James, one of Mansoor's tutees, becomes upset during the activity. In order to support James, and instead of excluding him from this activity, Mansoor suggests that he will get involved in the activity himself so that they can work through it together. When they feed back to the class, Mansoor offers a number of personal experiences about the subject which informs the group discussion. In a subsequent personal tutorial with James, Mansoor finds out that James greatly appreciated his efforts and that working through the activity together had helped them to come to terms with the subject matter. Mansoor recommends the Student Well-being Office as a source of further support and offers details of his colleague who works in student services.

2. Mansoor is delivering a strength and conditioning class to a group of level six students (including several of his tutees), where, in order to achieve a first-class mark on their assignment, the students need to work in groups. The purpose of the group activity is for the students to demonstrate leadership by planning and delivering their own conditioning session to the rest of the class. A heated argument begins within a student team where accusations arise that one of the group is not getting involved or making an effective contribution. The other students believe that this is damaging their chances of getting good marks. There are a number of options which Mansoor quickly considers, but he opts to informally mediate the situation. He speaks to the students individually to get their perspective, taking a non-directive approach, particularly using the question 'why?' repeatedly. This helps Mansoor to quickly get to the crux of the issue. Using exploratory questions helps him to dig deeper rather than accepting superficial responses from the students, many of whom are reluctant to speak up initially. Once Mansoor is clear about the issues from both sides, he works with the students collectively to develop a consensus between the group members. This helps them to focus effectively on the task. Mansoor later asks the students to reflect upon this as part of a group tutorial.

3. During a level 5 module at the end of the academic year, Mansoor sets a mock examination paper, under timed conditions, which will be peer-assessed using the exam grading criteria. Instead of watching the students take the test, he explains to the class that he will also sit the exam under the same conditions and put forward his paper to be assessed too.

Critical thinking activity 2

» *In each case decide which core value (from the personal tutor core values list at the start of this section) you believe Mansoor is embodying, and identify the positive benefit being created from this approach.*

Discussion

In the previous scenarios, Mansoor can be said to display the following core values of the personal tutor.

1. Compassion – this required Mansoor to put himself in James' position and to take action to ensure a positive outcome. Even though the action taken may not work effectively with all students, the tutor must appear to be concerned, caring and supportive (Rhodes and Jinks, 2005; Stephen et al, 2008; Ross et al, 2014). If students feel their tutor does not care the relationship is given no value and can feel like a waste of time (Yale, 2017). In this case, Mansoor's compassion enabled James to participate in the activity inclusively. It allowed James to continue to engage in the learning activity at the time, developed his relationship with Mansoor as personal tutor and enabled him to contact Student Well-being if he needs further support.

2.   Diplomacy – instead of Mansoor taking punitive action against the students, he demonstrated solid communication skills in order to sensitively and tactfully mediate the situation. By becoming skilled in the art of diplomacy, de-escalating a tense situation and reflecting upon the experience with the students later, Mansoor found a very useful way to engage and work positively with the students for whom he has responsibility (Wootton, 2007).

3.   The 'equal partner, not superior' approach – institutions and academics are beginning to conceive of students as partners in the education more than ever before (Thomas et al, 2015; McIntosh and Cross, 2017). The tutor–tutee partnership is a two-way relationship with a shared and negotiated agenda founded upon mutual recognition and respect (Wootton, 2006; Stephen et al, 2008; Yale, 2017). This relationship can be further facilitated by displaying to students that you understand the pressures they face, that you too have been a student and, on occasion, you also have challenges to overcome in your work (for example when receiving negative feedback about a proposed journal article submission). This approach also allows you to role model good behaviour and demonstrate a positive attitude in response to stressful situations.

The remaining core values from the list are explored in Table 2.1.

Table 2.1 *Remaining core values of the effective personal tutor*

Core value	Explanation	Typical context
High expectations	To challenge your students by demanding maximum effort and application as well as expecting a level of independence (Chickering and Gamson, 1987; Wootton, 2007; Thomas et al, 2015).	Student achievement is closely linked to the expectations that tutors place on them. Students who are expected to learn more or perform better generally may be more likely to do so, while those held to lower expectations may achieve less. Lowering expectations of students can become a self-fulfilling prophecy. The way to avoid this is to raise expectations for all areas of a student's life and ensure they receive the support they need to reach those high expectations. This is linked to the notion of independent learning (see Chapter 5) and will positively affect their grades and career prospects, as well the success rates of the institution.
Approachability	Being seen as friendly and easy to talk to is an essential skill for a personal tutor (Owen, 2002; Braine and Parnell, 2011; Ghenghesh, 2017; Yale, 2017). Without approachability, students may find interactions disappointing and hurried, they may be discouraged from seeking support from a tutor who appears to be busy and even drop out if they feel they are not able to engage meaningfully with them (Owen, 2002; Wilcox et al, 2005; Dobinson-Harrington, 2006).	When an experienced tutor works with students on a one-to-one basis, they can often see when something isn't quite right. It is possible to use verbal or non-verbal cues to explore this, for example a lack of eye contact, negative body language and/or demeanour. Tutors can become more approachable to a student and encourage them to open up by focusing on the following: • having open and welcoming body language; • having the confidence to ask how students are, using general and open questions, for example, 'how are you?', 'how are things?'; • reiterating the importance of trust in the tutor–tutee relationship. This can take time to establish so clear boundaries and a focus on confidentiality should be paramount and should include a frank discussion about disclosure and a duty to declare (for example if the tutee is at risk of harming themselves or others).

Table 2.1 (*Cont.*)

Core value	Explanation	Typical context
Being non-judgemental	As part of their training, tutors should be encouraged to avoid making judgements about students' lives based on their own values and university experiences (Wheeler and Birtle, 1993; Swain, 2008, Wisker et al, 2007; Stenton, 2017). The UK HE sector is built upon the belief that all students, regardless of background, should be supported so they can access, progress within and succeed in HE, and the tutor should embrace this wholeheartedly (Department for Education, 2017).	It can be challenging for a tutor, no matter how experienced they are, to completely reserve judgement when it comes to students. The core value of being non-judgemental means striving to overcome the need to label students, giving them the opportunity to engage with you and develop a healthy rapport. In order to be successful in their own right, students need to be given autonomy, the freedom to make mistakes and to learn from them, and be provided with the tools and support to cope with setbacks. Unfortunately, tutors often witness students struggling and feel powerless to prevent their distress. However, being an effective personal tutor involves motivating and inspiring students to achieve their potential. In order for a student to achieve this, and hopefully improve their behaviour or attitude, it is important to engage with them, individually and in groups, as often as you are able to do so.
Authenticity	Students must see their personal tutor as someone who appears authentic. This includes the appetite to support students selflessly and is essential when developing a healthy tutor–student relationship (Wisker et al, 2007; Yale, 2017).	Students are perceptive and can tell when a personal tutor is authentic and that their concern for them is genuine. Tutors are likely to have greater impact upon students if they feel that the help, advice and support the tutor is providing is honest and given as objectively as possible.
Valuing students as individuals	It is important to students that universities are student-focused and personal tutoring is an important element of that (Higher Education Academy, 2017). Students want to feel that they matter and are known to, and supported by, the university, are valued as individuals and not as 'just another student'. Students are not homogenous and it is important to differentiate between students' values, interests, background and goals (Hudson, 2006 in Stephen et al, 2008; Swain, 2008; Higher Education Academy, 2017; Thomas and Jones, 2017; Calcagno et al, 2017).	As tuition fees have risen so have student expectations of tutors and support services. At the same time student numbers have grown and resources have become stretched. Tutors often struggle to meet demand and to balance the needs of all their students, particularly when class sizes are large and the curriculum is packed with assessments. There is a danger that the massification of HE will involve treating students like a number, or as 'customers' who are paying for the privilege of being at university. An effective personal tutor is aware of this challenge and can work towards bridging this gap by valuing students as individuals, even if student–staff ratios are high. There are ways of managing this workload effectively, via group tutorials, which will be discussed later.

Individual and shared core values

Having established what the core values of the personal tutor are, you are hopefully thinking 'I believe I have a lot of these values (or similar ones) and I believe I show them through my actions a lot of the time when working with students'. To really have an impact on student support and, ultimately, students achieving their potential, these values need to be shared and showed consistently by other staff, as well as being recognised and promoted by middle and senior managers.

Core values directly affect employee actions, behaviour and organisational culture. Therefore, having positive and shared core values that everyone buys into (staff and students) is one of the key ways to improve consistency of performance. An academic study (Guiso et al, 2013) *'found that there is a relationship between a culture of strong values ("high integrity") as perceived by employees and organisational performance. That is to say, the values need to be "lived" throughout the organisation'* (The Great Place to Work Institute, 2014, p 5).

Critical thinking activity 3

» *What three actions could you take to embed the core values of the personal tutor into your work with students either within the class, in a group tutorial or working one-to-one?*

Discussion

Compare your answers to the following suggested ideas for embedding the core values of the personal tutor into your work with students:

- explain the core values to your students;

- display the core values in your module handbooks or Virtual Learning Environment (VLE) sites, with examples of actions that embody them;

- tell students what they can expect from you (in other words, to display the core values).

Section 2: What are the core skills of the effective personal tutor?

Now that you have a firm grasp on effective personal tutoring using core values, let's examine core skills. The core skills of the effective personal tutor are:

- building genuine rapport with your students;

- active listening and questioning;

- challenging;

- reflecting back and summarising;

- developing independence and resilience;
- teamwork;
- decision-making and problem-solving;
- role modelling;
- proactivity, creativity and innovation;
- working under pressure;
- consistency;
- critical thinking;
- digital literacy.

What is a core skill?

A skill refers to the ability to do something well. In addition, examples of synonyms for skill include expertise, adeptness, mastery, competence, efficiency, experience and professionalism, to name but a few. These highly descriptive words are connected with taking action or doing something, but also ensuring you do it well.

Core skills are the day-to-day actions you take to support your students. Having the right skills is important to be able to carry out your job, but it is your core values that drive you to take those actions repeatedly. So, to have the greatest impact and to develop into an effective personal tutor, you need to have and use both the core values and skills together.

Different categories of personal tutor core skills

The core skills of the personal tutor can be broken down into different subgroups as seen in Figure 2.1.

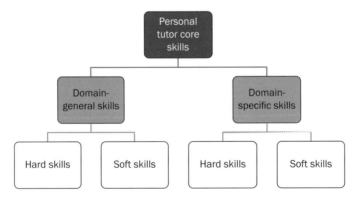

Figure 2.1 *Different categories of personal tutor core skills*

The first way to divide the core skills is into domain-general and domain-specific. Domain-general are common skills that may not necessarily be directly related to your personal tutor role and which you would find useful for most jobs, for example good communication, time management, problem-solving and organisational skills. Domain-specific skills are those that are more directly related to your personal tutor role.

Hard and soft skills

A further way to divide the core skills is into 'hard' and 'soft' skills. Table 2.2 gives examples of these.

Table 2.2 *Hard and soft skills examples*

Hard skills	Soft skills
Effective curriculum planning.	Building rapport.
Conducting effective research.	Decision-making.
Effective scheduling and time management.	Reflecting back and summarising.
Help students develop applications for postgraduate study.	Active listening and questioning.

Zepke and Leach (2010) argue for curriculum outcomes to include key skills which are hard (communication, application of numbers, information technology, problem-solving, improving personal performance and working with others) and soft (social skills, coping with authority, organisational skills such as personal planning, analytical skills such as exercising judgement and personal skills such as insight, motivation, confidence, reliability and awareness of health). Soft outcomes do not measure success objectively; they measure it according to students' perceptions of the progress made towards their own goals or that of their programme (Zepke and Leach 2010). Hard skills are normally related to a specific task or action, for example planning a group tutorial or undertaking a one-to-one, and we look at both of these in detail in Chapter 4. In terms of recruitment and selection, the hard skills are essential for getting an interview, but it is usually the soft skills (which are personality driven) that will get you the job because educational institutions target practitioners who will be a good fit within the department and make a good impression on students.

How to develop the personal tutor core skills

This section focuses on developing the core skills that are required when delivering effective personal tutoring. Table 2.3 outlines some background or explanation to the personal tutor core skills.

Table 2.3 *Core skills of the effective personal tutor*

Core skills	Explanation and/or example
1. Building genuine rapport with your students	Developing a harmonious relationship with a student in which each person is able to communicate effectively and understand the other's feelings or ideas.
2. Active listening and questioning	Asking intelligent questions and listening to/observing the responses is integral to ensuring that tutoring aids retention (Wilcox et al, 2005; Dobinson-Harrington, 2006; Wisker et al, 2007; Thomas, 2017; Stenton, 2017). It is also important to the student that their tutor listens actively and is able to interpret clear verbal and non-verbal messages.
3. Challenging	Students are more likely to succeed if tutors challenge them to achieve more (Mayhew et al, 2010). Challenging may be possible in discussion sessions, when setting goals and milestones or when encouraging them to embrace autonomous and independent learning (Rhodes and Jinks, 2005; Mayhew et al, 2010; Thomas et al, 2015; Ralston and Hoffshire, 2017). Guiding students to think more carefully about their situation and challenging the assumptions that they make may help them to see things they may otherwise fail to recognise.
4. Reflecting back and summarising	It is important to help students to reflect upon their motivations, aspirations and needs alongside their assessment feedback in order to make sense of their academic progress (Hughes, 2004; Stephen et al, 2008; Stenton, 2017; Calcagno et al, 2017). Showing students you understand what they have said by listening actively and paraphrasing it back to them will not only help your students to learn but also help you to continually reflect upon your own experience as a practitioner (Schön, 1983; Wisker et al, 2007; Small, 2013).
5. Developing independence and resilience	The quality of the academic environment is critical in helping students foster the resilience they need to succeed. The ability to embrace and learn from failure can be developed by personal tutors if they possess the innovative pedagogies required to do so (McIntosh and Shaw, 2017). As nurturing strong, independent learners is a traditional value and mission of HE, academics need the skills and knowledge required to help students understand and practise effective independent learning (Thomas et al, 2015; McIntosh and Shaw, 2017).
6. Teamwork	The ability to work effectively with your fellow tutors is paramount. It is also likely to grow in importance as you progress throughout your career and develop your academic programme (McCabe and McCabe, 2010). The challenges of working as part of a tutorial team and good practice in doing so are explored in Chapter 3.
7. Decision-making and problem-solving	Thinking through and making difficult decisions, even when there doesn't appear to be a clear consensus or solution.

Core skills	Explanation and/or example
8. Role modelling	Serving as a role model, academically, professionally and in terms of reflective practice, is an important part of being a personal tutor (Small, 2013). Embracing positive core values sets a healthy precedent for students; it also maintains professional boundaries and helps students to see what professionalism looks like.
9. Proactivity, creativity and innovation	Creativity is a requirement to succeed as a tutor and innovative practices are an indicator of success in student retention. Effective personal tutoring needs to be proactive because students prefer any interaction to be instigated by the tutor (Malik, 2000; Whittaker, 2008; Stephen et al, 2008; McCabe and McCabe, 2010; Thomas and Jones, 2017). However, a balance between proactive tutoring and student choice/autonomy is also required, especially in the face of competing daily pressures faced by both tutors and students (Stephen et al, 2008; Whittaker, 2008). The management of boundaries and the discussion of expectations is very important here. Boundaries and independent learning are explored in Chapter 3.
10. Working under pressure	Tutors are often exposed to many emotional situations, including listening to some distressing circumstances involving their students. This may leave both tutors and students feeling anxious and overwhelmed (Earwaker, 1992; Stephen et al, 2008; McFarlane, 2016). The time to support students in this way may not necessarily be included in their timetable or the time allocated may not be sufficient, forcing tutors to work beyond their contract to provide the best support they can (Hart, 1996; Owen, 2002; Havergal; 2015). In the face of these significant challenges tutors need to remain calm in order to stay effective and be sure to ask for help and support from others in order to perform their role.
11. Consistency	Tutors need to be a consistent and reliable point of contact and so must be transparent in letting students know when and how to contact them. If tutors advertise certain times when they will be available to students in their office they have to make sure that these times are consistent and communicated to students properly. If these circumstances change they must offer a clear alternative (Swain, 2008; Ross et al, 2014).
12. Critical thinking	It is vital that academics demonstrate and model to students a critical thinking approach to the management of information and help them to appreciate the dialectic processes of constructing knowledge (Wingate, 2007; Thomas et al, 2015).
13. Digital literacy	Digitally fluent tutors use technology to support their tutoring. This can promote innovative pedagogical practice and can lead to richer interactions with students, validating particular aspects of digital literacy and recommending these practices to them (Bennett, 2013; Higher Education Academy, 2017; Grey and McIntosh, 2017).

As a personal tutor, you need to choose which of these core skills, or which skill combinations, are appropriate for particular contexts and specific students. It is through practice and reflection that tutors can develop the experience to understand when one skill is more appropriate than another. The next two critical thinking activities explore two particular skills.

1. Building genuine rapport

Students place great importance on the quality of the relationship with their personal tutor and this can have a positive effect on their learning and progression (Braine and Parnell 2011; Small, 2013). Focusing on cultivating a healthy rapport can help to focus a student's attention, improve their enjoyment in learning and increase the time they spend engaging in study. It can also help to improve their attendance (Buskist and Saville, 2004; Benson et al, 2005, cited in Wilson and Ryan, 2013). Tutor–student rapport can increase student engagement levels both inside and outside of the classroom, including developing confidence in public speaking and asking questions of tutors, as well as improving student motivation levels (Starcher, 2011).

Building this relationship and establishing a rapport with students is therefore an essential part of being an effective personal tutor (Rhodes and Jinks, 2005; Wisker et al, 2007; Swain, 2008; Braine and Parnell, 2011). If students have a strong, positive rapport with their tutor and with their cohort they are more likely to understand, and be responsive to, tutor opinions and influence. Relationships should be close, supportive, personal, safe, confidential (unless appropriate to disclose), trusting and empowering (Stephen et al, 2008; Small, 2013; Calcagno et al, 2017; Thomas et al, 2017). This may be something that comes naturally to some practitioners but can take more time and effort for others. Rapport is affected by the tutor's natural personality as well as the student's nature and the context within which they work together. For example, exploring and understanding the difference between seeing students in classes and also meeting them in one-to-ones and group tutorials can greatly affect how rapport is developed. It is important to realise that the skill of building rapport can be learned and improved over time. This is an important skill to develop because a student's relationship with their personal tutor is the embodiment of a student's overall relationship with the institution (Yale, 2017).

Critical thinking activity 4

» *Some techniques for building rapport with your students follow. Think about them in general terms and from your own opinion and experience, rank the strategies one to six, with one being the technique you view as the most effective and six as the least effective. Are there any more techniques that you can add?*

Building rapport techniques	Rank 1–6
Making and maintaining sensitive eye contact	
Reinforcing and affirming the student's gestures	
Subtly matching and mirroring body language	

Building rapport techniques	Rank 1–6
Varying the tone of your voice	
Picking up on favourite phrases or key words and subtly building these into the conversation	
Validating through active listening and asking open-ended questions	

Now that you have your personalised rank of techniques, start with number one and work through the list by practising and reflecting on the impact with your students.

2. Decision-making and problem-solving

As you develop your career as an academic and personal tutor, you may find that sometimes you can find yourself 'between a rock and a hard place', facing conflicting pressures. Using creative problem-solving to make difficult decisions can be one of the most challenging parts of the tutor role, even when decisions are clouded by feelings and seemingly without clear consensus or solution (McCabe and McCabe, 2010). Conflicting tutoring ideologies may exist when seeking to meet the needs of the student, your career (by focusing on high-profile research activity), and the institution (Dobinson-Harrington, 2006; Watts, 2011).

Below are some scenarios. It is possible that you could find yourself in similar situations as students progress through their studies. These scenarios are deliberately described as being at specific points in the student lifecycle, as identified in Morgan's (2012) *Student Experience Practitioner Model*, presented and discussed in Chapter 5.

1. It is December and one of your level 5 joint honours Photography and Creative Writing students wants to leave the university because her wedding photography business has begun to take off. She has been doing well with taking bookings alongside her studies but has begun to find it difficult to concentrate on both work and study. The money she has raised through these weddings has been helpful but, having turned away good business to focus on assignments, has not been enough to avoid mounting levels of student debt. This is making the student question the value of her degree in terms of both its necessity for her business and the impact on her finances. She is a very capable student and you expect her to complete the course with a good honours degree. In the last two academic years, the graduation and degree outcomes across the institution (including this programme specifically) have been deemed unsatisfactory by the university's senior leadership team.

2. It is January and one of your level 4 Mechanical Engineering students is behind. She has missed the deadline to hand in a number of assignments to your colleagues for marking but she has managed to submit the assessment for your particular module. She has relatively low attendance and poor punctuality, and your colleagues report that she has appeared disengaged in classes even though you find that she works well in yours. However, in your opinion, she is quite vulnerable and you believe she would struggle to get on another course or to get a job if she left the course without achieving her qualification or progressing to the next level. As her

personal tutor you have been trying to support her development during your one-to-ones but this appears to be getting worse. Most of your colleagues openly state that she should be removed from the course. The retention rates on this programme have been very poor for the last three years.

3. It is February and one of your level 6 Early Childhood Studies students has poor attendance (71 per cent and the institution's target for all students is over 80 per cent) and also poor attainment (his average mark is 45 per cent). He has given you reasons for this, including ongoing dental work that he is having. He also reports that his two young children, for whom he is the sole carer, have been experiencing repeated bouts of illness over the last few weeks, including chicken pox and tonsillitis. The student has emailed on only a few occasions to explain these events and, as such, has a mixture of authorised and unauthorised absences on his record, as defined in the university's attendance policy. You are also aware that his family have serious money issues, he has limited time to work to fund his studies and the family rely upon his student loan. At an exam board at the end of the autumn semester you have been asked by the chair to recommend whether he should be allowed to re-sit the two modules he has failed, and do so alongside taking his spring modules, or whether he should either interrupt/suspend his studies or terminate them completely.

Critical thinking activity 5

1. For each scenario, consider the following questions.

    a. What decisions or actions would you take?

    b. What factors would you need to consider?

As you hopefully appreciate, there isn't always a perfectly correct answer; there is only what is the best option for that context at that time. Doing what is right for the student should be your first priority. However, this is easy to say. Your views may be in conflict with those of the institution. The ideal situation is when the institution always puts the students' interests first through its shared values, policies and decisions. The institutional self-assessment system at the end of this chapter and those that follow illustrate ways in which 'bigger picture' issues can be influenced and prompt you to act.

Summary

The core values of the effective personal tutor are your guiding principles which shape your priorities and, in many cases, dictate your day-to-day behaviours and approach to people and work. These principles are about putting your own agenda aside to focus on the best method(s) of supporting your students. They can be seen in the actions you take with students and can be shared by your colleagues, department and institution. When positive values are shared, this improves the organisational culture and ultimately the institution's key performance indicators.

Learning checklist

Tick off each point when you feel confident you understand it.

☐ *I understand that effective personal tutoring requires the adoption of particular core values and that it is important to take time to reflect on whether my current values and educational philosophy are consistent with my students' best interests.*

☐ *I understand that core skills are the day-to-day actions I take to support my students. Having the right skills is important to be able to carry out my job, but it is my core values which will drive me to take those actions consistently.*

☐ *I realise that all personal tutor core skills can be learned and improved with practice and reflection.*

Critical reflections

1. Compare and contrast the similarities and differences between your own values as an academic and the core values of the personal tutor.

2. To what extent do you believe your PG Cert in Teaching and Learning in Higher Education or induction focused on improving your core skills? What, if anything, do you think could be done to improve this?

3. Evaluate whether effective hard skills or soft skills have the greatest impact upon students' success.

4. How well do your students display the core values of the personal tutor or similar positive values? What factors do you believe are influential in this?

5. To what extent does your current institution explain and promote its shared core values to its staff? If you have experience of more than one institution, compare and contrast the two institutions' approaches to its shared core values, using examples.

Personal tutor self-assessment system

What it is for

The personal tutor self-assessment system is designed for you and your institution to self-score current performance and identify targets for improvement against each of the book's chapter themes. You can use it to continually reflect and judge where you and your institution are against particular standards. You will achieve a score at the end of each chapter leading to a cumulative score at the end of the book. This final score will rate you and your institution separately.

How to use it

To identify current standards you should choose the level that best describes you and your educational institution. These can then be used to set targets for future development. Bear in mind when doing this that the levels are sequential and incremental. The content of the level below is not repeated and it is assumed this has already been achieved. For example, to achieve the intermediate level you will have achieved the minimum standard and beginner level.

The personal tutor core values and skills are repeated below to aid this chapter's self-assessment.

Core values:

- high expectations;
- approachability;
- diplomacy;
- being non-judgemental;
- compassion;
- the 'equal partner, not superior' approach;
- authenticity;
- valuing students as individuals.

Core skills:

- building genuine rapport with your students;
- active listening and questioning;
- challenging;
- reflecting back and summarising;
- developing independence and resilience;
- teamwork;
- decision-making and problem-solving;
- role modelling;
- proactivity, creativity and innovation;
- working under pressure;
- consistency;
- critical thinking;
- digital literacy.

PERSONAL TUTOR SELF-ASSESSMENT SYSTEM : Chapter 2 Core values and skills of the personal tutor

	Minimum standard 1 star	Beginner level 2 star	Intermediate level 3 star	Advanced level 4 star	Expert level 5 star
Individual (core values)	My day-to-day actions with students generally display over half of the core values.	I am conscious to display all of the core values through my interactions with students in lessons, group tutorials and one-to-ones.	I often reflect upon the impact that the core values have on the performance of my students. The reflections inform my personal development targets.	Feedback I receive on my classes, group tutorials and one-to-ones reflect the core values.	I explain and promote the impact the core values have on my students, both within and outside of my curriculum team.
Individual (core skills)	I regularly use over half of the core skills in classes, group tutorials and one-to-ones, as well as with colleagues.	I use all of the core skills. They have a clear and positive impact on the relationships with my students and colleagues.	I often reflect upon the impact that the core skills have on the performance of my students. The reflections inform my personal development targets.	Feedback I receive on my classes, group tutorials and one-to-ones reflect the core skills.	I explain and promote the impact the core skills have on my students both within and outside of my programme team.
Institutional (core values)	My institution's values are similar to, or in some cases the same as, the core values. These are shared with new and existing staff at least twice within an academic year.	Deans and Heads of School discuss the core values in meetings. Discussions take place about how staff can embed these into their day-to-day activities, for example in schemes of work, lesson plans and one-to-ones.	All staff have a constructive appraisal which, in part, reviews how the core values are being embedded into every employee's activities.	All staff have a clear understanding of the core values and the importance of embedding them into their day-to-day work.	Student voice feedback shows that the majority of students feel the core values have a positive impact on their learning, progress and well-being.
Institutional (core skills)	Most staff use over half of the core skills with students. Evidence of this is shown through student voice feedback.	All staff receive regular training to develop the core skills and are encouraged to take ownership of this process.	Feedback from line managers routinely comments on employees' use of the core skills with students and colleagues. This feedback informs the appraisal process.	The core skills are consistently and routinely improved through varied strategies. Staff are encouraged to implement ways of assessing how effective the core skills are at improving student outcomes.	Student voice feedback shows the majority of students feel that the core skills employed by staff benefit their learning, progress and well-being.

The self-assessment system is available as a free download from the publisher's website and the authors' websites (all listed at the start of the book).

References

Bennett, L (2013) Learning from the Early Adopters: Developing the Digital Practitioner. *Research in Learning Technology*, 22. [online] Available at: https://journal.alt.ac.uk/index.php/rlt/article/view/1450/html (accessed 30 June 2018).

Braine, M E and Parnell, J (2011) Exploring Students' Perceptions and Experience of Personal Tutors. *Nurse Education Today*, 31: 904–10.

Buskist, W and Saville, B K (2004) Rapport-Building: Creative Positive Emotional Contexts for Enhancing Teaching and Learning, in Perlman, B, McCann, L I and McFadden, S H (eds) *Lessons Learned: Practical Advice for the Teaching of Psychology* (vol 2; pp 149–55). Washington, DC: American Psychological Society.

Calcagno, L, Walker, D and Grey, D J (2017) Building Relationships: A Personal Tutoring Framework to Enhance Student Transition and Attainment. *Student Engagement in Higher Education Journal*, 1(2): 88–99.

Chickering, A W and Gamson, Z F (1987) *Principles of Good Practice for Undergraduate Education.* Racine, WI: Johnson Foundation.

Department for Education (2017) *Securing Student Success: Risk-Based Regulation for Teaching Excellence, Social Mobility and Informed Choice in Higher Education – Government Consultation on Behalf of the Office for Students.* London: Department for Education. [online] Available at: https://consult.education.gov.uk/higher-education/higher-education-regulatory-framework/supporting_documents/HE%20reg%20framework%20condoc%20FINAL%2018%20October%20FINAL%20FINAL.pdf (accessed 30 June 2018).

Dobinson-Harrington, A (2006) Personal Tutor Encounters: Understanding the Experience. *Nursing Standard*, 20(50): 35–42.

Earwaker, J (1992) *Helping and Supporting Students.* Buckingham: Open University Press.

Ghenghesh, P (2017) Personal Tutoring from the Perspective of Tutors and Tutees. *Journal of Further and Higher Education*, 42(4): 570–84.

Grey, D and McIntosh, E (2017) Top Tips for Effective Personal Tutoring. [online] Available at: www.ukat.uk/blog/posts/2017/july/10-top-tips-for-effective-personal-tutoring (accessed 30 June 2018).

Guiso, L, Sapienza, P and Zingales, L (2013) *The Value of Corporate Culture.* Chicago Booth Research Paper No. 13–80; Fama-Miller Working Paper. [online] Available at: https://ssrn.com/abstract=2353486 or http://dx.doi.org/10.2139/ssrn.2353486 (accessed 30 June 2018).

Hart, N (1996) The Role of the Personal Tutor in a College of Further Education: A Comparison of Skills Used by Personal Tutors and by Student Counsellors When Working with Students in Distress. *British Journal of Guidance and Counselling*, 24(1): 83–96.

Havergal, C (2015) Is 'Academic Citizenship' Under Strain? [online] Available at: www.timeshighereducation.com/features/is-academic-citizenship-under-strain/2018134.article (accessed 30 June 2018).

Higher Education Academy (2011) UK Professional Standards Framework. York: Higher Education Academy. [online] Available at: www.heacademy.ac.uk/system/files/downloads/ukpsf_2011_english.pdf (accessed 30 June 2018).

Hudson, R (2006) cited in Stephen, D E, O'Connell, P and Hall, M (2008) 'Going the Extra Mile', 'Fire-fighting', or Laissez-faire? Re-evaluating Personal Tutoring Relationships within Mass Higher Education. *Teaching in Higher Education*, 13(4): 449–60.

Malik, S (2000) Students, Tutors and Relationships: The Ingredients of a Successful Student Support Scheme. *Medical Education*, 34: 635–41.

Mayhew, M J, Vanderlinden, K and Kim, E K (2010) A Multi-Level Assessment of the Impact of Orientation Programs on Student Learning. *Research in Higher Education*, 51: 320–45.

McCabe, L L and McCabe, E R B (2010) *How to Succeed in Academics* (2nd ed). Berkeley, CA: University of California Press.

McFarlane, K J (2016) Tutoring the Tutors: Supporting Effective Personal Tutoring. *Active Learning in Higher Education*, 17(1): 77–88.

McIntosh, E and Cross, D (2017) Who Sets the Agenda on Student Engagement? *Opinions Journal of Educational Innovation, Partnership and Change*, 3(2). [online] Available at: https://journals.gre.ac.uk/index.php/studentchangeagents/article/view/540 (accessed 30 June 2018).

Morgan, M (2012) *Improving the Student Experience: The Practical Guide for Universities and Colleges*. London: Routledge.

Owen, M (2002) 'Sometimes You Feel You're in Niche Time': The Personal Tutor System, a Case Study. *Active Learning in Higher Education*, 3(1): 7–23.

Quality Assurance Agency (2018) *Revised UK Quality Code for Higher Education*. Gloucester: QAA. [online] Available at: www.qaa.ac.uk/docs/qaa/quality-code/revised-uk-quality-code-for-higher-education.pdf?sfvrsn=4c19f781_6 (accessed 30 June 2018).

Ralston, N C and Hoffshire, M (2017) An Individualized Approach to Student Transition: Developing a Success Coaching Model. In Cintron, R, Samuel, J and Hinson, J (eds) *Accelerated Opportunity Education Models and Practices* (pp 34–50). Hershey, PA: IGI Global.

Rhodes, S and Jinks, A (2005) Personal Tutors' Views of Their Role with Pre-registration Nursing Students: An Exploratory Study. *Nurse Education Today*, 25(5): 390–7.

Ross, J, Head, K, King, L, Perry, P M and Smith, S (2014) The Personal Development Tutor Role: An Exploration of Student and Lecturer Experiences and Perceptions of That Relationship. *Nurse Education Today*, 34(9): 1207–13.

Schön, D (1983) *The Reflective Practitioner. How Professionals Think in Action*. New York: Basic Books.

Small, F (2013) Enhancing the Role of Personal Tutor in Professional Undergraduate Education. *Inspiring Academic Practice*, 1(1): 1–11.

Starcher, K (2011) Intentionally Building Rapport with Students. *College Teaching*, 59(4): 162.

Stenton, A (2017) *Why Personal Tutoring is Essential for Student Success*. [online] Available at: www.heacademy.ac.uk/blog/why-personal-tutoring-essential-student-success (accessed 30 June 2018).

Stephen, D E, O'Connell, P and Hall, M (2008) 'Going the Extra Mile', 'Fire-fighting', or Laissez-faire? Re-evaluating Personal Tutoring Relationships within Mass Higher Education. *Teaching in Higher Education*, 13(4): 449–60.

Swain, H (2008) *The Personal Tutor*. [online] Available at: www.timeshighereducation.co.uk/news/the-personal-tutor/210049.article (accessed 30 June 2018).

The Great Place to Work Institute (2014) *Organisational Values. Are They Worth the Bother? How Values Can Transform Your Business from Good to Great.* London: Great Place to Work Institute.

Thomas, L, Hockings, C, Ottaway, J and Jones, R (2015) *Independent Learning: Student Perceptions and Experiences.* York: Higher Education Academy.

Thomas, L and Jones, R for The Student Engagement Partnership (2017) *Student Engagement in the Context of Commuter Students.* [online] Available at: http://tsep.org.uk/student-engagement-in-the-context-of-commuter-students (accessed 30 June 2018).

Watts, A G (2011) Supporting Undergraduate Nursing Students through Stuctured Personal Tutoring: Some Reflections. *Nursing Education Today*, 31: 214–18.

Wheeler, S and Birtle, J (1993) *A Handbook for Personal Tutors.* Buckingham: Society for Research into Higher Education and Open University Press.

Whittaker, R (2008) *Quality Enhancement Themes: The First Year Experience – Transition to and During the First Year.* Glasgow: Quality Assurance Agency Scotland.

Wisker, G, Exley, K, Antoniou, M and Ridley, P (2007) Working One-to-One with Students: Supervising, Coaching, Mentoring, and Personal Tutoring (Key Guides for Effective Teaching in Higher Education). London: Routledge.

Wilcox, P, Winn, S and Fyvie-Gauld, M (2005) 'It Was Nothing to Do with the University, It Was Just the People': The Role of Social Support in the First-Year Experience of Higher Education. *Studies in Higher Education*, 30(6): 707–22.

Wilson, J H and Ryan, R G (2013) Professor–Student Rapport Scale: Six Items Predict Student Outcomes. *Teaching of Psychology*, 40(2): 130–3.

Wingate, U (2007) A Framework for Transition: Supporting 'Learning to Learn' in Higher Education. *Higher Education Quarterly*, 61(3): 391–405.

Wootton, S (2006) Changing Practice in Tutorial Provision Within Post-Compulsory Education. In Thomas, L and Hixenbaugh, P (eds) *Personal Tutoring in Higher Education* (pp 115–25). Stoke-on-Trent: Trentham Books.

Wootton, S (2007) An Inductive Enquiry into Managing Tutorial Provision in Post-Compulsory Education. PhD. Sheffield Hallam University.[online] Available at: https://search-proquest-com.proxy.library.lincoln.ac.uk/pqdtglobal/docview/1913902798/fulltextPDF/5B739D42F2A846B6PQ/1?accountid=16461 (accessed 30 June 2018).

Yale, A (2017) The Personal Tutor–Student Relationship: Student Expectations and Experiences of Personal Tutoring in Higher Education. *Journal of Further and Higher Education.* 1–12. doi:10.1080/0309877X.2017.1377164

Zepke, N and Leach, L (2010) Beyond Hard Outcomes: 'Soft' Outcomes and Engagement as Student Success. *Teaching in Higher Education*, 15(6): 661–73.

3 Setting boundaries

Chapter aims

This chapter helps you to:

*   identify the following types of boundaries along with their rationale
    *   expertise and referral;
    *   temporal (time);
    *   independence and engagement;
*   establish the necessary boundaries between
    *   personal tutors and students;
    *   personal tutors and academic colleagues;
    *   personal tutors and central departments;
    *   students and their peers.

Introduction

To perform the personal tutor role effectively it is vital you know your limits and establish firm, clear boundaries to guide your tutoring practice (Luck, 2010; Shaw, 2014; Stenton, 2017). When carrying out tutorial support you are nurturing individuals and small groups of students and this inevitably means that, at times, you will become closely associated with students' emotional and overall well-being. While this type of support is undoubtedly what will make you an effective personal tutor, it does come with a 'health warning'. It exposes you to some of the dangers of getting 'too close' to the issues and by implication, at times, to the students themselves (Luck, 2010). Also, if boundaries are not considered and adhered to, your role as tutor may sometimes feel as though it is morphing into that of social worker or even counsellor. This is especially so since academics are increasingly called upon to support students experiencing mental health problems and increasing levels of stress. It is at times like this that boundaries are critical and must be discussed and enforced appropriately. Support for the academic to cope with this pressure and to perform their tutoring role effectively must also be forthcoming (Tinklin et al, 2005; Robotham and Julian, 2006; Jordá, 2013; Hughes et al, 2018). Different institutions may place varying boundaries around the tutoring role. You may find the boundary lines drawn by your institution may differ from the examples given here. While the location of the boundary may be important the manner in which it is agreed, communicated and embedded is even more so.

Clear boundaries, wherever they lie, apply to both academics and to students themselves. In other words, an understanding and articulation of boundaries is absolutely necessary for the benefit and protection of both the student and the tutor. On the student side, recognising boundaries can avoid over-dependency. Good tutoring should always provide comprehensive support for students while also ensuring they take responsibility for themselves and develop as autonomous and independent learners. A tutor who is overly involved with a student's progress, and who attempts to remove some or all of the challenges they face, potentially stifles opportunities for them to learn to solve their own problems and develop the coping strategies necessary to navigate their learning journey and wider student life. These skills are essential for a student's growth and are key to helping the student develop in confidence, self-esteem and autonomy.

From a tutor's perspective, boundaries can help you to achieve a healthy balance. They can ensure that you are looking after yourself and are able to compartmentalise both your personal and professional responsibilities. This is even more crucial when you are exposed, on a regular basis, to students' distressing or emotional circumstances (Shaw, 2014; McFarlane, 2016). If you do not consider or enforce healthy boundaries then you risk compromising your own emotional well-being and this can easily lead to exhaustion and/or impact on your energy levels, sleep patterns and home life (Hughes et al, 2018). If you feel that this is something you are struggling with then it is important to acknowledge your feelings by confiding in a colleague in order to 'offload' in a constructive way and seek reassurance (Luck, 2010; Small, 2013). A mentor or trusted colleague can provide you with support to unpack these issues and this is discussed in more detail in Chapter 7.

It is necessary for you, and your students, to know where your sources of support begin and end (Earwaker, 1992; Luck, 2010; Hughes et al, 2018). However, this may not be easy to establish and maintain, not least because institutional personal tutor policies, processes and established practices can be ambiguous, exist only in theory and differ considerably from lived experience (Smith, 2008; Stephen et al, 2008; Hughes et al, 2018). The examples and case studies provided in this chapter aim to give you an insight into the subtleties needed to enable you to navigate institutional tutoring provision and to put policy and theory into practice. The chapter also explores and navigates the boundaries between you and your students, among you and your colleagues and between the different aspects of your academic role.

What are boundaries?

Boundaries can be best understood by grouping them into different types and by examining examples alongside their rationale (see Table 3.1).

Table 3.1 Boundary types

Boundary type	Rationale	Examples
Expertise and referral boundaries (Grant, 2006; Wisker et al, 2007; Swain, 2008; Whittaker, 2008; Aultman et al, 2009; Thomas et al, 2017; Hughes et al, 2018)	Tutors may lack certain levels of expertise or training and so may not feel comfortable in providing specific types of information, advice, guidance and support. At the same time, colleagues elsewhere in the institution may be employed specifically for these purposes (Hughes et al, 2018).	Student Counselling/well-being: Self-harm, (sexual) abuse, (domestic) violence, suicidal tendencies, traumatic bereavement, severe depression, alcohol or substance abuse or anything which strays from the normal student experience and would benefit from professional mental health support (Smith, 2008; Luck, 2010; Watts, 2011; Hughes et al, 2018). Student Funding: A student whose loan has not come through so cannot afford to both eat and travel to campus that week. Accommodation: A student who needs to escape their home for a place of safety so seeks advice (Luck, 2010). Disability Support: A student discloses that they feel they may be dyslexic but has no previous diagnosis.
Temporal (time) boundaries (Gidman et al, 2000; Wilcox et al, 2005; Aultman et al, 2009, p 639; Hughes et al, 2018)	Time is a major determinant in how the personal tutor role is undertaken and how effective it will be (Gidman et al, 2000, p 406). Tutors have limited time to support struggling students due to competing or even conflicting demands (Rhodes and Jinks, 2005; Luck, 2010; Watts, 2011; Gubby and McNab, 2013).	A tutee's complex individual pastoral needs take up excessive amounts of tutor time leading to increased pressure and work hours (Dobinson-Harrington, 2006; Luck, 2010). Several students approach tutors who are known to be helpful instead of their allocated personal tutor who appears more focused on their research and its link to potential promotions (Stephen et al, 2008; Morris, 2015). To be fair and equitable to all students the institution applies strict time limits to tutorial meetings but some students state that they feel rejected and that the support is hurried and disappointing (Owen, 2002; Dobinson-Harrington, 2006; Luck, 2010).

Table 3.1 *(Cont.)*

Boundary type	Rationale	Examples
Independence and engagement boundaries (Wisker et al, 2007; Thomas et al, 2015)	The quality of learning in HE can depend on the correct balance of scheduled contact and directed independent learning (Soilemetzidis et al, 2014). If students become overly dependent the relationship can become damaging and the consequences severe (Luck, 2010; Thomas et al, 2015; Hughes et al, 2018). Students generally accept the idea of independent learning but require support to learn autonomously and reflect upon this learning (Dobinson-Harrington, 2006; Harvey et al, 2006).	A tutor strays too far in their support, becomes overconfident in their ability to help and even provides their personal contact details to students, leading to constant phoning/messaging at all hours or even stalking (Luck, 2010; Hughes et al, 2018). It becomes clear that late enrolling students who were not inducted into a shared understanding of independent learning disengage or become disruptive in classes (Luck, 2010; Thomas et al, 2015). You find that those students who are clearly and actively engaged in their studies benefit from their active involvement on the programme (Thomas and Jones, 2015).

Expertise and referral boundaries

Ideally, tutors might prefer to advise only on academic matters, not seeing pastoral advice and guidance as part of their overall tutoring remit or role (Wilcox et al, 2005; Smith, 2008; Hughes et al, 2018). Many tutors have reported feeling uncomfortable, inadequate, anxious and exhausted by this part of their role, leaving them reluctant, or even unable, to offer students any degree of support on personal issues (Smith, 2008; Stephen et al, 2008; Gardner and Lane, 2010; Luck, 2010; Ghenghesh, 2017).

The increasing prevalence of student mental health problems means that complicated emotional and pastoral issues are becoming an inevitable part of the tutor's role (Hughes et al, 2018). Situations like this can result in an imbalance between the support that students need and expect compared with the support that tutors can realistically offer (Grey and Lochtie, 2016; Yale, 2017; Hughes et al, 2018). It is impossible to completely dissociate academic and pastoral issues. Invariably, many academic problems may have a non-academic cause, and vice versa (Owen, 2002; Wilcox et al, 2005; Smith, 2008, Hughes et al, 2018). In this context it is often helpful to look at what issues may be presenting as symptoms of a situation and those which are the likely cause. It is vital then that you acknowledge the wider factors affecting students, especially those relating to all-important social integration, beyond the curriculum, that 'spill over' into the academic context (Cartney and Rouse, 2006; Stephen et al, 2008; Race, 2010; McFarlane, 2016).

Legal advice suggests that, if you provide ongoing support and this goes wrong, you will be judged not against the qualities of a well-meaning academic but as that of a trained and experienced counsellor (Hughes et al, 2018). Many tutors have navigated this by stressing that they are not mental health professionals and stating they are more comfortable listening to a student and then signposting and referring, as appropriate, to other central, professional student services (Wilcox et al, 2005; Smith, 2008; Hughes et al, 2018). Your work as a professional is not sustainable alone so it is vital that you and your institution acknowledge the limits of the role and encourage students to seek help or access resources from central services (Wisker et al, 2007; Smith, 2008; Luck, 2010; Hawkins and Shohet, 2012; Thomas, 2012; Small, 2013). If students do not act on this advice then it may hinder their development, preventing them from receiving the best advice and support available (Wootton, 2006).

Clear and effective referral

In order to maintain clear boundaries of expertise, a robust referral system to direct students towards appropriate pastoral support is key (Grant, 2006; Wisker et al, 2007; Swain, 2008; Thomas et al, 2017; Grey and McIntosh, 2017). As a tutor you are a gatekeeper to specialist support and it is essential that you find out about the services your university offers to students (Owen, 2002; Grant, 2006; Shaw, 2014). Signposting can be more complex than it initially appears, often involving proactive engagement that identifies the student's needs and matches this with the correct support service before encouraging them to access it (Hughes et al, 2018). It can be particularly difficult to distinguish between regular stress levels, low motivation or academic anxiety and more severe mental health problems, so it is vital that you conduct an effective preliminary listening exercise and, if you do refer on, ensure it is done sensitively without appearing to 'pass the buck' (Owen, 2002; Grant 2006, p 17; Hughes et al, 2018).

The relationship between tutors and central services can be problematic and academics can worry when students do not return or come back frustrated by long wait times (Hughes et al, 2018). Clear and efficient routes of support and referral require effective communication between services as exact boundaries may be negotiable (Whittaker, 2008; Luck, 2010; Small, 2013; Hughes et al, 2018). Active referrals are recommended whereby you, as tutor, proactively refer students on for specialist support to colleagues, including passing on any important information the student has agreed can be shared (in accordance with data protection regulations), ensuring they do not have to recount their circumstances again fully to another member of staff. We suggest you retain details of specific services on hand and, where possible, ask the student to arrange an appointment while you are there with them (so that you are not just pointing students to another part of campus). Limited, targeted follow-ups that fit within your, and the student's, time constraints are also critical (Smith, 2008; Swain, 2008; Shaw, 2014; Grey and McIntosh, 2017).

The development of stronger partnerships between tutors and central services should provide greater support for you in your role. It is likely that you remain the first person students turn to for advice if they feel less confident approaching centrally based staff that they do not know (Sosabowski et al, 2003; Grant, 2006). Calls for closer and greater collaboration between academic programmes and central services are growing in number and volume (see Table 3.1), and this may prove to be essential in meeting the evolving challenges that students and tutors face (Zepke and Leach, 2010; Thomas, 2012; Grey and McIntosh, 2017; Thomas et al, 2017).

Temporal (time) boundaries

Academics are often expected to simultaneously perform several high pressure roles, such as lecturer, assesor, researcher and administrator, each of which carry multiple obligations and responsibilities. This tension can lead academics to make difficult decisions as to how they allocate their time and develop their career (Whittaker, 2008; Ghenghesh, 2017; Hughes et al, 2018). In some institutions, research output is prestigious and therefore regularly takes precedence over teaching expertise in the criteria for academic promotion. In cases like this, students often complain that their education is only a secondary priority to academic research (Morris, 2015).

Academics can easily spend more time on recording metrics or producing a paper trail for tutorials in order to justify their efforts and this starves them of the time they can spend actually supporting learning or struggling students (Rhodes and Jinks 2005; Luck, 2010; Gubby and McNab, 2013; The Guardian, 2015). Tutors often feel responsible for the approximately 30 students (or in extreme cases more than 100) they have been assigned as tutor. On top of this, tutors who feel that they are not well supported may find it particularly difficult to strike the right balance between being accessible to students, when needed, and being too available. This can mean that they become overwhelmed (Ridley, 2006; Grey and Lochtie, 2016). The time spent on tutoring may seem invisible to other colleagues, particularly those in management positions, when it is not properly considered in workload planning models (Hart, 1996; Owen, 2002; Hughes et al, 2018). Even if the support required falls outside the clear boundaries of their role, tutors may find that referring on conflicts with their core values and natural responsibility that they feel towards students (Hughes et al, 2018). However, to effectively support students' well-being tutors must first take care of and protect their own needs and this includes maintaining these boundaries wherever possible (Levy et al, 2009; Shaw, 2014).

Boundaries with academic peers

Early on in your academic career, you may gain advice and reassurance from your academic peers and/or a mentor. Nevertheless, effective tutoring means that you also need to be firm in establishing boundaries with your academic colleagues and to work with them effectively as a tutorial team (Small, 2013). In a time of significantly increased workloads and institutional change, tutoring can be seen by some as a low-priority task and merely an inconvenient add-on to the important business of teaching and research (Myers, 2008; Calcagno et al, 2017). If students do not receive the support they require from their designated lecturer they may approach you instead, potentially overloading you as any time spent on this will not be factored into your workload (Owen, 2002; Stephen et al, 2008; McFarlane, 2016; Hughes et al, 2018). Finding the correct balance (on an individual, department and institutional level) is an important element of maintaining temporal boundaries.

Independence and engagement boundaries

Given that time is a priority for tutors, it is perhaps unsurprising that you may become frustrated by apparent disengagement or levels of non-attendance among your student cohort, particularly in the face of their increasing academic and pastoral needs (Hargreaves,

2000; Rhodes and Jinks, 2005; Stephen et al, 2008). In order to be an effective personal tutor, and maintain a balance between the different aspects of the academic role, student–tutor boundaries are essential (Grey and McIntosh, 2017). It is advised that ground rules, boundaries, guidelines and expectations for the relationship are set at your first meeting so that both parties may be held accountable (Swain, 2008; Stevenson 2009; Ralston and Hoffshire, 2017). It is important to explore these boundaries in a group as well as in a one-to-one context given that students need to work well with one another in order to settle into student life and develop autonomy.

Boundaries are as important to the student as they are to you because they will need to be an active participant in their own enlightenment (Habermas, 1973 in Cook, 2017). Tutoring exists to help students become independent and promote a shared understanding of independent learning which can be vital to supporting their success (Broad, 2006; Thomas et al, 2015; Grey and McIntosh, 2017). It is advisable that tutors do not suggest options to students but instead ask probing questions that facilitate engagement and ultimately help the individual make a transition from passivity to ownership (Gurbutt and Gurbutt, 2015). Egan's well-established *Skilled Helper Model* (Figure 3.1) can help you to help students manage their own problems and empower them to better help themselves (Egan and Reese, 2018). Egan's model is used frequently in coaching and counselling situations where the aim is to ensure that students are empowered to manage their own problems more effectively and also explore any opportunities available to them. It can be a very useful and productive framework to use in a tutorial context. The model has three main stages: (1) current scenario, (2) preferred scenario and (3) action strategies. The first exploratory stage is to ensure that you are able to gather the facts about a given situation and reflect those back to the student in a non-judgemental way. This requires positive body language, active listening, acceptance and empathy as well as the ability to summarise, focus and ask questions. You should begin to challenge the student's viewpoint in a way which gets them to consider their situation from a variety of different perspectives. There are a number of reasons for this. The second stage is to consider some of the options that are available to them and to help them to commit to a preferred scenario. At this stage it might be helpful for you, as tutor, to consider a change agenda, helping the student to explore their feelings and to unpack the issues so that they are not too overwhelming. The third 'action strategies' stage involves encouraging the student to look at the ways forward and to commit to action. The intention is to motivate the student to take action and take realistic steps to improve their situation. There are alternative frameworks that you can use in addition to Egan's model and these are explored in more detail in Chapter 6.

The rate at which students become independent may be influenced by their previous educational experiences. These can be negotiated and overcome via open conversation and supported by reflection early on in their course (Dobinson-Harrington, 2006; Bates and Kaye, 2014; Grey and McIntosh, 2017). The role you may play in discovering the aspirations of students and setting their expectations as part of their induction (Morgan, 2012) is explained further in Chapter 4.

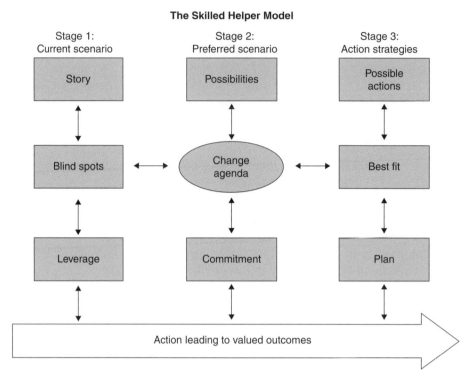

Figure 3.1 *Skilled Helper Model*
Reproduced with permission, Egan and Reese (2018)

Tutor support is important in facilitating student engagement, not only with you as a tutor but with the institution, their peers and their course which, according to a significant body of international evidence, leads to various benefits including higher motivation and commitment, improved mental health and greater levels of well-being (Schlechty, 2002; Thomas and Jones, 2017; McIntosh, 2017). While 'student engagement' has no fixed definition, it can be broadly themed into academic engagement, social engagement and student enhancement. Examples of these include student representation, student consultation, student involvement in curriculum design and peer-learning initiatives. Such opportunities have increased in significance in recent years and are part of the partnership approach to education endorsed by students, academics and the HE sector in general (Little et al, 2009; Thomas and Jones, 2017). Various methods of engaging with students and measuring student engagement are covered further in Chapter 4. The ultimate aim is that students fulfil their role and obligations, as may be outlined in your institutional student charter, potentially including taking *'responsibility for managing their own learning: actively engaging in their course; ensuring they spend sufficient regular time in private study, and partici-pating fully in group learning activities'* (Department for Business, Innovation and Skills, 2011, p 11).

Student peer boundaries

While a good working relationship with a tutor is something students feel is important, their relationship with their peers is where they feel they gain most support (Wilcox et al, 2005; Thomas et al, 2015). Both types of relationship need to be present in order for a student to thrive (McIntosh, 2017). Tutors can play a key role in establishing peer-learning communities which provide support and outline boundaries for students when working with each other (Fergy et al, 2011; Calcagno et al, 2017; McIntosh, 2017). Peer interaction can be encouraged by engaging students with, and endorsing sections of, your student charter or student learning agreement, which typically refers to diversity, inclusion, respect and communication. Although not all institutions have these, those that do should use them to set clear mutual expectations concerning courtesy and professionalism while emphasising the need to treat fellow students equally and respectfully (Department for Business, Innovation and Skills, 2011). The development of these attributes is important in preparing students for the workplace, as well as combatting the challenges of group work tensions and peer to peer plagiarism. Rather than assuming that students know how to act towards each other, it should be acknowledged that they are likely to be at various stages of development in these areas. Student charters should be embedded into the institution as living documents and should be referred to continually, not just when they are violated. These charters are open to ongoing review with active student involvement (including in induction) to encourage ownership (Department for Business, Innovation and Skills, 2011). If your institution does not have a student charter, or similar document, consider conducting a group exercise at an early stage in the student journey which encourages students to work with each other to devise a set of statements to which they are all happy to subscribe. These statements should be broad and outline mutual expectations, roles and responsibilities. They should encourage students to work in partnership with their peers and also establish boundaries for working with you as tutor. If this document is co-created, with the tutor as facilitator, then it becomes easier for students to understand, and adhere to, these boundaries. Group tutorials can play a significant role in supporting this activity and are discussed further in Chapter 4.

The difficulty of letting go and when to do it

Inevitably, in some tutoring contexts, there is a limit to the involvement that tutors have in working with a student to provide the support that they need. The key to this is understanding what level of support can be realistically provided, your capacity to provide this support and knowing when this limit has been reached. At this point, letting go and handing over to colleagues in specialist support services is necessary, especially when you feel you have exhausted all of your own supportive measures. The question is, how do you know when this is the case?

Critical thinking activity 1

» *When did you last think that your own capacity to support students had been reached? Did you notice at the time that this had reached a limit? How did you know and what did you do about it?*

Discussion

The answer you provide to the critical thinking activity will typically relate to the type of boundary you have reached. If it is a boundary of 'expertise', it could be that your level of knowledge, skill or experience is not sufficient enough to provide the student with further help and support. Your capacity to manage these issues can be improved and informed by guidance from central services, and with increasing experience over time, but this requires an honest conversation about whether you are comfortable enough to continue providing advice and guidance to the student. If the boundary relates to 'independence' it could be that you have given the student every opportunity, and significant support, to succeed but they have consistently either not acted upon that opportunity or not fulfilled their responsibilities to act on the advice that has been given. This might be due to inactivity, disengagement or even inability. When reviewing 'temporal' (time) boundaries, your limit could be harder to pinpoint. Here it is important to engage in regular conversations with your line manager, academic peers or a mentor, and central services about the amount of time you are involved in tutoring, as a finite resource, and the boundaries between yourself and colleagues or central services as well as the teaching/tutoring/research boundaries within your role.

Some of the issues and challenges shown in the final column of Table 3.1 may negatively affect institutional performance indicators such as retention, success, attendance, punctuality, persistence and graduation rates. Indeed, there can be a tension between individual student issues and institutional influences. You may find yourself in the middle of these competing pressures. However tempting it is to try and tackle such issues yourself, the boundaries we have been discussing need respecting for the good of all parties, particularly students. These boundaries need to be clear and consistent and should be reviewed continually throughout your career, responding to your experience and interactions with students as their needs change. It is also important to remember that it can be beneficial to work as part of a tutorial team which provides consistent advice and support. This may be out of your control as an individual tutor but it is advisable that you encourage the sharing of best practice with colleagues wherever possible.

CASE STUDY

Jenny's one-to-one with Andrew

The following dialogue is an excerpt taken from a one-to-one meeting between Jenny, a level 4 Human Biology student, and her personal tutor, Andrew.

ANDREW: *Hello Jenny, how are you?*

JENNY: *I'm ok thanks.*

[Jenny is using closed body language and Andrew notices that she appears tense and on edge.]

ANDREW: *Come in and have a seat. So, we've got your one-to-one today. We're going to talk about your attendance and how you're doing with completing your outstanding assignments.*

JENNY: *You know why I am behind with those things, I've told you a million times, I can't help it...*

[Jenny looks visibly upset and it appears that she might become more emotional.]

ANDREW: *Okay, I don't want you to get upset. I'd like us to talk things through calmly and to see how I can support you to make some progress. In a minute I'll ask you to update me on what is happening from your point of view. First though, you're right, you have told me about things in your past that have affected your studies. My aim is to work with you to reduce the impact of those challenges and to support you to do some proactive things that are going to help improve the situation.*

JENNY: *Yeah but no one's had the difficulties I've had...*

ANDREW: *It's important to remember that many people do have difficulties and have also had bad past experiences... also, we all feel different on different days, some days are good, some are bad... but on the bad ones it can help you to move forward if you focus on what can be done to improve the situation.*

JENNY: *But you get paid to be here – I pay to be here.*

ANDREW: *That's true* [smiles] *but your course is similar to a job in that you've agreed to abide by the principles in the student charter by accepting a place at the institution, just like myself and my colleagues do when we take a job here. As tutors, we work in partnership with students to support their success.*

JENNY: *Suppose so...*

ANDREW: *As outlined in the charter, it is your responsibility to attend classes regularly and to let us know if there are any reasons that might prevent you from doing this. So we need to talk about the practical barriers preventing you from engaging with your course. I can see you have missed seminars on your Anatomy and Physiology module. Is there a problem with that specific class?*

JENNY: *It's Dr Joseph. He speaks so fast and only has time for the smartest students – he just assumes the rest of us get it. I got a rubbish mark in my first assignment and his comments are really brief so I don't even know why. I am so worried about failing again that I haven't even started my next essay.*

ANDREW: *Have you asked him for further feedback?*

JENNY: *I tried to after the seminar – I approached him two weeks in a row but he always rushes off. Could you take a look at it for me instead?* [handing over a paper]

ANDREW: *Well... I want to help but the feedback you need may be specific to that class. I recommend you email Dr Joseph asking to schedule an appointment as soon as possible, so there is a written record that you have made contact... from a quick glance at his feedback I can quickly see that some of the issues highlighted may be about academic writing more generally than just Anatomy. Have you considered attending some learning development workshops? Here are the details of the study skills advisors in the library [Andrew shows Jenny his screen]. I'd like you to sign up for an appointment with one of them now, okay? They can help you to structure your assignments so that you can improve your writing skills and to develop a strong argument.*

JENNY: *Okay, I can make that one.*

ANDREW: *I look forward to hearing about it the next time I see you. In terms of the difficulties you mentioned right at the beginning, I remember putting you in contact with student services about your accommodation and I believe she's talked to you... how did that go?*

JENNY: *Alright, we've sorted something.*

ANDREW: *Good. And what about talking to someone else – Lyn, the counsellor – about the difficulties and feelings you have... like we mentioned in our last meeting. Have you had any more thoughts on that?*

JENNY: *But I don't know those people, I only like talking to you because I know you... I don't want to talk to them.*

ANDREW: *I want to support you but remember that I am not an expert or trained mental health professional and my colleagues in Student Services are specialists in this kind of thing. Talking about it can help make it clearer in your mind and problems can seem smaller if you talk about them rather than ignoring them in the hope they will resolve themselves. I can put you in touch with Lyn directly so you don't have to tell your story from the beginning and I can help you manage the impact of any difficulties you are having on your studies, but I am unable to help you address the source of them. A dedicated amount of time is required to sit down with you and help you work through these things and Lyn has that capacity as part of her workload. Remember, too, that she's supported many students in the past and will have insight into a whole range of potential solutions that might not be too obvious to me. I don't always have the time that is needed to talk through all these things at the length they deserve and I don't want this to disadvantage you.*

JENNY: *Suppose so.*

ANDREW: *How about if I introduce you to Lyn myself and take you to her when you arrange a first meeting?*

JENNY: *Dunno.*

ANDREW: *I'm not abandoning you. My role is not to solve your problems but to provide you with the tools, resources or contacts – in this case Lyn – to help you address them. I can then continue to talk you about how you manage any impact on your studies. Want to think about it and let me know by the end of today?*

JENNY: *Yep, okay.*

ANDREW: *Okay, good. I have another student who's been waiting for a bit and I'll wait to hear from you later on today.*

Critical thinking activity 2

1. List which type of boundaries (contained within the chapter and in Table 3.1) are set or recognised by Andrew and explain how he does this.

2. How easy was it to identify which boundaries were established and how did you do so?

Discussion

You may have your own thoughts about the manner in which Andrew conducted the one-to-one meeting with Jenny. There are no fixed rules and regulations governing how tutorial meetings are conducted and it's important to develop your own style and acknowledge that this may change depending on the situation and the issues up for discussion. Also, body language (referenced in the transcript) can be a useful cue when listening and responding to a student during a tutorial. Your initial thoughts and reactions to what is discussed in these meetings are useful insights into your own tutorial approach. You should review all the example dialogues presented in the book in this way, aligning them to your own experiences and clarifying whether you would have acted in a similar or slightly different way. It might be helpful to do this with a mentor or colleague and discuss your views. The topic of practice in one-to-one tutorials is covered in more detail in Chapter 5.

In terms of the boundary types established, we have identified the following examples.

Expertise and referral

ANDREW: *Here are the details of the study skills advisors in the library* [Andrew shows Jenny his screen]. *I'd like you to sign up now for an appointment with one of them now, okay? They can help you to structure your assignments so that you can improve your writing skills and to develop a strong argument.*

Andrew has a good awareness of the support services available across the institution. Not only does he have the information to hand, he also endorses the services by drawing on the experience of other students, making it a more positive option for Jenny.

ANDREW: *...and what about talking to someone else – Lyn, the counsellor – about the difficulties and feelings you have... I want to support you but remember that I am not an expert or trained mental health professional... and they are specialists in this kind of thing.*

Again, Andrew is aware of the limits of his expertise. He reassures Jenny that he's very much interested in providing her with support but that in order to discuss things further she should seek the help of a trained colleague.

Temporal (time)

ANDREW: *...I don't always have the time that is needed to talk through all these things at the length they deserve and I don't want this to disadvantage you.*

Andrew is managing Jenny's expectations. He is clear that the time required to unpack these issues is not available to him as he has a journal article submission due that afternoon. He ensures Jenny doesn't rely on his support alone and provides an opportunity for her to become more independent.

ANDREW: *...I have another student who has been waiting for a bit.*

Andrew sets healthy limits on the conversation to ensure that Jenny does not become over-reliant on lengthy conversations with him. He is attempting to divide his time equitably between Jenny and his other tutees.

Independence and engagement

ANDREW: *...As outlined in the charter, it is your responsibility to attend classes regularly and to let us know if there are any reasons that might prevent you from doing this. So we need to talk about the practical barriers preventing you from engaging with your course.*

Andrew reminds Jenny of her own roles and responsibilities in the learning process. He sticks to the facts, has knowledge of the classes that she has missed, notifies her that there are agreements in place to support her continued engagement with the course and makes her aware that her level of engagement has fallen below the acceptable level.

ANDREW: *Have you asked him for further feedback? I recommend you email Dr Joseph asking to schedule an appointment as soon as possible.*

Andrew uses specific questions to assess Jenny's engagement with another tutor. He uses these to determine whether or not she has sought feedback and encourages her to take further action.

We have highlighted some boundaries that were recognised and set between Andrew and Jenny. The case study also contained examples of boundaries with academic peers, central services and between tutoring/research alongside examples of effective referral arrangements.

It is important to pay attention to the manner in which Andrew approaches this conversation. How does he get these messages across to Jenny and is his approach grounded in the personal tutor core values of Chapter 2? In the context of the conversation as a whole, Andrew approaches his tutorials supportively and exhibits the core values of approachability, compassion, being non-judgemental and embodying 'equal partner, not superior' approach. It may be useful to consider the dialogue you might use in a similar situation as well as the tone and body language you would employ to deliver it.

There is always room for improvement. One observation is that Andrew talks a lot more than Jenny. The use of open questions could have elicited more information from her. It is also important to avoid coming across as too patronising, especially if you are encouraging a student to commit to action. This is critical in the context of an adult learning environment where you are empowering and championing students to take ownership of their learning. The comment *'As outlined in the student charter, it is your responsibility to attend class'* could be re-phrased as *'Can you remind me what the student charter says about attendance?'* The latter gives Jenny an opportunity to talk as well as checking if she actually remembers any initial conversations in class about the charter.

Another strategy is to encourage the student to identify and adhere to defined tutorial boundaries. This can be done with effective use of active listening and open questioning (considered in more depth in Chapters 5 and 6) but it does require a degree of confidence and commitment to practising this approach over time. This approach helps to reframe the situation and encourages the student not only to talk more in the meeting but also, more importantly, to understand better their role and responsibilities, which supports greater student autonomy and ownership. The overarching rationale for setting student boundaries is that for the student to truly engage they should be encouraged to take responsibility and be independent. A conversation about boundaries can also be used in the context of a small group tutorial where students can work together to discuss how to access support, advice and guidance. This often works well as part of a discussion about expectations, roles and responsibilities.

Summary

This chapter has demonstrated the importance of setting healthy boundaries, both for yourself and for your students. These boundaries promote well-being and protect both parties. The aim of setting these boundaries is to ensure that your students are aware of how to access the support they need and are also supported to become more responsible, autonomous and independent. The chapter identifies and defines the different types of boundaries that are most relevant to the personal tutoring process, alongside specific examples and rationale for adhering to these, including how to make effective referrals to centralised and specialist support services. The chapter also considers how boundaries can be set and reinforced in practice through an example of a one-to-one conversation with an individual student.

Learning checklist

Tick off each point when you feel confident you understand it.

☐ *I understand the need to set boundaries in the tutorial process, especially for the benefit and protection of both students and myself.*

☐ *I understand and can articulate the different types of boundaries most relevant to the personal tutoring process and the rationale for each one:*

- ○ *expertise and referral – at times I recognise that I need to refer to other 'experts';*

- ○ *temporal (time) – I am a limited resource with competing demands on my time;*

- ○ *independence and engagement – I can empower students to take responsibility for their own learning and encourage them to become more independent.*

☐ *I know how to set and recognise boundaries between myself and others (students, academic peers or central services) through careful management of my interactions with them.*

Critical reflections

1. In your personal tutor role, to what extent do you believe you, your students and your colleagues know and recognise the boundaries that should exist between one another?

2. Can you think of particular students (individuals and groups) who would benefit from having a clear conversation about boundaries? What types of boundaries would this conversation include? How will you go about doing this and will you need to make reference to any other institutional documents such as the student charter?

3. To what extent did you have the opportunity to discuss boundary setting (those boundaries examined in this chapter or others) as part of your induction, staff development programme or PG Cert in Teaching and Learning in Higher Education course?

4. How much emphasis does your current institution (and your colleagues within it) place on setting boundaries and conducting referrals? What do you think could be done to improve this?

Personal tutor self-assessment system

As a reminder, the main boundary types are: expertise and referral, temporal (time) and independence and engagement, as detailed in the following table.

PERSONAL TUTOR SELF-ASSESSMENT SYSTEM : Chapter 3 Setting boundaries	Minimum standard	Beginner level	Intermediate level	Advanced level	Expert level
	1 star	2 star	3 star	4 star	5 star
Individual	I clearly outline the various sources of support available to students, and set boundaries between myself and them, at the outset of their course. I keep to these expertise/referral, temporal (time) and independence/engagement boundaries in my everyday practice.	I revisit these boundaries in group tutorials. Through one-to-ones and other support meetings, students have a clear idea of these key boundaries.	Through individual meetings, my students are progressively becoming more able to recognise the boundaries. My students benefit from clarity on a range of boundaries that help them to take responsibility and succeed.	My students are becoming responsible and independent as a result of these boundaries. I continually review the boundaries I keep in my own work and with students, colleagues and central departments for the benefit of all.	Effective boundary setting is embedded in all of my work and interactions with my students. As a result of this and other factors, my students take responsibility and are independent while I maintain a healthy balance in my work.
Institutional	My institution ensures that all students are given clear information on the various sources of support that are available and what is expected of them in terms of independent learning.	My institution provides clear guidance to staff on the necessary boundaries within academic roles, between staff and students and between support services. Referrals are managed effectively.	Departments and/ or support functions allocate and review resources relating to setting boundaries. Line managers discuss boundary setting and referrals with staff individually for the purposes of student and staff welfare.	Departments or support functions actively seek students' views in boundary setting and integrate these into resources. Academics are supported in maintaining a balance between all aspects of their role.	A range of different types of boundaries are set by departments or support functions which are informed by students themselves. As a result of this and other factors, students take responsibility and are independent.

References

Aultman, L P, Williams-Johnson, M R and Schutz, P A (2009) Boundary Dilemmas in Teacher–Student Relationships: Struggling with 'The Line'. *Teaching and Teacher Education*, 25(5): 636–46.

Bates, E A and Kaye, L K (2014) 'I'd Be Expecting Caviar in Lectures': The Impact of the New Fee Regime on Undergraduate Students' Expectations of Higher Education. *Higher Education*, 67(5): 655–73.

Broad, J (2006) Interpretations of Independent Learning in Further Education. *Journal of Further and Higher Education*, 30(2): 119–43.

Calcagno, L, Walker, D and Grey, D J (2017) Building Relationships: A Personal Tutoring Framework to Enhance Student Transition and Attainment. *Student Engagement in Higher Education Journal*, 1(2): 88–99.

Cartney, P and Rouse, A (2006) The Emotional Impact of Learning in Small Groups: Highlighting the Impact on Student Progression and Development. *Teaching in Higher Education*, 11(1): 79–91.

Cook, B (2017) Paulo Freire and the De-commodification of Higher Education in the 21st Century. Presentation at *Education and Transformative Practice – International Paulo Freire Conference,* Cyprus, 5–7 September 2017. [online] Available at: www.paulofreireconference.com/index. php/ipfc/education-transformativepractice/paper/view/34 (accessed 30 June 2018).

Department for Business, Innovation and Skills (2011) *Higher Education: Students at the Heart of the System*. London: Department of Business, Innovation and Skills.

Dobinson-Harrington, A (2006) Personal Tutor Encounters: Understanding the Experience. *Nursing Standard*, 20(50): 35–42.

Earwaker, J (1992) *Helping and Supporting Students*. Buckingham: Open University Press.

Egan, G and Reese, R (2018) *The Skilled Helper: A Problem-Management and Opportunity-Development Approach to Helping*. Boston: CENGAGE Learning Custom Publishing.

Fergy, S, Marks-Maran, D, Ooms, A, Shapcott, J and Burke, L (2011) Promoting Social and Academic Integration into Higher Education by First Year Student Nurses: The APPL project. *Journal of Further and Higher Education*, 35(1): 107–30.

Gardner, L D and Lane, H (2010) Exploring the Personal Tutor-Student Relationship: An Autoethnographic Approach. *Journal of Psychiatric and Mental Health Nursing*, 17(4): 342–7.

Ghenghesh, P (2017) Personal Tutoring from the Perspective of Tutors and Tutees. *Journal of Further and Higher Education*, 42(4), 570–84.

Gidman, J, Humphreys, A and Jennys, M (2000) The Role of the Personal Tutor in the Academic Context. *Nurse Education Today*, 20(5): 401–7.

Grant, A (2006) Personal Tutoring: A System in Crisis? In Thomas, L and Hixenbaugh, P (eds) *Personal Tutoring in Higher Education* (pp 11–20). Stoke-on-Trent: Trentham Books.

Grey, D and Lochtie, D (2016) Comparing Personal Tutoring in the UK and Academic Advising in the US. *Academic Advising Today*, 39(3). [online] Available at: www.nacada.ksu.edu/Resources/ Academic-Advising-Today/View-Articles/Comparing-Personal-Tutoring-in-the-UK-and-Academic-Advising-in-the-US.aspx (accessed 30 June 2018).

Grey, D and McIntosh, E (2017) Student Dashboards – The Case for Building Communities of Practice. Presentation at *UK Advising and Tutoring Conference*, Leeds, 12 April 2017.

The Guardian (2015) Our Obsession with Metrics Turns Academics into Data Drones. [online] Available at: www.theguardian.com/higher-education-network/2015/nov/27/our-obsession-with-metrics-turns-academics-into-data-drones (accessed 30 June 2018).

Gubby, L and McNab, L (2013) Personal Tutoring from the Perspective of the Tutor. *Capture*, 4(1): 7–18.

Gurbutt, D J and Gurbutt, R (2015) Empowering Students to Promote Independent Learning: A Project Utilising Coaching Approaches to Support Learning and Personal Development. *Journal of Learning Development in Higher Education*, 8: 1–17.

Habermas, J (1973) *Theory and Practice*. Viertel, J (trans). Boston: Beacon.

Hargreaves, A (2000) Mixed Emotions: Teachers' Perceptions of their Interactions with Students. *Teaching and Teacher Education*, 16: 811–26.

Hart, N (1996) The Role of the Personal Tutor in a College of Further Education: A Comparison of Skills Used by Personal Tutors and by Student Counsellors When Working with Students in Distress. *British Journal of Guidance and Counselling*, 24(1): 83–96.

Harvey, L, Drew, S and Smith, M (2006) *The First Year Experience: A Review of Literature for the Higher Education Academy*. York: Higher Education Academy.

Hawkins, P and Shohet, R (2012) *Supervision in the Helping Professions*. Maidenhead: Open University Press.

Hughes, G, Panjwani, M, Tulcidas, P and Byrom, N (2018) *Student Mental Health: The Role and Experiences of an Academic.* [online] Available at: www.studentminds.org.uk/theroleofanacademic.html (accessed 30 June 2018).

Jordá, J M M (2013) The Academic Tutoring at the University Level: Development and Promotion Methodology through Project Work. *Procedia – Social and Behavioral Sciences*, 106: 2594–601.

Levy, J, Tryfona, C, Koukouravas T, Hughes, N and Worrall, M (2009) Cardiff School of Management Personal Tutors: Building Student Confidence. *Widening Participation and Lifelong Learning*, 11(3): 36–9.

Little, B, Locke, W, Scesa, A and Williams, R (2009) *Report to HEFCE on Student Engagement.* [online] Available at: http://oro.open.ac.uk/15281/1/Report_to_HEFCE_on_student_engagement.pdf (accessed 30 June 2018).

Luck, C (2010) Challenges Faced by Tutors in Higher Education. *Psychodynamic Practice*, 16(3): 273–87.

McFarlane, K J (2016) Tutoring the Tutors: Supporting Effective Personal Tutoring. *Active Learning in Higher Education*, 17(1): 77–88.

McIntosh, E (2017) Working in Partnership: The Role of Peer Assisted Study Sessions in Engaging the Citizen Scholar. *Active Learning in Higher Education*, 1–16. https://doi.org/10.1177%2F1469787417735608

Morgan, M (2012) *Improving the Student Experience: The Practical Guide for Universities and Colleges*. London: Routledge.

Morris, D (2015) *Teaching and Research: A Zero-sum Game?* [online] Available at: http://wonkhe.com/blogs/teaching-research (accessed 30 June 2018).

Myers, J (2008) Is Personal Tutoring Sustainable? Comparing the Trajectory of the Personal Tutor with that of the Residential Warden. *Teaching in Higher Education*, 13(5): 607–11.

Owen, M (2002) 'Sometimes You Feel You're in Niche Time': The Personal Tutor System, a Case Study. *Active Learning in Higher Education*, 3(1): 7–23.

Race, P (2010) *Making Personal Tutoring Work.* Leeds: Leeds Met Press.

Ralston, N C and Hoffshire, M (2017) An Individualized Approach to Student Transition: Developing a Success Coaching Model. In Cintron, R, Samuel, J and Hinson, J (eds) *Accelerated Opportunity Education Models and Practices* (pp 34–50). Hershey, PA: IGI Global.

Rhodes, S and Jinks, A (2005) Personal Tutors' Views of Their Role with Pre-registration Nursing Students: An Exploratory Study. *Nurse Education Today*, 25(5): 390–7.

Ridley, P (2006) 'Who's Looking After Me?' Supporting New Personal Tutors. In Thomas, L and Hixenbaugh, P (eds) *Personal Tutoring in Higher Education* (pp 127–36). Stoke-on-Trent: Trentham Books.

Robotham, D and Julian, C (2006) Stress and the Higher Education Student: A Critical Review of the Literature. *Journal of Further and Higher Education*, 30(2): 107–17.

Schlechty, P (2002) *Working on the Work: An Action Plan for Teachers, Principals, and Superintendents.* San Francisco: Jossey-Bass.

Shaw, C (2014) *How Academics Can Help Ensure Students' Wellbeing.* [online] Available at: www.theguardian.com/higher-education-network/blog/2014/oct/01/university-academic-support-student-welfare-wellbeing (accessed 30 June 2018).

Small, F (2013) Enhancing the Role of Personal Tutor in Professional Undergraduate Education. *Inspiring Academic Practice*, 1(1): 1–11.

Smith, E (2008) *Personal Tutoring: An Engineering Subject Centre Guide.* Leicester: Higher Education Academy.

Sosabowski, M H, Bratt, A M, Herson, K, Sawers, G W J, Taylor, S, Zahoui, A and Denyer, S P (2003) Enhancing Quality in the M.Pharm Degree Programme: Optimisation of the Personal Tutor System. *Pharmacy Education*, 3(2): 103–8.

Soilemetzidis, I, Bennet, P, Buckley, A, Hillman, N and Stoakes, G (2014) *The HEPI-HEA Student Academic Experience Survey 2014.* York: Higher Education Academy.

Stenton, A (2017) *Why Personal Tutoring is Essential for Student Success.* [online] Available at: www.heacademy.ac.uk/blog/why-personal-tutoring-essential-student-success (accessed 30 June 2018).

Stephen, D E, O'Connell, P and Hall, M (2008) 'Going the Extra Mile', 'Fire-fighting', or Laissez-faire? Re-evaluating Personal Tutoring Relationships within Mass Higher Education. *Teaching in Higher Education*, 13(4): 449–60.

Stevenson, N (2009) Enhancing the Student Experience by Embedding Personal Tutoring in the Curriculum. *Journal of Hospitality, Leisure, Sport and Tourism Education*, 8(2): 117–22.

Swain, H (2008) *The Personal Tutor.* [online] Available at: www.timeshighereducation.co.uk/news/the-personal-tutor/210049.article (accessed 30 June 2018).

Thomas, L (2012) *Building Student Engagement and Belonging in Higher Education at a Time of Change: Final Report from the What Works? Student Retention and Success Programme.* London: Paul Hamlyn Foundation.

Thomas, L, Hockings, C, Ottaway, J and Jones, R (2015) *Independent Learning: Student Perceptions and Experiences.* York: Higher Education Academy.

Thomas, L and Jones, R (2017) *Student Engagement in the Context of Commuter Students.* [online] Available at: http://tsep.org.uk/student-engagement-in-the-context-of-commuter-students (accessed 30 June 2018).

Thomas, L, Hill, M, O'Mahony, J and Yorke, M (2017) *Supporting Student Success: Strategies for Institutional Change. What Works? Student Retention and Success Programme. Final Report.* London: Paul Hamlyn Foundation.

Tinklin, T, Riddell, S and Wilson, A (2005) Support for Students with Mental Health Difficulties in Higher Education: The Students' Perspective. *British Journal of Guidance and Counselling*, 33(4): 495–512.

Watts, T (2011) Supporting Undergraduate Nursing Students through Structured Personal Tutoring: Some Reflections. *Nursing Education Today*, 31: 214–18.

Whittaker, R (2008) *Quality Enhancement Themes: The First Year Experience – Transition to and During the First Year.* Glasgow: Quality Assurance Agency Scotland. [online] Available at: http://dera.ioe.ac.uk/11595/1/transition-to-and-during-the-first-year-3.pdf (accessed 30 June 2018).

Wisker, G, Exley, K, Antoniou, M and Ridley, P (2007) *Working One-to-One with Students: Supervising, Coaching, Mentoring, and Personal Tutoring (Key Guides for Effective Teaching in Higher Education).* London: Routledge.

Wilcox, P, Winn, S and Fyvie-Gauld, M (2005) 'It Was Nothing to Do with the University, It Was Just the People': The Role Of Social Support in the First-Year Experience of Higher Education. *Studies in Higher Education*, 30(6): 707–22.

Wootton, S (2006) Changing Practice in Tutorial Provision within Post-Compulsory Education. In Thomas, L and Hixenbaugh, P (eds) *Personal Tutoring in Higher Education* (pp 115–25). Stoke-on-Trent: Trentham Books.

Yale, A (2017) The Personal Tutor–Student Relationship: Student Expectations and Experiences of Personal Tutoring in Higher Education. *Journal of Further and Higher Education.* doi:10.1080/0309877X.2017.1377164

Zepke, N and Leach, L (2010) Beyond Hard Outcomes: 'Soft' Outcomes and Engagement as Student Success. *Teaching in Higher Education*, 15(6): 661–73.

4 Key activities: identifying and supporting student populations

Chapter aims

This chapter helps you to:

- identify the various student populations you may encounter as a personal tutor and methods and good practice to support them.

This includes:

- clarifying the terms that may be used to describe 'at risk' students;

- identifying different student populations, understanding different risk factors and putting plans in place to support vulnerable students;

- exploring effective ways of working with students with additional needs including potential safeguarding considerations;

- understanding the tracking, monitoring and supporting of student progress in terms of rationale, methods (including dashboard-based learning/engagement analytics) and benefits.

Introduction

In this chapter and the next we cover all of the key activities that a student is likely to benefit from, either directly or indirectly, if they are given effective tutorial support. We offer you a toolkit of actions to identify student needs, increase their motivation to learn and achieve or exceed their targets. Furthermore, to help each student to achieve these aims, we look at tracking and monitoring strategies that you can use to ensure that all of your students receive the necessary support from the wider institution.

Personal tutoring tools that cover all aspects of a student's experience are illustrated through several key personal tutoring activities, including tracking and monitoring students, identifying their support needs and providing activities which enable effective support for them as they progress through the key lifecycle stages which are identified in Chapter 5.

What is the purpose of the personal tutor key activities?

You will spend your time supporting students in a variety of ways. The main reason you assess the needs of your students along with tracking and monitoring them is to provide support so that each student has the best chance of succeeding on their course, and also to help them successfully progress on to their next step. To do this you will be implementing individual actions to increase students' motivation, supporting them to overcome or reduce as many of their barriers to learning as possible and developing their employability skills. The activities and strategies within this chapter and the next are designed to facilitate student success, student engagement, progression and learning gain. A sector-wide definition of 'learning gain' has not yet been agreed but appears in government policy-making documents. It refers to the impact that higher education has on a student's development, their attitude to learning and the acquisition of higher level skills. Related terms include 'value-added' and 'distance travelled'.

The tracking and monitoring of students

The close, regular, ongoing and systematic tracking and monitoring of student progress and performance is widely considered as a necessity in any successful student intervention or support system (Owen, 2002; Rhodes and Jinks, 2005; Hixenbaugh et al, 2006; Smith, 2008; Stephen et al, 2008; Swain, 2008; Shaw, 2014; McFarlane, 2016; Thomas et al, 2017). Literature suggests that students welcome this close attention, commonly referred to as personalised learning, and regular, proactive follow-up contact. A lack of contact and/or follow up can diminish a student's perception of the importance of the tutor–tutee relationship (Hixenbaugh et al, 2006; Braine and Parnell, 2011; Stephen et al, 2008; Small, 2013; Ghenghesh, 2017; Yale, 2017). Though it is important to be aware of the limits and boundaries involved in effective tutorial relationships (see Chapter 3), a close monitoring of students is generally recommended (Naidoo and Jamieson, 2005). This is particularly the case for students who may be categorised as at risk or vulnerable (Calcagno et al, 2017).

What do we mean by non-traditional, vulnerable, disadvantaged and at risk students?

While the sector aims to address inequality so that all students (regardless of background) are supported to access, succeed in, and progress from HE, outcomes for all student groups have not always been equal (Department for Education, 2017; Stenton 2017). In 1983, an article entitled *A Nation at Risk*, published by the National Commission on Excellence in Education, used the term 'at risk' and the term has since been used to refer to certain groups of HE students over the last 25 years (Jones and Watson, 1990). Within HE institutions and general HE discourse, the expression 'at risk' is sometimes connected to other terms or used interchangeably with them. We have made some subtle distinctions between these different, but potentially related, concepts below. It is critical to understand that while various terms are used to describe certain student characteristics, backgrounds and behaviours, they must not be used to label, homogenise, or place limits on a student's ability. Instead, appreciating a student's context can help you to understand how to support them to succeed.

The term 'non-traditional' students generally refers to those students from low-participation neighbourhoods where, historically, fewer people have gone on to pursue HE opportunities. The term may also be used when referring to the changing profile of students as a result of demographic and sociocultural factors, related to widening participation (Jones and Watson, 1990; Small, 2013; Webb et al, 2017). Factors affecting, but not exclusive to, non-traditional students include disadvantage, for example low income levels or an educational background which has restricted acquisition of knowledge, abilities and skills (Stephen et al, 2008; Reay et al, 2010; See et al, 2012; Department for Education, 2017; McIntosh, 2017; Webb et al, 2017). These disadvantages may, in some cases, make them more vulnerable, impacting negatively on attendance, behaviour or completion of their course (McIntosh and Shaw, 2017). They may also increase the risk of non-completion or under-achievement against target grades (Thomas et al, 2017; McIntosh and Shaw, 2017). There are other student groups, for example those from Black, Asian and Minority Ethnic (BAME) backgrounds, those with disabilities and mental health issues and mature students (those who are over 21 years of age) who may also experience barriers to success and become especially vulnerable (Mountford-Zimdars et al, 2015; Million Plus, 2018). At the time of writing, there is a renewed focus on these students nationally and universities have to put in place arrangements to ensure that students from particular groups are not disadvantaged further when they progress to HE. These arrangements are enshrined in the *Access and Participation Plans* (The Office for Students, nd, online) which replace the *Access Agreements* that have been a feature of university access and participation strategies for several years, governed by the former Office for Fair Access (OFFA). The new *Access and Participation Plans*, which take effect from the academic year 2019–20, are a requirement of registration (in the Office for Students' regulatory framework) for providers of HE in England that charge the highest level of tuition fees. These documents will be published and publically available.

What characteristics might mean a student is at risk or vulnerable?

So, how might you identify whether your students could be deemed at risk or vulnerable? The following characteristics are not exhaustive (for example, gender and sexuality, which are not covered, may be important factors) but they should deliver a reminder of the diversity of the student population. To enable you to think more broadly about where these influences may stem from we have grouped them under the headings of student characteristics, home life and cultural/economic factors. We have used a Venn diagram to show how these groupings are closely interlinked and how any given at risk/vulnerable student can be within one, two or all three groupings (see Table 4.1 and Figure 4.1).

Table 4.1 Characteristics of at risk or vulnerable students

Student characteristics	Home life	Cultural/economic factors
A student who: • has a history or signs of alcohol and/or substance misuse (Shaw, 2014; Harrison, 2017); • has a disability, learning or mental health difficulty (Smith, 2008; Whittaker, 2008; Department for Education, 2017; McIntosh and Shaw, 2017; Hughes et al, 2018); • is a part-time student (Department for Education, 2017; Thomas et al, 2017; Webb et al, 2017); • is a mature student (Baxter and Britton, 2001; Wilcox et al, 2005; Thomas et al, 2017); • has displayed offending behaviour and/or has had contact with the police or justice system (Harrison, 2017).	A student who: • has a history of abusive relationships, safeguarding issues or domestic violence within the family (Wootton, 2007; Watts, 2011); • is a care leaver, estranged from their parents or the first generation in their family to attend university (Thomas, 2006; Lochtie, 2015; Harrison, 2017; McIntosh and Shaw, 2017); • has a history of homelessness or is living in unsafe housing (Harrison, 2017); • is pregnant, a student parent or responsible for dependents (McFarlane, 2016; Department for Education, 2017); • is a commuter student or lives with a parent (Wilcox et al, 2005; Thomas and Jones, 2017).	A student who: • is from socio-economic groups D and E (semi-skilled, unskilled manual and workless households) (McIntosh and Shaw, 2017; Webb et al, 2017); • is from an ethnic minority (Department for Education, 2017; Thomas et al, 2017; Webb et al, 2017); • is an asylum seeker (McIntosh and Shaw, 2017); • is an international student, particularly if English is an additional language (Lamont, 2005); • has been previously identified as being at risk or vulnerable by a former educational institution or local authority.

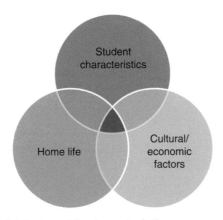

Figure 4.1 Groupings of at risk/vulnerable characteristics

Tailored support or student profiling?

While we advise against homogenising students, as discussed previously, we do acknowledge that it is important to understand student contexts and to develop an awareness of why and how certain students might struggle while in HE. It may therefore be beneficial to tailor support or allocate specific tutoring expertise to individuals or groups according to the type or number of risk factors applicable (Beatty-Guenter, 1994; Smith, 2008; Lochtie, 2015). However, it is important to remember that every student needs to be understood and treated equitably as an individual rather than profiling them and simply supporting only according to a generalised set of characteristics (Priest and McPhee, 2000; May and Bridger, 2010; Gurbutt and Gurbutt, 2015; Calcagno et al, 2017). Just because students may have one or more of the background characteristics listed above does not mean this will necessarily have a negative impact on their progress. Likewise, it is important to remember that you may have students who do not display any of these characteristics and may be at significant risk of dropping out. Exercising your own knowledge and intuition is critical here.

Most students do struggle at some point in their programme of study. Generally, students who possess any of the various characteristics listed above may have barriers to overcome and find adapting and transition into university life more difficult than others or be hesitant to ask for assistance (Cooke et al, 2004; Thomas, 2006; Small, 2013; McIntosh and Shaw, 2017). They may be disengaged from mainstream forms of support, face specific practical challenges which impact on their academic and social engagement or initially lack the tools and environment required to succeed (Whittaker, 2008; Thomas and Jones, 2017; McIntosh and Shaw, 2017). Calcagno et al (2017) suggest identifying at risk students during the 'getting to you know you' stage of tutoring while building a relationship with the student. It is generally acknowledged that this approach is good practice. These decisions inform at risk meetings where further exploration can occur and support be provided if required (as discussed later in this chapter). In some institutions, particular tutors are assigned to work with these students.

The tools to keep your students on track to succeed

This section aims to provide a good practice model for student tracking and monitoring. You may not recognise some of the terms used in the Table 4.2 – for example 'staff comments about students', 'cause for concern or congratulations' – as these differ depending on the institution you work for. However, even though the terms may differ, the meaning behind them is usually the same, whichever student you work with or institution you work for. Table 4.2 outlines some of the key activities you can use to ensure students succeed.

Table 4.2 Tracking and monitoring activities

Method	Explanation
At risk meetings	• Formal meetings where you discuss the progress of each of the students in your cohort in turn. • Discussion focuses on each student's progress in relation to SMART targets. • Discussion takes place with other staff and support staff who work with those students.
At risk categorisation	• Where you identify the likelihood that students may not pass the course or achieve their target grade. • You will take a holistic view of each student's progress and profile. • Remember, the role of the tutor can include improving intellectual and academic ability as well as nurturing the emotional well-being of your students. These factors can influence the student's at risk category (discussed in detail later in this chapter).
At risk documentation	• Methods by which you record the reasons for your students' at risk categories. • At risk documents should be seen as 'live', in other words they should be added to and updated accordingly over the academic year. • The method for recording isn't as important as actually going through the process of identifying the at risk category and support needs of every student with the relevant lecturers, support staff and managers. • It is good practice for you to notify all staff who work with a student on a regular basis of the student's at risk category, reasons for this and supportive interventions (with an awareness of data protection regulations). This establishes a more informed and co-ordinated approach to each student's individual needs.
One-to-ones with students	• Arranged and structured conversations that allow you to discuss the progress the student is making. • Where SMART targets are agreed along with actions for improvement and dates when these will be reviewed.
Course progress feedback	• This can be discussed with the student within the classroom or in a one-to-one situation. • How well (or not) students are doing on their course will affect their at risk category.

Table 4.2 (*Cont.*)

Method	Explanation
Staff comments about students	• The majority of institutions now have a dashboard-based analytics system for monitoring individual student progress. • Usually these systems allow lecturers and support staff to make comments (positive or developmental) about every student's progress. • This information is usually visible to all staff (and students in some institutions) and is vital to inform the at risk category and supportive actions.
Cause for concern or cause for congratulations	• Dashboard tracking and monitoring systems usually allow staff to share when students are causing real concern or when they have really excelled. • These things need to be recognised and sometimes discussed with the students and will partly inform their at risk category and the supportive actions you will take.

Critical thinking activity 1

1. In relation to the tracking and monitoring activities in Table 4.2:

    a. How many of these have you explored during your induction, PG Cert in Higher Education or continuing professional development (CPD) courses?

    b. How many of these have you discussed with your course leader, mentor and/ or line manager?

    c. How many of these have you used in your practice as a personal tutor?

2. Rank the seven activities listed in Table 4.2 in order of what you feel has the greatest impact on your ability to track and monitor whether all of your students are on track to succeed (1 = greatest impact).

3. The seven activities listed are only *some* examples of tracking and monitoring activities. What others can you think of?

Feedback to the student

To be truly effective, all tracking and monitoring activities must inform timely and effective feedback to the student. To achieve this, depending on the time you are given within the institution, the aim is to have regular discussions with every student in your cohort to convey how they are progressing against their SMART targets. Discussions can take place at any time, for example in the seminar room or corridor, or on the phone. However, usually the most effective method is through an arranged one-to-one.

For student feedback to be effective it must:

- be a two-way conversation in which, where appropriate, you employ many of the core skills discussed in Chapter 2, for example active listening and questioning, challenging, reflecting back and summarising;

- involve the student doing the majority of the thinking and talking. Ineffective feedback is where you do the majority of the talking and the student is disengaged. You should be trying to get the students to think and reflect about their own progress and develop agreed targets with you.

Critical thinking activity 2

» *Think of the most useful face-to-face feedback you have ever had which you acted upon and which helped you to improve. List the factors which made that feedback so effective.*

How risk is assigned to a student

When you start to work with your students within the classroom, through group tutorials and one-to-ones, you will be creating a picture in your mind of the type and level of support each will need in order to be successful on their course. Regularly speaking to colleagues and using the institution's dashboard student tracking and monitoring system are of equal importance to inform your view of each student's progress. So that you and everyone who works with individual students are clear about the support they need, it is useful to assign an at risk category to each of them if your institutional dashboard does not already do this automatically.

The at risk category helps you and other colleagues to have a clear overview of your cohort and to decide the actions needed to support each student effectively. As the academic year progresses and each student's situation changes, so should their at risk status and the level and type of support you provide. It is good practice to review each student through formal at risk meetings at regular intervals to ensure that you are tracking and monitoring that each is on course to succeed. Table 4.3 illustrates suggested at risk categories and criteria by which students can be categorised.

Table 4.3 At risk categories and criteria

At risk category	Criteria				
	Student progress against SMART targets, including target grades	**Attendance and punctuality**	**Engagement in class/ tutorials**	**Submission records**	**Background characteristics**
Outstanding	*The student is making exceptional progress above their SMART targets and target grade.*	*100%*			
No risk					
Medium risk					
High risk					

Critical thinking activity 3

1. Table 4.3 provides general at risk categories along with the main criteria that determine them. Thinking about your institution, complete the table with phrases or statistics that describe particular features for each at risk category under each criterion. An example of a phrase and a statistic is provided in italics for you.

2. Pick a group of your tutees and allocate each student an at risk category based on a holistic view of their progress so far. Then:

   a. calculate the percentage of students who fall into each category currently;

   b. estimate the percentage you would like in the outstanding or no risk category by the end of the course/academic year.

Discussion

The reason we have asked you to provide your own specific criteria is because each institution is different and therefore will use different criteria to determine what factors put a particular student at a particular level of risk. For example, one institution may consider that a student who has below 85 per cent attendance is at high risk, but another may only consider that student to be at medium risk. Also, it is important to note that institutions may have created their own at risk categories with associated criteria (different to those shown in Table 4.3) and indeed they may use a different term for 'at risk'. Additionally, some institutions are moving away from using the language of risk to inform their student support systems. Therefore, it will be useful for you to ascertain, if you don't know already, what terminology is used in your own institution and what definitions are provided.

Another aspect that you should consider is how these categories are used. Are they to be used to simply reflect whether students will pass or fail their course or should they incorporate a more holistic view (for example, including background characteristics)? In this chapter, we are proposing the holistic view because personal issues are strongly linked to a student's success. However, senior managers may only want to use it to reflect whether students will pass or fail their course, and you may find it useful to reflect on why this might be.

A final point to consider is, to what extent should you share the categories with the student? Although institutions may use this categorisation primarily for their own purposes, arguably it is useful for students to be aware of their progress, and any factors that may be impeding this, so that they can gain a realistic view of their routes to progression.

At risk meetings

Once an at risk category has been assigned to each of your students, it is important to regularly review the reasons for the at risk category and the actions being taken to support every student. Where regular at risk meetings are a requirement or are common practice, they are usually most effective when they are:

* undertaken on a regular cycle;

* run as formal meetings in which anecdotal comments, gossip and any 'moans' are kept to an absolute minimum;

* attended by staff who work closely with the students in question, including lecturers, support staff and managers where appropriate.

If at risk meetings are not a requirement, or common practice, at your institution, then an alternative strategy that you could adopt is to regularly hold informal discussions with your colleagues about students who are deemed *most* at risk. The purpose of these discussions should be to evaluate the impact of current supportive actions and to agree future actions.

Within formal at risk meetings, your role as personal tutor is to lead the conversation and discuss each student in turn to review the reasons for their at risk category. You should discuss what actions have been, and need to be, taken to support that student to be successful (in other words, to ensure that they are supported to keep on track and realise their potential), with dates when these actions will be reviewed. It is important to remember that this method of tracking and monitoring is not solely focused on students who may be at risk of failing or withdrawing from their course; it should be equally focused on students who may be at risk of not achieving their target marks. The former helps to improve retention and success rates whereas the latter helps to improve the experience of students who need to be continually stretched and challenged. Together, they improve the overall student experience.

The name and format given to at risk meetings will differ between institutions and some may not have them at all. If this is the case, it is not your role to formally implement this system. Experience suggests that this is a good practice model that achieves positive results both for the students and the institution. Again, it must be emphasised that these systems are only indicative of the most appropriate types of tutorial support that may be offered to students and must not be used to place subjective judgments or limits on their ability or potential.

Critical thinking activity 4

»   *Table 4.4 is an excerpt from a live at risk monitoring document. This is an overview of students with the at risk category for each, which includes reasons for the category and support actions taken. It is completed by you as personal tutor and is an example of at risk documentation as mentioned in Table 4.2. Read the document and write down what actions you would take to support these students. The names used here are fictional*

Table 4.4 *Example at risk monitoring document (excerpt; actions omitted)*

Student name	At risk category	Reasons for the category
Tim Bentley	High risk	Tim displays a poor attitude to learning and is at risk of not achieving his target grades, as well as potentially being withdrawn from his course due to non-submission of work. He struggles with his written expression but is very good in presentations and seminar discussions when he focuses. He has had a number of positive learning conversations (covered in detail in Table 4.5) and is being taken through the formal disciplinary procedure.
Leanne Pickering	Outstanding	Leanne displays an excellent attitude to learning and has exemplary attendance and punctuality. She is working at her target degree outcome level. However, she wants to achieve higher than this to ensure a first-class degree classification.
Ahmed Osman	Medium risk	Ahmed is at risk of not achieving his target degree outcome. He started the course enthusiastically and did very well in all of his assignments in the first few months. Recently, he appears to have lost interest in his studies. He had good attendance and punctuality; however, this has now started to fall. He has a part-time job and works most evenings.
Rebecca Walters	High risk	Rebecca is a carer for her mother. She suffers from anxiety, which can lead to panic attacks in class. She is academically able and motivated; however, she has fallen behind with her assignments. Her target classification is upper second-class honours but due to poorly presented work as well as not submitting some of her assignments she is currently only achieving the pass mark. Attendance is currently 68 per cent, with poor punctuality.

Discussion

When documenting actions to support students, it is important to:

- keep previous actions on the at risk document as you progress through the academic year. This helps to show any progress and also gives a clear overview of the support given to each student;

- ensure that your actions to support the student include, for example, one-to-ones and SMART targets. Supportive actions should not be, for example, transferring or withdrawing the student from the course. These would be the final result, not the supportive actions taken;

- share this information with as many colleagues who will be supporting that student within your institution as possible, for example academic colleagues, support staff and managers. Ensure that anything sensitive or confidential is not mentioned within a document like this and that rules governing data protection are adhered to.

Critical thinking activity 5

» *Using the group you identified in critical thinking activity 3, complete an at risk monitoring document that includes all of your students. State the at risk category, reasons for assigning students that status, actions taken so far to support each student and future actions you will take.*

Tools to re-engage students

The specific tools to help you re-engage your students are explained in Table 4.5.

Table 4.5 Tools to re-engage students

Tool	Aim	Explanation	When to use
Positive learning conversation (PLC)	To uncover underlying reasons for poor attendance, engagement or completion of work and thus re-engage the student and effect a behavioural change.	An individual meeting between the personal tutor and student to discuss issues with attendance, engagement or completion of work. It could be one, a combination or all three of these. Use the key principles of an effective one-to-one with a student from Chapter 5 but with the added dimension of purposefully trying to effect a positive behavioural change. The SMART targets set should reflect this. You may wish to request a manager to be present if appropriate.	With a student whose standards of attendance, engagement or completion of work has fallen below the institution's expected standards. A useful guideline is to use after two or three 'causes for concern' from lecturers. Use before formal disciplinary stages at manager level.
Positive learning conversation review	To review whether the targets set in the PLC have been achieved.	If PLC review targets are repeatedly not met, the student can be referred to the formal disciplinary process at manager level. Again, you may wish to request a manager to be present if appropriate.	Shortly after the PLC, depending on the issue. A useful guideline is one to two weeks after the PLC.

Student progress report or review	To effect a change in engagement or attainment for a student whose progress needs monitoring.	A report, incorporating learning and engagement analytics combined with the views of (personal and module) tutors each semester reviewed by staff as part of the assessment process.	In isolation or can work well alongside a PLC or when a formal disciplinary meeting has taken place and where showing improvements from the report have been set as a condition of continuing on the course.
Informal mediation process	Restore justice/repair relationships/ heal hurt feelings between fellow students or between students and lecturers.	A meeting of students (or students and staff) between whom there has been disagreement/gossiping. You are present in a personal tutoring capacity and are joined by other colleagues. Rules of the meeting include: • only one person to talk at a time; • each person to be able to state their points; • all views respected; • no raising of voices; • keeping as calm as possible.	After a conflict situation between fellow students or students and lecturers.

The case for a positive approach to re-engagement

If a student appears to be disengaged from, or disinterested in, their course, it is important to try to dig down to the underlying reasons for this and to provide positive reinforcement to students (some of whom may have never experienced this before). Wallace (2013, p 95) states: *'What looks like simply a lack of respect may be a signal that something more complex needs addressing in terms of the learner's needs'*. Reading and interpreting student behaviour and seeing it as a way of communicating in order to understand what it is telling us (Wallace, 2013) is key. Although Wallace is talking about further education students, we can also apply this principle to HE students.

It is important to emphasise that this goes hand in hand with the aim of encouraging the student to become independent, take ownership and take responsibility. Positive strategies, which include conversations with the student to address these issues, can initiate behavioural change and can reduce the number of incidents in a more effective way than simple, punitive measures. You should still be robust when addressing issues of disengagement and have tight rules and clear procedures but know that ultimately it is a student's choice to join the course and, depending on your attendance policy, to attend and engage in class. The aim of these tools and strategies is not for us to control student behaviour but for students to eventually take ownership and control it themselves.

Despite all these efforts, even a highly effective personal tutor will inevitably sometimes have tutees that will fail and drop out. This can be one of the most challenging and unpleasant parts of the tutoring role as you may be the member of staff that has to explain to a student that they will not be able to complete their studies. All you can do is provide the best support you can, utilising the knowledge available to you and within the boundaries discussed in Chapter 3. You can do all you can to offer the student a fair opportunity to succeed but you cannot complete the course for them and must also afford them the freedom to fail. If and when they do, however, you have a responsibility to offer to support them on their next steps as best you can, again being mindful of the boundaries already discussed. Before a student gets to the stage of programme termination they might benefit from informed advice about course suspension or change (discussed in the next chapter). Often, there are trained student support colleagues within an institution who can speak with students about the options available to them.

Working with students who have additional support needs

There is plenty of information already out there on the topic of additional support needs themselves, in terms of the definitions, approaches, issues and support needs related to specific learning difficulties and disabilities. This section is specifically concerned with your role as a personal tutor regarding your students who have support needs and your relationship with other staff within the institution when it comes to monitoring these issues. UK-based HE institutions are required by law to make reasonable adjustments for students with disabilities in relation to learning, teaching and assessment and we will consider the role of the personal tutor in this (Wisker et al, 2007; Riddell and Weedon, 2014; Kendall, 2017).

First, a quick note on terminology. Some different terms are used within HE. Students can be referred to as having learning difficulties and disabilities (LDD) or special educational needs and disability (SEND) or ASN (additional support needs). As you can see from the title of this section, we are using the last of these but without the acronym ASN. The staff employed to work directly with these students may also have different titles. One of the most common for the relevant group of staff or department is 'professional support services', which is the term we use.

Critical thinking activity 6

You have a student, David, who has an additional support need. We have not specified the particular support need on purpose since we would encourage you to think about your role as personal tutor in terms of facilitating and providing appropriate support for students with additional support needs generally rather than specific actions related to a particular need, which can have a wide range of individual differences within them.

1. List what you think are the key actions to support David generally.

2. For each action, state whether it should be carried out by you as personal tutor, other members of staff or a combination of both.

3. Make notes that explain and discuss how you decided on your answers to question 2 and how important each action is.

4. Compare your answers to the suggestions in Table 4.6.

Table 4.6 *Additional support actions, roles and explanations*

Action	*Who to carry out?*	*Explanation and discussion*
With David, complete a referral to professional support services for assessment.	Any member of staff working with David	This may have already happened at an early stage of the year and David may have declared his need at enrolment, meaning an additional referral from you is not necessary. You may have other students who you feel might benefit from additional support but who haven't had any referral, and who you'll need to refer.
Talk to David in his first one-to-one meeting about support needs and whether he feels they are being met.	Personal tutor	This is an important part of your initial one-to-one and subsequent one-to-one meetings. It needs handling sensitively of course in that a student may not want undue attention being drawn to the additional support need. Also, it has been declared but is confidential between the student and relevant staff. David's support needs may also be flagged in the institutional dashboard or progression monitoring system.

Table 4.6 (Cont.)

Action	Who to carry out?	Explanation and discussion
Adapt my approach in one-to-ones and group tutorial for David.	Personal tutor	Like other academics, your own approach to a student such as David in face-to-face support and learning situations may need adapting (as informed by an individual support plan).
Use information about David's additional support need to inform at risk meetings, documentation and actions.	Personal tutor	Continuing with the holistic view, these issues need to inform at risk discussions and actions. Of course, David may be judged to be 'no risk' or 'low risk' if there is no negative impact on his chances of success and appropriate support is in place.
Communicate with the relevant professional support services staff member.	Personal tutor and other staff	Clear communication and conversations are paramount. Other academic staff should also be in regular communication with the relevant additional support staff, but as the primary support, much of this responsibility will rest with you.
Raise awareness of the support need to the department and academic staff.	Professional support staff; possibly the personal tutor	You can have a role in raising awareness of support needs and issues, particularly if you feel there is a need for this in the curriculum area. However, it is not your primary role on a formal level and professional services staff also need to be proactive in this. Again, the rules governing data protection and confidentiality apply here and David may have set limits on the number of people he wants to be informed about his additional support needs.
Advise other academic staff about how they need to adapt their teaching and approach to David.	Professional support staff; possibly the personal tutor	While you can have a role in this, the relevant professional support services member of staff is key here and this information should be on a shared individual support plan for a student such as David and, ideally, uploaded to the dashboard tracking and monitoring system.
Work with in-class support for David.	All academic staff including the personal tutor	If allocated, these are members of staff you need to work with in group tutorials (and possibly one-to-ones).
Ensure additional support information informs any PLCs and/or disciplinary meetings that David may have. Ensure a relevant professional support services member of staff is present in disciplinary meetings.	Personal tutor; relevant managers	This information should inform disciplinary meetings and it is good practice for a member of the professional support services team to be present as another advocate for the student in an appropriate way. The latter is not directly your role and the managers should initiate this; however, you can be useful in reminding those organising the meeting that this should happen.

Table 4.6 *(Cont.)*

Action	Who to carry out?	Explanation and discussion
Undergo training in David's specific support need.	Possibly the personal tutor and other academic staff	While many institutions will have specialist staff and are the 'experts', it is useful for personal tutors to undergo training in additional support needs and learning difficulties. It is not a prerequisite of working with a student with a particular need, but in order to provide holistic support you may request this or research and talk to others informally.
Allocate support staff.	Student services manager	It is not your role, but if you feel there's a need you can discuss the requirement for resourcing with your line manager or directly with the student services manager.

Discussion

To fulfil the aim of providing effective and holistic support to students, additional support needs have to be taken into account. You may be the first staff member to whom a student discloses details of their need or disability, but you are not the only source of support and student services have a key role to play. As such, and as we have seen, additional support issues are something you will have much involvement with while at the same time remembering expertise and temporal boundaries. You are not expected to be an expert in all of these needs, but you will inevitably gain more knowledge of these issues as you undertake the role and you may want to pursue an area of particular interest for your own development. A clear referral process, both internal and external, is key. Also, a connection is often needed between additional support and safeguarding, the next topic of this chapter.

Safeguarding

Cast your mind back to the beginning of the book. There we listed all of the different roles you have to play, thinking of them in terms of alternative job titles. Among them was therapist or counsellor. Once again, we need to remember the expertise and referral boundary. You are not a therapist or counsellor but a personal tutor. However, any social issues relating to a particular student will almost certainly impact upon the things you are given the task of ensuring: effective learning and assessment; 'stretch and challenge' and the retention of students in the institution. Moreover, you are often the individual with whom students build the most trusting relationship, meaning that they may often talk to you about such issues rather than speaking to other individuals either within or external to the institution.

You will no doubt be familiar with the term 'safeguarding'. 'To safeguard' has a generic definition of '*protect from harm or damage with an appropriate measure*' (Oxford Dictionaries, nd, online). While there is a statutory duty for further education colleges and schools to safeguard and protect children in their care, the same is not true for HE institutions. However, they have a common law duty to take steps to ensure reasonably foreseeable harm does not occur by way of careless acts or omissions by the institution, particularly in relation to a vulnerable adult (often referred to as an 'adult at risk'). This term is used to describe *'any person who is aged 18 years or over and at risk of abuse or neglect because of their needs for care and or support'* (National Health Service England, 2017, p 2). This tells us that it is the duty of all staff and the institution to safeguard vulnerable adults; but in the day-to-day language of the educational institution it is often used as an umbrella term for those students who have had, or are still undergoing, safeguarding issues. A typical statement when discussing a student may be 'she has a safeguarding file'. Among the issues involved could be domestic violence, abuse, sexual exploitation or neglect.

In a scenario where a student discloses information to you which suggests that they may be vulnerable to harm, it is usually a case of referring the information to the relevant member of staff at your institution – for example the 'safeguarding officers' – while also ensuring that the student feels supported and listened to at all times. Where safeguarding information is already held on a student within your cohort, this information should inform your approach from the beginning of the academic year, but it can be received in-year. The processes at your institution should ensure that you are a member of staff with whom relevant safeguarding information is shared.

Dashboards and learning/engagement analytics

As part of their academic support benchmarking tool, the National Union of Students suggest having some *'systems in place to alert staff to sudden drops in performance or attendance'* and that this should be a minimum requirement (2015, p 1). The use of learning and engagement analytics is becoming the norm in the majority of educational institutions because they can help identify those who may be at risk of withdrawal (McCluckie, 2014; Webb et al, 2017). These systems capture data from a range of 'touchpoints' and store this information in a data warehouse. This enables institutions to identify patterns and trends, inform their planning and decision-making, create predictive models and identify students who need, or are predicted to need, assistance and interventions. An early warning system may trigger when, for example, a student drops below 80 per cent attendance in the first few weeks of the semester, thus offering an opportunity for bespoke, targeted, and timely interventions (McCluckie, 2014). Figure 4.2 displays information on the data that may be gathered and the student support mechanisms it may inform. The results of analyses are often presented in dashboards for easy consumption. There are numerous companies in the marketplace that offer systems which, broadly, do a similar job. In this section we are not going to name all of the different systems or list their characteristics. However, we feel it is important to illustrate some of the most useful features for achieving the best outcomes for students.

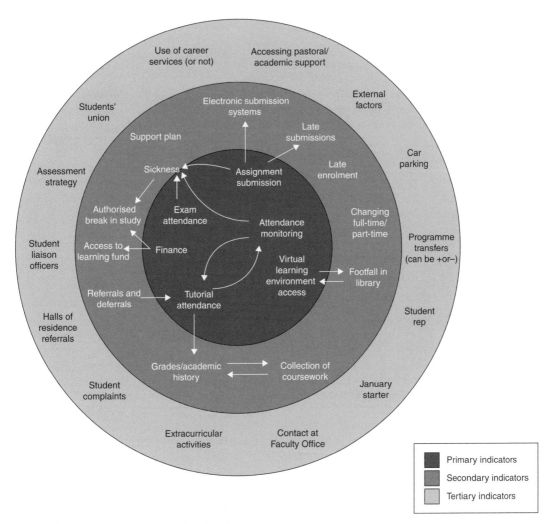

Figure 4.2 *Engagement Analytics Diagram*
Reproduced and adapted with permission, Mutton (2012)

Overall, the most important element of these electronic dashboards is that they are a 'one stop shop' for all information about every student. Information about individual students or groups should be updated by all tutors and support staff and is visible in real-time. These attributes are what make these systems so useful to your personal tutor role and key activities. Table 4.7 details useful features of dashboard systems relating to learning and engagement analytics.

Table 4.7 *Useful features of dashboard-based learning and engagement analytics*

Feature	Why it is useful
Additional support information	Students with additional support needs should have their support requirements available instantly, enabling more informed lesson planning and decision-making by academics, personal tutors and support staff.
At risk categories	Allows all staff to instantly see all students' at risk categories, usually by adopting a flagging or traffic light system. This enables quicker decisions to be made about support requirements and allocation of resources.
Attendance and punctuality data	Enables you and other staff to identify any issues or any patterns which will inform student meetings and inform SMART targets.
Centralised grades system	Provides a clear overview about the academic progress of students. This is particularly useful in one-to-ones to inform SMART target setting.
Staff comments about students	Provides instant feedback from any member of staff about a student, particularly his or her progress against attendance, engagement and completion of work standards. This qualitative information is useful in one-to-ones.
Student meetings	These meetings with students are useful for documenting progress against SMART targets. It also allows you to document and share discussions you have had (with students) with all colleagues to inform support.
Safeguarding information	Due to confidentiality it is unlikely to include any specific issues, rather, it acts as a 'flagging up' that a safeguarding file for a particular student is held and that staff can see the designated safeguarding officer for more information, if required. This section is vital for keeping every student safe. The previous 'staff comments about students' feature provides a good overview of the progress of every student, which, when twinned with safeguarding information clearly informs the at risk category, supportive actions and student meetings.
Target degree outcome or classification	Enables you to set and review effective SMART targets in order to help ensure students achieve their potential and/or stretch and challenge them to achieve more.

Good practice tips when using dashboards and learning/ engagement analytics

- Ensure you use clear language that students can understand and aim to avoid misinterpretation. This includes being clear about why you are putting information on the system. For example, if you include a comment that the student is having a difficult time then seek the student's permission to note this down and clarify that you are putting this on the system because you want other personal tutors and support staff to be sensitive around the student at this time.

- Use SMART targets where applicable.

- Ensure updating of information about students is done in a timely manner, particularly in relation to the features shown in Table 4.7.

- Where comments can be made about a student on your dashboard, try to not be *overly* critical of the student. In other words, try to turn a negative point into a positive action that could be taken by the student. For example, try not to say, 'Simone doesn't take part in seminars'; instead, say, 'We have agreed a target for Simone to contribute regularly to seminars'. This provides clear instruction on how improvements can be made.

It is prudent to be cautious about relying solely upon data, automated analysis or computer-generated information to drive your personal tutoring practice. For example, while some research indicates a positive correlation between attendance and academic achievement, other sources disagree. Student attendance may not necessarily equate to student learning and non-attendance does not necessarily indicate that learning is not taking place (Davis, 2011; Gurbutt and Gurbutt, 2015; Handley, 2016; Hughes et al, 2018). Attendance is one, but not the only, factor to consider when assessing what support a student requires. Some students may quickly learn how to play whatever system you might create; for example, we have experienced instances of students remaining logged on to appear active in a virtual learning environment. Again, face-to-face communication and knowledge, as well as using intuition, is critical here. This attendance data can be extremely insightful but it requires your interpretation to add significant value.

If data is analysed and contextualised in a careful, structured and considered way (in conjunction with strategic co-ordination between students, staff and senior management) it can be extremely valuable (Witt et al, 2016). As a personal tutor, it is important that you can identify patterns and accurately infer meaning from a variety of information sources. When considering this information it is essential that you take into account the wider context (which may vary considerably from one student, programme, department or institution to another) because this can both inform and improve your professional practice. When recording information, either in a dashboard system or elsewhere in a tutorial record or notebook, it is important to strike a balance and include the right level of detail to capture what was discussed and observed. Too much time spent behind the scenes recording information in great depth and detail can impact negatively on your ability to work with students face to face. Admittedly, in complicated situations, recording more detail might be necessary. As discussed previously, it is this contextual information that can be critical to providing the right support for students. Systems work well when they facilitate greater interaction with students rather than reducing the time you have available to do this properly. It may be worth discussing approaches to recording tutorials with other tutors in your team to ensure consistency of practice.

Critical thinking activity 7

1. With every student tracking and monitoring system, whether electronic or not, there can be problems or issues. Identify:

    a. what you think these are most likely to be;

    b. what actions you or the institution could take to overcome them.

2. If you as personal tutor are not permitted access to all the data your institution holds on your tutees (eg GCSE or A level grades), what issues does this raise?

Summary

In this chapter we have looked in detail at the various student populations you may encounter and outlined good practice in supporting them.

We have looked at the tracking and monitoring of students. Many factors will influence the effectiveness of your tracking and monitoring. One of them is the relationship you have with your colleagues. When you are developing actions for students who are underperforming, not all staff will have the same view. Some may think that a firmer approach is needed, while others may think a softer approach will work best. Agreeing a way forward isn't always a 'straight line' and this subjectivity is something you must learn to manage through your influencing skills. Remember, however, that everyone has the right to a view but not everyone's view will be right. It is your responsibility to allow these individual perceptions to inform your holistic interpretation of each student's performance and support needs, while ensuring that the actions that you and others take always have students' success and well-being at the centre of them.

Learning checklist

Tick off each point when you feel confident you understand it.

☐ *I recognise that regularly tracking and monitoring the progress of each of my students is one of the key activities in pursuit of improving their success.*

☐ *I understand the various terms that may be used to describe at risk students and the variations between them.*

☐ *I realise some of my students may have background characteristics (either from their past or which develop during their time in the institution) which may increase the chances of risk and vulnerability.*

☐ *I know that, as the academic year progresses and each student's situation changes, the at risk category and the support provided should change accordingly.*

☐ *I recognise that tracking and monitoring of students should not be solely focused on students who may be at risk of failing or withdrawing from their course; it should be equally focused on students who may be at risk of not achieving their target degree classification or assessment outcomes. It should also be used to stretch and challenge students.*

☐ *I recognise that regularly speaking to my colleagues and using the institution's dashboard-based learning/engagement analytics system is important to inform a holistic view of each student's progress.*

☐ *I understand the boundaries between tailored support and profiling so am able to make informed choices as to when additional support may be required for a student based upon grouped or individual characteristics.*

☐ *I understand my role with students in my cohort who have additional support needs. I understand what actions I can take for these students and the role of other staff within the institution.*

Critical reflections

1. Analyse the emphasis that your institution places on tracking and monitoring student progress (if you have taught at more than one institution, compare and contrast the two institutions' approaches, using examples). What are the positive points about the methods they use and what things could they improve?

2. Evaluate:

   a. how you feel dashboard-based analytics may have improved the tracking and monitoring of student progress compared to traditional paper-based systems;

   b. how this may have influenced the impact of the personal tutor role.

3. Using Figure 4.2 as a guide (whether you have a dashboard analytics system or not):

   a. identify your strengths and points for development in the tracking and monitoring of your students;

   b. set yourself two development targets to work on over the next six weeks. On completion, critically review your progress.

4. What are your views on the boundaries between tailored support and profiling students? Under what circumstances, and with what information, do you offer additional support to students?

Personal tutor self-assessment system

As a reminder, some key activities for the personal tutor are:

- tracking and monitoring your students;

- identifying the needs of your tutees on an individual and group level;

- working with students who have additional support needs.

PERSONAL TUTOR SELF-ASSESSMENT SYSTEM : Chapter 4 Key activities : Identifying and supporting student populations

	Minimum standard 1 star	Beginner level 2 star	Intermediate level 3 star	Advanced level 4 star	Expert level 5 star
Individual	I ensure that I consider the potential needs of various student populations before tutoring commences. I understand and can use any dashboard analytics systems that my institution utilises.	I regularly reflect on the needs of my tutee cohorts, based upon any information I have. I build these reflections into my future planning and discuss them with my head of department during appraisal meetings.	I regularly assess the needs, engagement and development of my students, recording any observations made on any dashboard systems my institution utilises.	Feedback from my students regarding the key activities is consistently very positive. Feedback from colleagues shows they regard them as having a strong impact on student progress and outcomes.	I have detailed plans in place to ensure I identify the needs of my students at an early stage and I monitor these needs as they evolve throughout their studies. I continually and thoroughly analyse the data provided by the dashboard system to seek new ways to improve my practice. I discuss consistency of practice with my fellow tutors.
Institutional	My institution ensures that any information held about students, which may affect or support them, is made available to tutors (in line with data protection regulations) and this is regularly utilised.	The strategy for supporting specific student populations is effectively communicated to all new staff and updates for existing staff are frequent. Where dashboard analytics systems are used there is basic uniformity in their application to record student interactions.	The identification and support of specific student populations is routinely discussed in all academic staff's appraisal meetings. Tutors and central support services regularly utilise analytics to inform practice.	The use of dashboard-based analytics is embedded into all relevant departments of the institution. Analysis of the data they produce informs programme and department-level student support planning.	Relevant data on key performance indicators is used to systematically review the institution's student support strategy. This analysis feeds into a rigorous departmental self-assessment system and the outcome is SMART quality improvement plans. Staff training and development includes discussion on how to use dashboard and analytics systems and promotes continuity of practice.

The self-assessment system is available as a free download from the publisher's website and the authors' websites (all listed at the start of the book).

References

Baxter, A and Britton, C (2001) Risk, Identity and Change: Becoming a Mature Student. *International Studies in Sociology of Education*, 11(1): 87–104.

Beatty-Guenter, P (1994) Sorting, Supporting, Connecting, and Transforming: Retention Strategies at Community Colleges. *Community College Journal of Research and Practice*, 18(2): 113–29.

Braine, M E and Parnell, J (2011) Exploring Students' Perceptions and Experience of Personal Tutors. *Nurse Education Today*, 31: 904–10.

Calcagno, L, Walker, D and Grey, D J (2017) Building Relationships: A Personal Tutoring Framework to Enhance Student Transition and Attainment. *Student Engagement in Higher Education Journal*, 1(2): 88–99.

Cooke, R, Barkham, K, Audin, K, Bradley, M and Davy, J (2004) How Social Class Differences Affect Students' Experience of University. *Journal of Further and Higher Education*, 28(4): 407–21.

Davis, A (2011) *The Correlation between Attendence* [sic] *and Achievement*. Dublin: Dublin Institute of Technology. [online] Available at: http://arrow.dit.ie/fellow/13 (accessed 30 June 2018).

Department for Education (2017) *Securing Student Success: Risk-Based Regulation for Teaching Excellence, Social Mobility and Informed Choice in Higher Education – Government Consultation on Behalf of the Office for Students*. London: Department for Education. [online] Available at: https://consult.education.gov.uk/higher-education/higher-education-regulatory-framework/supporting_documents/HE%20reg%20framework%20condoc%20FINAL%2018%20October%20FINAL%20FINAL.pdf (accessed 30 June 2018).

Ghenghesh, P (2017) Personal Tutoring from the Perspective of Tutors and Tutees. *Journal of Further and Higher Education*, 42(4): 570–84.

Gurbutt, D J and Gurbutt, R (2015) Empowering Students to Promote Independent Learning: A Project Utilising Coaching Approaches to Support Learning and Personal Development. *Journal of Learning Development in Higher Education*, 8: 1–17.

Handley, S (2016) Turning Up – Does it Matter? Presentation at *RAISE (Researching, Advancing and Inspiring Student Engagement) Conference*, Loughborough, 9 September 2017.

Harrison, N (2017) *Moving on Up: Pathways of Care Leavers and Care-Experienced Students into and through Higher Education*. Bristol: University of the West of England. [online] Available at: www.nnecl.org/file/HERACLESFinalreport.pdf (accessed 30 June 2018).

Hixenbaugh, P, Pearson, C and Williams, D (2006) Student Perspectives on Personal Tutoring: What Do Students Want? In Thomas, L and Hixenbaugh, P (eds) *Personal Tutoring in Higher Education* (pp 45–56). Stoke-on-Trent: Trentham Books.

Hughes, G, Panjwani, M, Tulcidas, P and Byrom, N (2018) *Student Mental Health: The Role and Experiences of an Academic*. Oxford: Student Minds. [online] Available at: www.studentminds.org.uk/theroleofanacademic.html (accessed 30 June 2018).

Jones, D J and Watson, B C (1990) High-risk Students and Higher Education: Future Trends. *ASHE-ERIC Higher Education Report*, 19(3): 83–90.

Kendall, L (2017) Supporting Students with Disabilities within a UK University: Lecturer Perspectives. *Innovations in Education and Teaching International*, 1–10. https://doi.org/10.1080/14703297.2017.1299630

Lamont, B J (2005) *East Meets West – Bridging the Academic Advising Divide.* NACADA Clearinghouse of Academic Advising Resources. [online] Available at: www.nacada.ksu.edu/Resources/Clearinghouse/View-Articles/East-meets-West--Bridging-the-advising-divide.aspx (accessed 30 June 2018).

Lochtie, D (2015) A 'Special Relationship' in Higher Education? What Influence Might the US Higher Education Sector Have in Terms of Support for International Students in the UK? *Perspectives: Policy and Practice in Higher Education*, 20(2–3): 67–74.

May, H and Bridger, K (2010) *Developing and Embedding Inclusive Policy and Practice in Higher Education*. York: Higher Education Academy.

McCluckie, B (2014) Identifying Students 'At Risk' of Withdrawal Using ROC Analysis of Attendance Data. *Journal of Further and Higher Education*, 38(4): 523–35.

McFarlane, K J (2016) Tutoring the Tutors: Supporting Effective Personal Tutoring. *Active Learning in Higher Education*, 17(1): 77–88.

McIntosh, E (2017). Working in Partnership: The Role of Peer Assisted Study Sessions in Engaging the Citizen Scholar. *Active Learning in Higher Education*, 1–16. https://doi.org/10.1177%2F1469787417735608

McIntosh, E and Shaw, J (2017) *Student Resilience: Exploring the Positive Case for Resilience.* Students Unite. [online] Available at: www.unite-group.co.uk/sites/default/files/2017-05/student-resilience.pdf (accessed 30 June 2018).

Mountford-Zimdars, A, Sabri, D, Moore, J, Sanders, J, Jones, S and Higham, L (2015) *Causes of Differences in Student Outcomes*. Bristol: HEFCE.

Million Plus: The Association for Modern Universities (2018) *Forgotten Learners: Building a System that Works for Mature Students*. London: Million Plus. [online] Available at: www.millionplus.ac.uk/policy/reports/forgotten-learners-building-a-system-that-works-for-mature-students (accessed 30 June 2018).

Mutton, J (2013) *Student Engagement Traffic Lighting Project Case Study*. [online] Available at: http://repository.jisc.ac.uk/5028 (accessed 30 June 2018).

Naidoo, R and Jamieson, I (2005) Empowering Participants or Corroding Learning? Towards a Research Agenda on the Impact of Student Consumerism in Higher Education. *Journal of Education Policy*, 20(3): 267–81.

National Health Service England (2017) *Safeguarding Adults*. [online] Available at: www.england.nhs.uk/wp-content/uploads/2017/02/adult-pocket-guide.pdf (accessed 30 June 2018).

National Union of Students (2015) *Academic Support Benchmarking Tool*. [online] Available at: www.nusconnect.org.uk/resources/academic-support-benchmarking-tool/download_attachment (accessed 30 June 2018).

Office for Students (nd) *Access and Participation Plans*. [online] Available at: www.officeforstudents.org.uk/advice-and-guidance/promoting-equal-opportunities/access-and-participation-plans (accessed 30 June 2018).

Owen, M (2002) 'Sometimes You Feel You're in Niche Time': The Personal Tutor System, a Case Study. *Active Learning in Higher Education*, 3(1): 7–23.

Oxford Dictionaries (nd) Terms searched for: to safeguard. [online] Available at: https://en.oxforddictionaries.com (accessed 30 June 2018).

Priest, R and McPhee, S A (2000) Advising Multicultural Students: The Reality of Diversity. In Gordon V N and Habley, W R (eds) *Academic Advising: A Comprehensive Handbook* (pp 105–15). San Francisco, CA: Jossey-Bass.

Reay, D, Crozier, G and Clayton, J (2010) 'Fitting In' or 'Standing Out': Working-class Students in UK Higher Education. *British Educational Research Journal*, 36(1): 107–24.

Rhodes, S and Jinks, A (2005) Personal Tutors' Views of Their Role with Pre-registration Nursing Students: An Exploratory Study. *Nurse Education Today*, 25(5): 390–7.

Riddell, S and Weedon, E (2014). Disabled Students in Higher Education: Discourses of Disability and the Negotiation of Identity. *International Journal of Educational Research*, 63: 38–46.

See, B H, Gorard, S and Torgerson, C (2012) Promoting Post-16 Participation of Ethnic Minority Students from Disadvantaged Backgrounds: A Systematic Review of the Most Promising Interventions. *Research in Post-Compulsory Education*, 17(4): 409–22.

Shaw, C (2014) *How Academics Can Help Ensure Students' Wellbeing.* [online] Available at: www.theguardian.com/higher-education-network/blog/2014/oct/01/university-academic-support-student-welfare-wellbeing (accessed 30 June 2018).

Small, F (2013) Enhancing the Role of Personal Tutor in Professional Undergraduate Education. *Inspiring Academic Practice*, 1(1): 1–11.

Smith, E (2008) *Personal Tutoring: An Engineering Subject Centre Guide.* Leicester: Higher Education Academy.

Stenton, A (2017) *Why Personal Tutoring is Essential for Student Success.* [online] Available at: www.heacademy.ac.uk/blog/why-personal-tutoring-essential-student-success (accessed 30 June 2018).

Stephen, D E, O'Connell, P and Hall, M (2008) 'Going the Extra Mile', 'Fire-fighting', or Laissez-faire? Re-evaluating Personal Tutoring Relationships within Mass Higher Education. *Teaching in Higher Education*, 13(4): 449–60.

Swain, H (2008) *The Personal Tutor.* [online] Available at: www.timeshighereducation.co.uk/news/the-personal-tutor/210049.article (accessed 30 June 2018).

Thomas, L (2006) Widening Participation and the Increased Need for Personal Tutoring. In Thomas, L and Hixenbaugh, P (eds) *Personal Tutoring in Higher Education* (pp 21–31). Stoke-on-Trent: Trentham Books.

Thomas, L and Jones, R (2017) *Student Engagement in the Context of Commuter Students.* London: The Student Engagement Partnership. [online] Available at: http://tsep.org.uk/student-engagement-in-the-context-of-commuter-students (accessed 30 June 2018).

Thomas, L, Hill, M, O'Mahony, J and Yorke, M (2017) *Supporting Student Success: Strategies for Institutional Change. What Works? Student Retention and Success Programme. Final Report.* London: Paul Hamlyn Foundation.

Wallace, S (2013) When You're Smiling: Exploring How Teachers Motivate and Engage Learners in the Further Education Sector. *Journal of Further and Higher Education*, 38(3): 346–60.

Watts, T (2011) Supporting Undergraduate Nursing Students through Structured Personal Tutoring: Some Reflections. *Nursing Education Today*, 31: 214–18.

Webb, O, Wyness, L and Cotton, D (2017) *Enhancing Access, Retention, Attainment and Progression in Higher Education*. York: Higher Education Academy. [online] Available at: www.heacademy. ac.uk/system/files/resources/enhancing_access_retention_attainment_and_progression_ in_higher_education_1.pdf (accessed 30 June 2018).

Whittaker, R (2008) *Quality Enhancement Themes: The First Year Experience – Transition to and During the First Year*. Glasgow: Quality Assurance Agency Scotland.

Wilcox, P, Winn, S and Fyvie-Gauld, M (2005) It Was Nothing to Do with the University, It Was Just the People': The Role of Social Support in the First-year Experience of Higher Education. *Studies in Higher Education*, 30(6): 707–22.

Wisker, G, Exley, K, Antoniou, M and Ridley, P (2007) *Working One-to-One with Students: Supervising, Coaching, Mentoring, and Personal Tutoring (Key Guides for Effective Teaching in Higher Education)*. London: Routledge.

Witt, N, McDermott, A, Kneale, P and Coslett, D (2016) *Effective Learner Analytics: A Senior Leadership–Staff–Student Informed Approach (Plymouth University)*. [online] Available at: www.heacademy.ac.uk/about/news/hea-event-shares-innovative-strategies-he-institutions (accessed 30 June 2018).

Yale, A (2017) The Personal Tutor–Student Relationship: Student Expectations and Experiences of Personal Tutoring in Higher Education. *Journal of Further and Higher Education*, 1–12. doi:10.1080/0309877X.2017.1377164.

5 Key activities: effectively supporting all stages of the student lifecycle

Chapter aims

This chapter helps you to:

- identify the importance of transitions in HE and how they relate to the personal tutor role;

- understand the following typical stages in the student lifecycle, your role within them and their impact upon students:

  - pre-arrival;

  - induction and first year;

  - internal progression (getting students back on track, course changes or suspension of studies);

  - external progression (preparation for graduation and beyond).

It will explore these stages through the application of the key tutoring activities, helping you to:

- understand the purpose of one-to-ones with students and strategies for conducting them effectively;

- identify the reasons for, benefits of, and best practice in group tutorial planning and teaching;

- reflect upon what an effective curriculum of personal tutoring might look like at your institution.

Introduction

Chapter 4 looked at some of the key activities of the personal tutor in the context of the various student populations you may encounter in your role. This chapter explores further key activities within the context of supporting students through the recognised stages of their journey. As an educator, one of the greatest pleasures you may enjoy is seeing how an individual progresses from applicant to graduate, overcoming various challenges along the way. The student lifecycle includes the stages of profiling students (as we explored in Chapter 4), supporting them, connecting them and finally helping them to transform and transition into autonomous, independent learners (Beatty-Guenter, 1994). The *Student Experience Practitioner Model* breaks down the stages as shown in Figure 5.1.

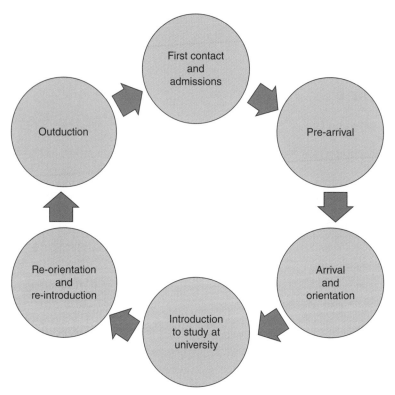

Figure 5.1 *Student Experience Practitioner Model*
Reproduced with permission, Morgan (2012, p 16)

This chapter guides you through these stages and the transitions that students typically experience as they progress through them, building upon transition theory and pedagogy (Schlossberg, 1981; Kift, 2009). The role of the tutor in supporting students during each phase is explored, including one-to-one and group tutorials, as part of a tutoring curriculum, tailored to the needs of students at each stage of the lifecycle.

Transitioning to university life

The process of transition that students undergo before and at the start of their course can cause psychological distress, anxiety, depression, sleep disturbance and a reduction in self-esteem (Hicks and Heastie, 2008; Palmer et al, 2009). The first 12 months of HE is widely recognised as the highest point of attrition in post-secondary education with approximately 10 per cent of students leaving their programme and as many as 42 per cent considering leaving HE generally (Tinto, 1987; Yorke, 2001; Thomas, 2012). The first eight to ten weeks are clearly the most difficult period of transition when students are at their most vulnerable. They can feel overwhelmed by new responsibilities and expectations that can leave them feeling confused, panicked, lost or isolated (Gutteridge, 2001; Mortenson, 2005; Hixenbaugh et al, 2006; Hicks and Heastie, 2008; Small, 2013). Student attrition in the early part of the course is usually caused by a lack of social and/or academic integration and often linked to difficulties in making friends or homesickness (Wilcox et al, 2005). New students need support to deal not only with the academic culture shock of adapting to HE but also with other material factors such as the emotional shock of moving away from the familiar home environment to a very different life at university (Wilcox et al, 2005). For students juggling a multitude of commitments outside of university, such as part-time work, family and caring responsibilities, these factors can impact considerably on their ability to cope with student life. Adequate arrangements need to be put in place to support them to manage these conflicting commitments. While the individual student is responsible for making this work, they require support in order to do so.

Effective transitional support

Schlossberg's *Transition Theory* and model, a vehicle for analysing human adaptation, suggests that the support available at the time of transition is critical to an individual's sense of well-being (Schlossberg, 1981; Schlossberg, 2011). The establishment of the Office for Students and the regulatory framework in UK HE presents a unique opportunity to take a fresh look at the sector's approach to enhancing student retention on campus and supporting important transition points (Tinto, 1993; Department for Education, 2017).

Comprehensive and easily accessible pre-entry information and interaction are required via a combination of email, social media and events (Parmar and Trotter, 2005; Whittaker, 2008; Calcagno et al, 2017). This can inform expectations, develop academic skills and foster early engagement with peers, current students and staff (Thomas, 2012). Once students arrive, immediate programme involvement and induction adds purpose, direction and structure, which makes students less vulnerable to drift (Walker, 2010). Throughout the student lifecycle, transition pedagogy should support students to adapt their previous learning experiences to HE. This should be followed by supporting and facilitating their transition into later years and future employment (Beatty-Guenter, 1994; Kift, 2009). First-year curriculum design should have interconnected organising principles embedded into it, including enabling effective transition/engagement, developing academic/personal skills and generally supporting any subject, attendance or independent study-related issues (Wilcox et al, 2005; Yorke and Longden, 2008; Kift, 2009; Fergy et al, 2011). It is important to bear in mind that students are consistently in transition, given that every year of study involves a new set of considerations and expectations. These should be consistently negotiated. Applying Kift's six principles of transition pedagogy when designing student success interventions may prove highly beneficial: (1) transition; (2) diversity; (3) design; (4) engagement; (5) assessment and (6) impact and evaluation (2009, p 2).

The social dimension

In the initial transitional phase, students have an urgent need to find a safe place, belong, identify with others and negotiate their new identities as university students (Wilcox et al, 2005). In fact, social integration, relationship forming, stress management and the development of non-academic skills were found to be as influential as academic skills in ensuring successful transition (Richardson, 2000; Stephen et al, 2008; Richardson et al, 2012). It has been suggested that the sector pay greater attention to social aspects of student integration, including peer support arrangements, since students have to manoeuvre through a number of cultures in order to be successful (Lea and Street 2000; Wilcox et al, 2005; McIntosh, 2017).

An induction centred around helping students to settle in, connect to friends and get to know each other is recommended (Parmar and Trotter, 2005; Whittaker, 2008). This might include supporting social and personal issues, overcoming difficulty in making friends or connecting with their personal tutor (Wilcox et al, 2005). The first week of university requires specific attention as it is a key time for students to form relationships and gain a sense of group and cohort identity (Hartwell and Farbrother, 2006). The impact of effective early transition can play a key role in transforming students in terms of their skills, active learning and engagement. It can therefore help determine and support future persistence and success (Thomas, 2002; Palmer et al, 2009).

The role of the tutor in transition

The actions of others, such as trained facilitators, can help (or hinder) how an individual progresses through these transitional stages. Therefore, the enabling role that tutors play is key to ensuring the quality of the early student experience (Leibowitz and Schlossberg, 1982; Sargent and Schlossberg, 1988; Lago and Shipton 1999; Brinkworth et al, 2009; Stevenson, 2009; Zepke and Leach, 2010). A personal tutor's observation, support and instincts can inform a proactive early warning system, contribute towards a sense of belonging, 'buffer' against key first-year challenges and develop group identity (Thomas, 2006; Smith, 2008; Stevenson, 2009; Yale, 2017). For these reasons, the quality of relationships and frequency of interactions between academic staff and students is a key influence on their retention, progression and performance (McGivney, 1996; Thomas, 2002; Thomas, 2006; National Audit Office, 2007; Small, 2013).

Student engagement is key. Effective personal tutoring involves getting to know, and building a relationship with, your tutees before they arrive and then serving as a first point of contact very early on during their induction (Thomas, 2012; Calcagno et al, 2017). A favourable first impression of you formed by a face-to-face meeting with your tutees during the first week of study is of significant importance and value to them. It is also key to an ongoing successful relationship (Dobinson-Harrington, 2006; Wisker et al, 2007; Swain, 2008; Yale, 2017). If your tutees do not meet you, or find you intimidating, uncaring or cold, they may feel rejected and reconsider the value and financial implications of their decision to go to university (Yorke and Longden, 2008; Yale, 2017).

To be effective as a personal tutor, it is important to understand the intense anxiety and fear new students experience in relation to the social aspects of transition to university and convey to them that this feeling is perfectly normal and they are not alone (Wilcox et al, 2005). Also critical is understanding that students may have varying expectations of tutoring and support based on previous experiences so these will need to be discussed and managed (Yale, 2017). Your main focus when tutoring new students should be connecting and settling them into the institution while also helping them adjust to university-level study – essentially facilitating both academic and social integration (Barefoot, 2000; Thomas, 2006; Calcagno et al, 2017).

In order to provide robust academic support, it is necessary to encourage students to reflect upon their needs, motivations and aspirations for studying at university, while also familiarising them with the range of support services available and the role personal tutors play as part of those services (Calcagno et al, 2017). It is important to support your students, at a very early stage, to develop their awareness, curiosity and academic skills. At the same time it is necessary to encourage them to explore healthy study habits as well as gain assessment literacy (including reflecting on feedback and planning improvements). All of these things can help them develop a higher academic self-efficacy and increase their motivation (Calcagno et al, 2017; Yale, 2017). Academic well-being can also be promoted through educational socialisation, including peer-learning initiatives such as Peer Assisted Study Sessions (PASS) or student representation, which links academic and social integration together (Yorke, 2001; McIntosh, 2017). If you have an understanding and appreciation of the challenges that students may face, for example, living away from home for the first time, striving for financial independence and navigating a new environment, you are in a better position to assist them with social integration (Lee and Robinson, 2006). It is also important to champion extra-curricular activities (such as student clubs and societies) as these can be instrumental in establishing a renewed sense of belonging and connectedness with the institution. As part of this, you can encourage them to engage in these activities for their own well-being and benefit (Calcagno et al, 2017; Grey and McIntosh, 2017). Finally, if students feel that you understand their context then they are more likely to engage with you and follow your advice.

It is widely agreed that induction and transitional support, particularly for specific populations, should continue past the first few weeks after arrival. This is because students benefit significantly from information given at the point of need and this includes reinforcing information about the support they can access when they truly need it. This support should be 'live' and ongoing, not just buried in a handbook or an induction talk (Owen, 2002). It is recommended that your institution develop a curriculum or framework for personal tutoring which provides a structured programme of activities for tutors to use to support transitions and encourage student development (Calcagno et al, 2017). An example framework for the first year of study is displayed later in the chapter in Table 5.2. Support for students as they go through the different stages of their lifecycle can be delivered via a range of key tutoring activities including one-to-one and group tutorials. These frameworks must be informed by the student lifecycle and be based on the delivery of 'just-in-time' information.

Key tutoring activities

One-to-ones with students

Students increasingly value one-to-one time with their tutors and this can be an effective way to support and empower them in their learning (Wootton, 2007; Wisker et al, 2007). Students would like to see their tutors more frequently and routinely but, as discussed in Chapter 3, this becomes more challenging as the profile of the student body changes and student numbers rise (Owen, 2002; Sosabowski et al, 2003; Stephen et al, 2008; Thomas et al, 2017). Both students and tutors have called for more structured and focused support for their one-to-ones to reflect the complexity of their relationship (Blythman et al, 2006; Small, 2013; Thomas et al, 2017). It is important that meetings have an explicit purpose and structure to ensure students and tutors do not resort to guesswork or trial and error to figure out what personal tutoring is for (Thomas et al, 2017).

While many tutors believe students would benefit from taking responsibility for making appointments, students have called for tutors to be proactive and to schedule tutorials in advance. Here there is a danger that those who need support the most may not seek it and slip through the net (Malik, 2000; Owen, 2002; Neville, 2007; Wisker et al, 2008; Stephen et al, 2008). It is therefore important that tutorial support is proactive and seen as an integral part of all students' education rather than a safety net or as part of a deficit model (Owen, 2002; Whittaker, 2008; Stenton, 2017).

CASE STUDY

One-to-one meeting between Anita and Claire

The following dialogue is taken from an arranged one-to-one meeting between Claire, a level 5 Business Studies student, and her personal tutor Anita.

ANITA: *Come in and sit down Claire.*

CLAIRE: *Thanks.*

[Anita is sitting at a table with her back to the door. Claire sits in the only chair available at the other end of the table.]

ANITA: *Are you well?*

CLAIRE: *Er... yeah, I guess so.*

ANITA: *Good! So are you getting on okay with your studies?*

CLAIRE: *...Erm, I'm okay I think. I'm not sure... I'm trying my best to get all of the work done but I've had so much to do lately... I've been struggling a bit to get all of my coursework in on time.*

ANITA: *You've been struggling? What's gone wrong?*

CLAIRE: *Nothing's gone wrong as such... I've just had a lot on with my Human Resource Management (HRM) coursework and revising for my marketing exam... I've also been having some problems at home.*

[Anita turns her back to Claire to face her computer]

ANITA: *Hang on, I need to make sure I get all of this down onto the one-to-one part of our system.*

CLAIRE: *Okay.*

ANITA: *So, just say again, what's gone wrong?*

CLAIRE: *Erm... I'm doing okay, but I've felt like I've been getting a bit behind with my work.*

ANITA: *Okay, do you remember your targets from our last one-to-one meeting?*

CLAIRE: *I think it was to revise for my Marketing mock exam, complete my HRM coursework and... something else, I can't remember.*

ANITA: *I can't either. I'll check in a minute. What other modules do you do?*

CLAIRE: *Business and Applied Operations Management.*

ANITA: *Oh yes, I remember. So, did you revise for your Marketing exam?*

CLAIRE: *I tried to get as much done as possible at home, but it wasn't easy... I did much better than I thought I would though. I was really pleased, I got 66 per cent.*

ANITA: *Right. Did you get your HRM coursework in as well?*

CLAIRE: *It was late, but yes.*

ANITA: *Good... I can also see that you've had a few causes for concern from your Operations Management lecturer, Matt. Tell me what you did wrong.*

CLAIRE: *Nothing, I haven't done anything wrong... I had to have some time off because of the problems I've had with my housemate.*

ANITA: *Okay, did you see Matt about this though? Because you need to tell him if you're going to be off.*

CLAIRE: *No, I didn't, sorry.*

ANITA: *Well you need to make sure you do next time... we're not mind readers! You have to tell us if you've got a problem.*

So, the targets I want you to achieve by the next time we meet are full attendance, no causes for concern from your lecturers and make sure you get all of your work in on time. Okay?

CLAIRE: *Alright.*

ANITA: *Okay, great! I've got an important meeting I need to get to now, so I'll let you know when our next one-to-one meeting is. Okay?*

CLAIRE: *Yes... fine.*

Critical thinking activity 1

» *How would you evaluate this meeting? Note down three points about the meeting which you feel would make useful areas for development for Anita.*

CASE STUDY

One-to-one meeting between Anita and Claire — take two

ANITA: *Come in and sit down Claire, it's nice to see you.*

CLAIRE: *Thank you.*

[Anita is sitting near Claire, partly facing her at an angle; in other words, not sitting directly facing her. There is no table between them and Anita is not blocking the route to the door.]

ANITA: *Thank you for attending our one-to-one to review your progress, I'm interested to find out how things are. So, how are you?*

CLAIRE: *I'm not bad... I'm trying my best to get all of the work done but I've had so much to do lately... that I've been struggling a bit to get all of my coursework in on time, but I got it in, just a bit rushed.*

ANITA: *It sounds like it's been hard going for you. But as you say, you did get it in, so well done!*

CLAIRE: *Thanks, it has been a bit of a struggle for me lately.*

ANITA: *What are the reasons for it being a struggle?*

CLAIRE: *Well to be honest, I've been having some problems at home which have been affecting my studies.*

ANITA: *Okay, do you want to tell me about them?*

CLAIRE: *Erm, well... okay. I've been having lots of arguments with my housemate... and it's been really upsetting the dynamic of the house. We've been falling out a lot and I've not been able to concentrate on my studies all of the time when I've needed to.*

[Anita and Claire continue to discuss these issues. They both agree some small actions that Claire can take to help her situation and her studies. They agree to review these in the next one-to-one meeting.]

ANITA: *Okay, let's review your previous agreed targets. For HRM, you had a target of handing in two exam questions for marking as well as achieving over 60 per cent in the test. Did you get the assessment questions in?*

CLAIRE: *Yes, I've had them marked and have discussed the feedback with my teacher. I did okay in them but I now know what I need to do better next time.*

ANITA: *That's good, well done. Make sure you note all of this feedback down so you can refer back to it when you begin revision. I can see that you achieved 58 per cent in the test, how do you feel about that?*

CLAIRE: *I'm a bit disappointed to be honest. I did revise, but not as much as I probably could have. We have another test coming up in four weeks which I want to do better in.*

ANITA: *Okay, on a scale of one to ten, where ten is maximum effort, how much effort did you put into the revision?*

CLAIRE: *Erm... six.*

ANITA: *So, what can you do to bring that up to a seven?*

CLAIRE: *I think I could comfortably do an hour's revision for two evenings a week as I did before.*

ANITA: *Okay. How about we set you a more stretching target of doing an hour for three evenings a week? You've done really well so far to get the 58 per cent but I think you've got the potential to do even better next time.*

CLAIRE: *Er... okay. I'll give it a go, I guess.*

[Anita and Claire continue to agree SMART targets for the rest of her subjects. Anita asks Claire to summarise her targets after they have been agreed.]

ANITA: *Looking forward, we've agreed your targets and I'd like to see how you are getting on with these when we have our next one-to-one meeting on the 4th of March. Does this sound fair to you?*

CLAIRE: *Yes, that's fine.*

ANITA: *Well, thank you for this chat. I know you're facing a few obstacles but you've done really well so far and I believe in you. If you continue to push yourself, you can do even better.*

CLAIRE: *Thanks, I hope so.*

Critical thinking activity 2

»   *Examine whether your three points from Critical thinking activity 1 have been addressed.*

Dos and don'ts for one-to-ones

Table 5.1 Suggested dos and don'ts for one-to-ones

Dos	Don'ts
Prepare for them, for example by reading notes from previous one-to-ones, at risk meeting documents, 'staff comments about students' and speaking to other tutors and support staff about progress.	Be unprepared, because poor preparation or no preparation at all may lead to issues being missed, therefore reducing the impact of the meeting.
Appear pleased to see the students and have a sincere and calm approach (even if you are busy and have competing priorities; Dobinson-Harrington, 2006).	Let it appear to the students that you are just 'ticking off' your one-to-ones as an administrative duty you must fulfil.
Explain at the start of the meeting what things you would like to cover, but ensure you are clear that students can discuss anything that they have on their own agenda.	Go straight into reviewing the targets without some opportunity for discussion about how the students are feeling about their studies and any factors which might be affecting their progress.
Use more open questions to allow students and yourself to explore their thoughts and feelings.	Use more closed questions, because this will elicit only brief answers which don't help to build rapport or understand and explore issues deeply.
Record details of the conversation using the dashboard system for future reference.	Focus more on the recording of the conversation than on the quality and depth of the discussion.
Sit near and facing the student. Facing them slightly at an angle is preferable.	• Have tables between you. • Sit in a way that blocks access to the door. • Be too close so as to invade their personal space.

Table 5.1 (Cont.)

Dos	Don'ts
Display active listening, as well as body language and tone of voice that show you are genuinely interested. Also challenge, reframe, reflect back and summarise where appropriate.	Appear unengaged in the conversation.
Start with and praise the positive things that students have, or feel they have, tried or achieved.	Ignore their perspective or be too general.
Be honest about any areas that students need to improve.	Start with or ignore areas for development.
Be clear about the consequences of not improving.	Fail to explain the consequences of not improving.
Encourage the students to reflect and have a clear, open and honest discussion about progress against previous SMART targets (these may be academic, attendance, punctuality, engagement or personal).	Briefly mention previous SMART targets and offer no opportunity for discussion around these.
Allow the discussion to develop SMART targets that are stretching but are agreed between you and the students.	Set targets for the students which you have not discussed or agreed, because this will reduce the level of ownership that they feel for them.
Use scaling and solution-focused coaching techniques where appropriate (more of which in Chapter 6).	
Make clear your desire to help resolve any problems where it is possible.	
Ensure that the agreed targets are SMART.	
Finish on a positive and ask the student to summarise the agreed targets before the end of the meeting.	
Ensure dates for the review of these targets are agreed before the meeting finishes.	

Critical thinking activity 3

»   *Concentrating on the dos from Table 5.1, tick those that you use regularly and describe how you will employ the others from now on.*

A final thought on one-to-ones

As with teaching and curriculum planning, there isn't a secret formula for a perfect one-to-one. Within your busy personal tutor role, to avoid spending too much time on detailed planning or recording, it is useful to use the dos and don'ts as a helpful checklist (particularly the dos). As every student and educational institution is different, your one-to-ones will be different too. You will need to be adaptable to the needs and context of every student as well as the resources available, and to keep in mind the boundaries discussed in Chapter 3. Carrying out effective one-to-ones with students is a skill that can be learned through practice and reflection, and as you get better the impact on your students' progress and outcomes will improve.

Group tutorial planning and teaching

Group tutorial models are increasingly being used in response to resourcing issues in HE. Nevertheless, the benefits of group tutoring go beyond cost saving and include facilitating helpful student–student and tutor–student social integration (Wilcox et al, 2005; Whittaker, 2008; Stevenson, 2009). Small group tutorials can be central to effective transition and useful in formalising social relationships and networks (Tinto, 1993; McInnis, 2001; Yorke and Thomas, 2003; Cook and Rushton, 2008; Stevenson, 2009; Braine and Parnell, 2011; Richardson et al, 2012). Getting to know other students can help foster a sense of belonging, develop common experiences, support stress management and aid the development of peer-learning communities (Tinto, 1993; Stevenson, 2009; Fergy et al, 2011; Richardson et al, 2012; Calcagno et al, 2017). There are many issues regarding student transition that can be tackled via the group tutorial process, such as where to go to seek help and support, which normalises certain healthy student behaviours without singling out individual students. Group tutorials can also make support more accessible. Students have reported that the most positive aspects of group tutorials include getting to know their tutor. Students felt that they were more likely to approach tutors whom they had got to know in a group setting first, especially if they encountered problems later (Wilcox et al, 2005; Calcagno et al, 2017).

There are very few common definitions of group tutorials but a helpful way of thinking about them is as offering a 'secondary curriculum' for personal development including supporting active and independent learning, building study skills and enhancing graduate attributes (Barrie, 2007; Wootton, 2007; Calcagno et al, 2017). Tutorials are central to the delivery of an integrated curriculum, not separate from it, and should be seen as such. It is important to make the purpose of the group tutorial sessions clear to the students when they start and to explain the relevance to their course, career pathway (if they know it) and wider lives. Group tutorials provide another opportunity for you to co-ordinate the student journey, with the aim of enhancing the student experience and helping to improve student outcomes, such as retention, progression and performance as well as the National Student Survey (NSS).

We would recommend that, where possible, group tutorials are:

- **timetabled** for both tutors and students (Owen, 2002; Braine and Parnell, 2011; Thomas et al, 2017);

- **compulsory** for every first-year student (Owen, 2002);

- **credited** as students have an instrumental approach to their time so will commit to an activity more if credits are awarded for the time spent (Owen, 2002);

- **mainstream**, appearing to the student as a seamless part of the curriculum (Earwaker, 1992; Calcagno et al, 2017).

Critical thinking activity 4

Of course you, as an individual tutor, may not be able to directly influence some of the above considerations. There is no one correct way of doing things and the purpose and model for delivery can differ between institutions. Note down your answers to the following questions.

1. To what extent do you agree with each of the four previous recommendations and why?

2. Does making group tutorials compulsory for students increase their importance or make them an obligation that will lead to reluctant compliance? Why, or why not?

3. Does adding credits to tutorials (with assessed reflection) add importance or detract from other subjects? Why, or why not?

Discussion

You can hopefully see the potential benefits of making group tutorials timetabled, compulsory, credited and mainstream. You may find your group tutorials begin to feel more closely comparable to regular curriculum-based seminars.

The principles of good teaching are largely the same whether you are delivering core curriculum content or a group tutorial.

The key differences are as follows:

- Group tutorials tend to be shorter, therefore, this should be taken into account in your planning, particularly the learning objectives, activities and assessment methods.

- There is more opportunity to be flexible to the immediate needs of the group, for example allowing students to influence the content based upon the challenges they face at that time.

- There can be greater flexibility, meaning you may want to consider some different learning activities or room layout, for example:

  o have the room with the chairs in a circle and no tables. This can allow for open discussion. Be sensitive to those students who don't want to contribute. If they normally contribute but don't want to, this could be an indicator of an issue that you may want to approach later in a one-to-one discussion;

  o if group tutorials are used to provide or discuss feedback on assessments it is useful to provide an opportunity for them to reflect on the work they have done or the feedback from their module tutor (although this may have been done already in the lesson). Ways to do this include:

    – individual reflection – allow students time to reread their work and ask them to write down three things they did well and three things they need to do better next time;

    – peer reflection – pair students up and ask them to read each other's work and then discuss with their partner three things they did well and three things they could do better next time. This needs to be managed carefully in terms of the sensitivity of students analysing each other's work and usually works best when it isn't done with their friends and is undertaken in groups of mixed ability.

Group tutorial contextualisation

Group tutorial delivery (as well as the tracking and monitoring of students and one-to-ones) works best when it is embedded within the institution's strategy for learning, along with being tailored to the subject area the students are studying. Tailoring the content to be specific to particular industries or career pathways helps to improve the relevance and enjoyment for the student as well as the impact on their career prospects.

Differentiation

You may be familiar with the concepts of differentiation and inclusive learning and be employing some of these techniques already. These may include modification of:

- the dialogue and support you give to each student;

- the tasks you set them;

- the pace students can work at individually;

- the way you group the students;

- the resources you use;

- the outcomes you expect or find acceptable.

It is important to differentiate the content within group tutorials for two main reasons. To ensure:

1. it is accessible and relevant for the student populations you are working with;

2. that, as students progress through levels, the content and activities offer appropriate variety and depth, especially when there is a chance they may cover the same or a similar topic again.

Course suspension or change

At an early age, young people in the UK have to make fairly big choices affecting their future. In comparison to some other countries there is a greater specificity of subject. As a result, many students consider changing their course or institution at some point during their studies, with many stating they would apply to a different course or institution if they had the choice again (Department for Education, 2017). This may be because they entered HE without clear goals, their personal or employment circumstances changed or for a host of other reasons, academic or otherwise (Tinto, 1993; Department for Education, 2017). Dropping out or changing course can have significant financial and career implications for students and the rules governing these decisions are very complicated (Malcolm, 2013). A more flexible approach to study for both providers and students has been called for and this is something institutions will need to adjust to (Swain, 2008; Department for Education, 2017).

Students should have the option of taking a break from their studies and/or transferring to a different course or institution and be aware of the associated consequences (Department for Education, 2017). Your institution is likely to have a set of academic policies or regulations that refer to course suspension or change which may be complicated (there may be specific deadlines with various financial implications or specific procedures to adhere to). Students are likely to call upon trusted advisors, such as personal tutors, for guidance on these matters (Tinto, 1993; Bowden, 2008; Malcolm, 2013). While you do not need to know your academic regulations in their entirety, you should know how to access them, have a reasonable understanding of them and utilise them to inform your students, as and when this is required. Similarly, as an effective tutor, you do not need to be an expert in student finance but you should know where you can refer students to for support at an institutional or national level. Often, the person or department responsible for tutor training at an institutional level will have resources available to help you navigate the help on offer.

On occasion, the best course of action for an individual student may not be the ideal option for their institution. Universities are judged on their performance using specific metrics to assess student retention, satisfaction and persistence and this is discussed in more detail later. For example, a high-achieving student may want to withdraw because of a lucrative job offer or a struggling student may want to cut their losses rather than gamble further money on fees. In these cases all an effective tutor can do is try to ensure that the student makes a fully informed choice. This choice must be informed by the relevant support functions of the university offering appropriate support in line with any relevant boundaries or policies.

Critical thinking activity 5

»   *Look at the case study dialogue from a one-to-one meeting between Patrick and his personal tutor Linda, which is taking place in week 2. Identify helpful behaviours that enable Patrick to form a decision about the best way forward for him.*

CASE STUDY

Linda's one-to-one with Patrick

LINDA: *How's the course going so far?*

PATRICK: *Alright...*

LINDA: *Tell me two things you most enjoy about it.*

PATRICK: *Erm... dunno really... looking forward to the trip.*

LINDA: *But anything you've done so far that you've enjoyed?*

PATRICK: *(shrugs)*

LINDA: *How about two things you find hard or have not enjoyed then?*

PATRICK: *There's so much writing... and lots of units and topics to cover...*

LINDA: *Okay... it does take hard work to get a degree and academic writing is a significant part of that... what modules are you taking?*

PATRICK: *Health and Wellbeing, Chemistry and... Anatomy and Physiology.*

LINDA: *How do you feel about those classes?*

PATRICK: *Not much... not really enjoying the course to be honest.*

LINDA: *Okay, let's go back a step... what do you do at home when you're not at university?*

PATRICK: *Not a lot... work at Sportsworld, watch TV, look after my little brother and kick-boxing club once a week.*

LINDA: *I noticed your face lit up when you mentioned the club... what's so good about that?*

PATRICK: *It's just... I really enjoy the challenge, the competition and I'm not bad at it. The bloke who runs it gets me to teach the kids there some of the techniques.*

LINDA: *And you like that teaching part as well as the competition and the keeping fit?*

PATRICK: *Yeah, all of it really.*

LINDA: *Interesting. So if you had to list all the things you do outside university and had to say which you enjoy most what would your top two be?*

PATRICK: *Kick-boxing and... looking after my brother... well most of the time* [smiles].

LINDA: *I know what you mean* [smiles]. *Do you do much reading or writing at home?*

PATRICK: *Not really...*

LINDA: *What do your parents do?*

PATRICK: *My dad's a lab technician.*

LIZ: *And is that where the idea to do science came from?*

PATRICK: *Yes.*

LINDA: *Right, okay. If you had to say how much out of ten you enjoy practical and sporting subjects what would you say?*

PATRICK: *Probably nine...*

LINDA: *Wow... right, okay. Now do the same for factual, scientific or theory subjects... what would you say?*

PATRICK: *It depends...*

LINDA: *On what?*

PATRICK: *If the topic is something I'm interested in then I don't mind doing some theory...*

LINDA: *Ah, okay... can you give me an example?*

PATRICK: *Well, this guy at the club told me all about fitness.*

LINDA: *Right, well that's really interesting... You're right, it's not always a clear divide between theory and practical... often there's a mix. What do you think about Sports Science for example?*

PATRICK: *Sounds good... that's what attracted me to the course in the first place.*

LINDA: *On the Human Biology course there is the opportunity for you to partially concentrate on sports science. Your Health and Wellbeing module in the spring will introduce you to this and you can then specialise in Year 2 as part of the Nutrition and Metabolism for Sport and Exercise module. In Year 3 students can take Biomedical Implications of Exercise, Activity and Health, Advanced Nutrition for Sport and Sport Toxicology. Does that sound interesting?*

PATRICK: *A lot more, it's just the other stuff I'm not really into.*

LINDA: *Well it is a Human Biology course so you will have to take other modules as well. Did you think about the Sports and Exercise Science course?*

PATRICK: *Yeah but my parents said Biology was more academic than Sport.*

LINDA: *Well there are various merits and challenges involved in studying on each course and the potential career each one of them might lead to.*

PATRICK: *What modules make up Sport and Exercise?*

LINDA: *Well... Research and Academic Skills – so there would still be plenty of writing! Anatomy and Physiology as you would in Human Biology but with a different focus. You can do Coaching and Skill Acquisi...[Patrick interrupts]*

PATRICK: *That's what I really like to do. Coaching sport, elite sport but maybe kids' sport too?*

LINDA: *It's not really my area of expertise but the Strength and Conditioning pathway in the Sport Rehabilitation programme would seem to support that. Look, I'm not going to tell you what to do, it is your decision but you need to make an informed decision. What do you think you might need to know to make the choice?*

PATRICK: *Should I talk to my parents? Is there a tutor on that programme I could speak to?*

LINDA: *Yes and yes. Definitely speak to your parents. They know you far better than I do and will, I'm sure, have your best interests at heart.*

PATRICK: *Yeah, they support me... as long as I work hard!*

LINDA: *Good. I'm emailing my colleague Helen and copying you in now. She'll be able to tell you about that course, any admissions criteria and the sports science elements of Human Biology too. Look at the academic regulations here – when would you have to make a change?*

PATRICK: *It says the end of next week.*

LINDA: *I strongly recommend you go and see Helen now – even if she is teaching her office hours are written on the door. Have you spoken to careers at all?*

PATRICK: *Erm, they were in the induction talk weren't they?*

LINDA: *Yeah, I've sent you the link to sign up to meet with them too.*

PATRICK: *Thanks – do I really have to decide all this now?*

LINDA: *Well, look at this section of the regulations... 5.2.*

PATRICK: *If the two courses are linked, I could potentially move at the end of the year.*

LINDA: *Potentially, so you don't have to do anything rash... but it is more difficult to catch up on the second year of that course if you haven't taken all of the first-year content. The best thing you can do is fully inform yourself now. Talk to your parents, careers, Helen, your classmates, anyone else?*

PATRICK: *Sports Science students?*

LINDA: *Exactly. Then draw up a list of pros and cons? You may find that you're on the right course after all but it's good to check. There's a PASS, Peer Assisted Study Scheme, on that course too. Why not ask whether you can join them for one session to meet some of the other students and find out more about the course content?*

PATRICK: *Yeah... okay, I can do that. Can I let you know how it goes?*

LINDA: *Absolutely, shall we schedule a phone chat?*

Discussion

Some helpful behaviours that we can take from Linda's approach are:

* use of open questions, for example asking the student to list the most enjoyable and least enjoyable aspects of the course rather than closed questions such as 'are you enjoying your course?' which is likely to elicit a simple 'yes' or 'no';

* try a different tack when information is not forthcoming, for example appeal to life outside university in order to gain a picture of interests;

* use scaling, in other words where you get the student to mark a statement out of ten (scaling is discussed further in Chapter 6);

* link thoughts or actions to feelings;

* try to uncover underlying reasons for the student's choice of course;

* emphasise the positives and reassure, thus creating a supportive environment making honest discussion more likely;

* don't fix the student's issue or sway them with your opinion; just offer them the benefit of your knowledge and experience so they can make an informed choice for themselves.

Internal progression

Towards the end of the academic year, the module selection for the following year is usually introduced and explained in group tutorials or core module classes. Your role as a tutor may be to advise students about the options available to them, drawing upon their experience and attainment this year and linking this to their planned career destinations. The focus of personal tutoring for level 5 and 6 students is enhancing employability, professional skills and preparing for graduation (Calcagno et al, 2017). Although much of the research on attrition focuses on the first year, students' second year can be the stage when many feel most detached so it is recommended that level 5 students are required to meet with their personal tutors during induction week (Stephen et al, 2008; Jevons and Lindsay, 2018). It is also during the level 5 stage that other factors such as employment, health issues, financial problems, family challenges and relationship difficulties can have significant impact (Jevons and Lindsay, 2018). As an effective tutor you can advise students regarding these challenges, suggest they utilise all support available to them, help them remain focused and ensure they are aware of any extension or interruption procedures. As discussed above, expectations do change as a student progresses on their course and so regular conversations with students, in group and one-to-one settings, can help ease any transitional issues that they are experiencing.

External progression

Personal tutoring activities towards the end of a degree programme focus increasingly on support for completing dissertations and transitioning out of university. This includes information about whether students are acquiring and evidencing graduate attributes which will enhance their employment prospects (Calcagno et al, 2017). Your role is therefore to make the link between academic learning and professional careers, including serving as a professional role model, by showing you continually reflect on your own practice for example (Small, 2013). Working closely with the careers and employability service can help here.

A curriculum for tutorials

The content that you cover in tutorials is usually flexible (depending on your institution) and must be able to meet the needs of your students. Since all institutions are different and the students within them are divided by subject area and level, the following suggested tutorial content in Table 5.2 (adapted from Calcagno et al, 2017) covers themes that can be adapted and differentiated, as appropriate. Some institutions may favour individual tutorials for certain aspects while others may favour group tutorials so the delivery method may have some flexibility. You may already have tutorial content set; however, the following information acts as a useful guide.

You can use the information much as you would a course curriculum from which you can develop your own tutorial scheme of work. It is also necessary to recognise the natural overlap between the sections and the importance of revisiting topics or themes, just as you would do in the core curriculum.

The National Occupational Standards (NOS) for Personal Tutoring set out good practice in personal tutoring and thus are relevant to group tutorial content. The 11 standards are as follows.

- *Manage self, work relationships and work demands.*

- *Develop own practice in personal tutoring.*

- *Create a safe, supportive and positive learning environment.*

- *Explore and identify learners' needs and address barriers to learning.*

- *Enable learners to set learning targets and evaluate their progress and achievement.*

- *Encourage the development of learner autonomy.*

- *Enable learners to develop personal and social skills and cultural awareness.*

- *Enable learners to enhance learning and employability skills.*

- *Support learners' transition and progression.*

- *Provide learner access to specialist support services.*

- *Contribute to improving the quality and impact of personal tutoring and its reputation within own organisation.*

(UK Commission for Education and Skills, nd, online)

Each has its own 'knowledge and understanding' and 'performance criteria' descriptors which are too lengthy to state here, but they can be found in their entirety at http://nos.ukces.org.uk.

We revisit the standards in Chapter 8 (on measuring impact). The final column of Table 5.2 states the relevant standard for each theme.

Table 5.2 A suggested personal tutoring curriculum

Journey point	Theme	Aims	Outcomes By the end of this stage students will	Activities	Link to NOS
Pre-arrival	**Getting to Know You**	Building relationships Easing the transition to university Identifying 'at risk' students	Know who their tutor is and how to contact them Outline broad goals for their time at university Identify issues and areas of concern about moving to university	(Video) messaging with tutor via email, social media or virtual learning environment Complete pre-entry survey	NOS 3 NOS 4 NOS 5 NOS 9 NOS 10
Level 4, semester 1, first 4 weeks	**Getting Connected**	Becoming more informed Building relationships Social integration Settling in	Have familiarised themselves with: • the institution • the campus • their timetable • the location of programme information • tutorial policies, purposes and values • student voice and representation	Ice-breakers and team building Each student is given a passport with details of support services details and have to visit each to get a stamp before their next tutorial Note taking Library skills	NOS 3 NOS 7 NOS 9 NOS 10

| Level 4, semester 1, week 5 onwards | **Preparing for Success** | Establishing the rhythm of the student year

Support tutees to be prepared for their assessments

Study skills assessment | Be familiar with communication processes, complaints procedures, information systems, absence and attendance processes

Know how to submit coursework

Understand how to prepare effectively for exams | Planning and writing assignments

Using references and avoiding plagiarism

Revision guidance and exam technique

Reminder of relevant support services

Study skills self-assessment | NOS 3
NOS 4
NOS 6
NOS 8
NOS 9 |
|---|---|---|---|---|---|
| Level 4, semester 2 | **Making the most of University** | Working effectively

Action planning and using feedback

Establish effective independent learning

Engaging with extra-curricular opportunities to develop graduate attributes | Reflect on feedback on assessed work and use to plan for improvements

Know how to be independent, take responsibility and manage their time effectively

Understand the range of extra-curricular opportunities for developing graduate attributes available within the university | Using feedback for personal development – reflective learning and action planning

Time management, independent learning and organisation activities

Exploring sources of information on extra-curricular opportunities

SMART action planning | NOS 3
NOS 5
NOS 6
NOS 7
NOS 9 |

Table 5.2 (Cont.)

Journey point	Theme	Aims	Outcomes By the end of this stage students will	Activities	Link to NOS
Level 5, semester 1	**Refreshing, Reflecting and Developing**	Review of tutorial content covered at level 4 Review paid work/study/life balance Further action planning	Fully reflect on academic performance, social integration at level 4 to inform future action plans Ensure relevant support is in place for level 5	Return to previous assessment feedback and connect learning to upcoming assessments Action plan for level 5 including ongoing review	NOS 4 NOS 5 NOS 6 NOS 8 NOS 9 NOS 10
Level 5, semester 2 (including any time spent on work placement)	**Enhancing your Future**	Employability Developing graduate attributes Linking module and pathway selection to careers	Understand the importance of engaging with extra-curricular opportunities which develop graduate attributes Have developed a CV and covering letter Understand the process of finding and applying for jobs or future study Engage with the careers service	CV and job application exercise Career choice exploration and/or presentation Module and pathway selection guidance	NOS 8 NOS 9 NOS 10

Level 6, semester 1	**Becoming a Professional**	Reflect on any work placements Planning for the future Selling yourself/your skills	Have a plan for what they intend to do after graduation, with clearly identified actions for implementation Have a professional online profile and an effective CV Have provided information to their tutor to facilitate the production of effective references	Employability audit – to identify students who would benefit from interventions Mock interview and assessment day exercises with the careers service Reflection activities on work placements and what they mean for graduation Set SMART targets for post-graduation	NOS 5 NOS 6 NOS 7 NOS 8 NOS 9 NOS 10
Level 6, semester 2	**Moving On**	Transitioning out of university Staying connected Providing feedback	Understand the graduation process Appreciate the importance of providing feedback on their student experience	Explaining graduation and opportunities for remaining connected to the institution as Alumni	NOS 3 NOS 8

Adapted from Calcagno et al (2017, pp 96–9) and incorporating the National Occupational Standards (NOS) for Personal Tutoring.

Critical thinking activity 6

1. Using Table 5.2, identify any topics you think need adding and any you think are less important for your students.

2. Expand upon the content in the fifth column to develop student activities for each theme.

3. Using these student activities, with a particular individual or group in mind, plan a tutorial session on any topic from Table 5.2, which is fully contextualised within the (or a) subject area the individual or group is studying.

Summary

The personal tutor role can feel all-encompassing, as part of a busy academic workload of teaching and research. Students need support specific to the stage in the lifecycle they are in. Early in your career or in a new role you may not know what support they may need and how you might help. This chapter has, hopefully, assisted by informing you:

• what the key stages in the student lifecycle are;

• what key tutoring activities personal tutors can use to support students through these stages;

• what an effective tutoring curriculum might look like.

Moreover, you should now have the terminology in order to further understand and enquire about how things work in your institution.

If you want to be highly effective in the role and have ambitions to progress, you need to be a constructive enquirer of those around you including those in more senior roles. You'll need the appropriate knowledge and language to do this. There will be more on the higher-level support skills in the remaining chapters where we also discuss the bigger picture enquiries needed when you are aiming to be highly effective.

Learning checklist

Tick off each point when you feel confident you understand it.

☐ *I have developed understanding of transitions in HE and the stages of the student lifecycle.*

☐ *I can identify the key activities of the personal tutor and how they support the stages of the student lifecycle.*

☐ *I understand and can apply the tools to re-engage a student to aim to effect behavioural change without using punitive measures.*

☐ *I recognise the necessity for students to be on the right course from a student, personal tutor, departmental and institutional perspective. I understand and can advise regarding course changes, interruptions, suspensions or terminations of study as required.*

☐ *I recognise the elements of an effective one-to-one: that I should be well prepared and that it should be a two-way conversation where the student does the majority of the thinking and talking (in other words is active, not passive).*

☐ *I can identify the two main purposes for group tutorials, which are, firstly, the management of the student and, secondly, the development and support of the student, as well as focusing on more pastoral areas, such as emotional well-being.*

☐ *I appreciate that there are more common elements between a good curriculum lesson and group tutorial delivery than there are differences and that the principles of good teaching are very similar whether you are delivering a lesson or a group tutorial.*

☐ *I am aware of examples of content that might make up a tutoring curriculum and have an understanding of how they would fit into the policies and procedures of my institution.*

Critical reflections

1. How much knowledge do you have of the stages in the student lifecycle from your induction or PG Cert in Teaching and Learning in Higher Education?

2. Can you recognise a curriculum of personal tutoring in your institution that guides students through the various stages? How much does the example curriculum given reflect the practice of your institution?

3. What is your view on the relative importance of one-to-one meetings compared to group tutorials in enabling students to succeed? Do you think your colleagues, and more widely your institution, have a similar view?

4. From your experience of group tutorials, explain how much of your time is spent on managing the students and how much is spent on developing and supporting them, including pastoral activities. Which factors influenced how you divide your time?

Personal tutor self-assessment system

As a reminder, some key activities for the personal tutor are:

• supporting students through the challenges of their initial transition to HE;

• one-to-ones with students;

• group tutorial planning and teaching;

• supporting students through the stages of internal progression on their course;

• advising students regarding potential suspensions, course changes and terminations;

• supporting students' external progression by preparing them for the next step in their education or career.

PERSONAL TUTOR SELF-ASSESSMENT SYSTEM : Chapter 5 Key activities : effectively supporting all stages of the student lifecycle

	Minimum standard 1 star	Beginner level 2 star	Intermediate level 3 star	Advanced level 4 star	Expert level 5 star
Individual	I am aware of the key stages of the student lifecycle from pre-arrival support to graduation. I ensure that key activities, including individual and group tutorials, which support transition through these stages are fully thought through and planned before they begin. My students are aware of the transition support available and how they relate to them.	I regularly reflect to identify strengths and areas for development related to the key activities. I build these into my transition planning and discuss them with my head of department during appraisal meetings. This informs the support I provide for relevant students at an individual and group level.	I regularly ask for student feedback on how effective my individual and group tutorials are at supporting student transitions. I hold formal end-of-year reviews with relevant colleagues to identify strengths and areas for development.	My actions to support student transition put the student first and provide holistic and comprehensive support. Feedback from my students regarding individual and group tutorials is consistently very positive.	I identify and implement methods to measure the impact of individual and group tutorials on my students' progress and outcomes. I reflect and constructively question key activities with managers and others involved to review and improve them regularly. This is a significant factor in improving some key performance indicators.

Institutional			
My institution has an awareness of student transition into higher education and has the key activities embedded into its strategy for supporting it. Staff are aware of the key activities.	The strategy for supporting students through transitions is effectively communicated to all new staff and updates for existing staff are frequent. Recommended content and structure for one-to-ones and group tutorials are widely disseminated.	Sufficient hours for tutoring (one-to-one and group) are allocated in the timetable to send a clear message to tutors and students that the institution values the role/activity. Clear guidelines on the roles and responsibilities of both tutors and tutees are discussed at the outset.	The key activities (including individual and group tutorials) are routinely discussed in all delivery staff's appraisal meetings. All staff clearly know their roles in supporting transition and carry these out effectively.	The key activities are regularly reviewed involving all relevant student-facing staff and a selection of students. As a result, staff feel invested in them. There is a highly consistent approach to the key activities across my institution.

The self-assessment system is available as a free download from the publisher's website and the authors' websites (all listed at the start of the book).

References

Barefoot, B O (2000) The First-Year Experience. *About Campus*, 4(6): 12–18.

Barrie, S C (2007) A Conceptual Framework for the Teaching and Learning of Generic Graduate Attributes. *Studies in Higher Education*, 32(4): 439–58. [online] Available at: www.tandfonline.com/doi/abs/10.1080/03075070701476100 (accessed 30 June 2018).

Beatty-Guenter, P (1994) Sorting, Supporting, Connecting, and Transforming: Retention Strategies at Community Colleges. *Community College Journal of Research and Practice*, 18(2): 113–29.

Blythman, M, Orr, S, Hampton, D, McLaughlin, M and Waterworth, H (2006) Strategic Approaches to the Development and Management of Personal Tutorial Systems in UK Higher Education. In Thomas, L and Hixenbaugh, P (eds) *Personal Tutoring in Higher Education* (pp 103–12). Stoke-on-Trent: Trentham Books.

Bowden, J (2008) Why do Nursing Students Who Consider Leaving Stay on Their Courses? *Nurse Researcher*, 15(3): 45–58.

Braine, M E and Parnell, J (2011) Exploring Students' Perceptions and Experience of Personal Tutors. *Nurse Education Today*, 31: 904–10.

Brinkworth, R, McCann, B, Matthews, C and Nordström, K (2009) First Year Expectations and Experiences: Student and Teacher Perspectives. *Higher Education*, 58(2): 157–73.

Calcagno, L, Walker, D and Grey, D J (2017) Building Relationships: A Personal Tutoring Framework to Enhance Student Transition and Attainment. *Student Engagement in Higher Education Journal*, 1(2): 88–99.

Cook, A and Rushton, B S (2008) *Student Transition: Practices and Policies to Promote Retention.* London: Staff and Educational Development Association.

Department for Education (2017) *Securing Student Success: Risk-Based Regulation for Teaching Excellence, Social Mobility and Informed Choice in Higher Education – Government Consultation on Behalf of the Office for Students.* London: Department for Education. [online] Available at: https://consult.education.gov.uk/higher-education/higher-education-regulatory-framework/supporting_documents/HE%20reg%20framework%20condoc%20FINAL%2018%20October%20FINAL%20FINAL.pdf (accessed 30 June 2018).

Dobinson-Harrington, A (2006) Personal Tutor Encounters: Understanding the Experience. *Nursing Standard*, 20(50): 35–42.

Earwaker, J (1992) *Helping and Supporting Students.* Buckingham: Open University Press.

Fergy, S, Marks-Maran, D, Ooms, A, Shapcott, J and Burke, L (2011) Promoting Social and Academic Integration into Higher Education by First Year Student Nurses: The APPL Project. *Journal of Further and Higher Education*, 35(1): 107–30.

Grey, D and McIntosh, E (2017) Student Dashboards – The Case for Building Communities of Practice. Presentation at *UK Advising and Tutoring Conference*, Leeds, 12 April 2017.

Gutteridge, R (2001) Student Support, Guidance and Retention: Re-defining Additional Needs. Presentation at *Qualitative Evidence-Based Practice Conference*, Coventry, 14–16 May 2001. [online] Available at: www.leeds.ac.uk/educol/documents/00001709.htm (accessed 30 June 2018).

Hartwell, H and Farbrother, C (2006) Enhancing the First Year Experience through Personal Tutoring. In Thomas, L and Hixenbaugh, P (eds) *Personal Tutoring in Higher Education* (pp 59–71). Stoke-on-Trent: Trentham Books.

Hicks, T and Heastie, S (2008) High School to College Transition: A Profile of the Stressors, Physical and Psychological Health Issues That Affect First-year On-campus College Students. *Journal of Cultural Diversity*, 15(3): 143–47.

Hixenbaugh, P, Pearson, C and Williams, D (2006) Student Perspectives on Personal Tutoring: What do Students Want? In Thomas, L and Hixenbaugh, P (eds) *Personal Tutoring in Higher Education* (pp 45–56). Stoke-on-Trent: Trentham Books.

Jevons, C and Lindsay, S (2018) The Middle Years Slump: Addressing Student-reported Barriers to Academic Progress. *Higher Education Research and Development*. [online] Available at: www.researchgate.net/profile/Sophie_Lindsay2/publication/323507498_The_middle_years_slump_Addressing_student-reported_barriers_to_academic_progress/links/5ad326940f7e9b2859349cb0/The-middle-years-slump-Addressing-student-reported-barriers-to-academic-progress.pdf?origin=publication_detail (accessed 30 June 2018).

Kift, S (2009) Articulating a Transition Pedagogy (1st ed). Queensland: Australian Learning and Teaching Council.

Lago, C and Shipton, G (1999) *Personal Tutoring in Action* (2nd ed). Sheffield: University of Sheffield.

Lea, M and Street, B (2000) Student Writing and Staff Feedback: An Academic Literacies Approach. In Lea, M and Stierer, B (eds) *Student Writing in Higher Education* (pp 32–46). Buckingham: Open University Press.

Lee, B and Robinson, A (2006) Creating a Network of Student Support. In Thomas, L and Hixenbaugh, P (eds) *Personal Tutoring in Higher Education* (pp 83–90). Stoke-on-Trent: Trentham Books.

Leibowitz, Z B and Schlossberg, N K (1982) Critical Career Transitions: A Model for Designing Career Services. *Training & Development Journal*, 36(2): 12–16, 18–19.

Malcolm, D (2013) *I Have to Leave my Course Before The End – What Do I Do about my Higher Education Funding?* National Union of Students. [online] Available at: www.nus.org.uk/en/advice/money-and-funding/i-have-to-leave-my-course-before-the-end--what-do-i-do-about-my-higher-education-funding (accessed 30 June 2018).

Malik, S (2000) Students, Tutors and Relationships: The Ingredients of a Successful Student Support Scheme. *Medical Education*, 34: 635–41.

McGivney, V (1996) Staying or Leaving the Course. *Adults Learning*, 7(6): 133–5.

McInnis, C (2001) Researching the First Year Experience: Where to from Here? *Higher Education Research and Development*, 20(2): 105–14.

McIntosh, E (2017) Working in Partnership: The Role of Peer Assisted Study Sessions in Engaging the Citizen Scholar. *Active Learning in Higher Education*, 1–16. https://doi.org/10.1177%2F1469787417735608

Morgan, M (2012) *Improving the Student Experience: The Practical Guide for Universities and Colleges*. London: Routledge.

Mortenson, T G (2005) Measurements of Persistence. In Seidman, A (ed) *College Student Retention* (pp 31–60). Westport: Praeger Publishers.

National Audit Office (2007) *Staying the Course: The Retention of Students in Higher Education.* Report by the Comptroller and Auditor General, HC 616 Session 2006–2007. London: The Stationery Office.

Neville, L (2007) *The Personal Tutor's Handbook.* Basingstoke: Palgrave Macmillan.

Owen, M (2002) 'Sometimes You Feel You're in Niche Time': The Personal Tutor System, a Case Study. *Active Learning in Higher Education*, 3(1): 7–23.

Palmer, M, O'Kane, P and Owens, M (2009) Betwixt Spaces: Student Accounts of Turning Point Experiences in the First-Year Transition. *Studies in Higher Education*, 34(1): 37–54.

Parmar, D and Trotter, E (2005) Keeping Our Students: Identifying Factors That Influence Student Withdrawal and Strategies to Enhance the Experience and Retention of First Year Students. *Learning and Teaching in the Social* Sciences, 1(3): 149–68.

Richardson, A, King, S, Garrett, R and Wrench, A (2012) Thriving or Just Surviving? Exploring Student Strategies for a Smoother Transition to University. A Practice Report. *The International Journal of the First Year in Higher Education*, 3(2): 87–93.

Richardson, J (2000) *Researching Student Learning.* Buckingham: Open University Press.

Sargent, A G and Schlossberg, N K (1988) Managing Adult Transitions. *Training and Development Journal*, 42(12): 58–60.

Schlossberg, N K (1981) A Model for Analyzing Human Adaptation to Transition. *Counseling Psychologist*, 9(2): 2–18.

Schlossberg, N K (2011) The Challenge of Change: The Transition Model and its Applications. *Journal Of Employment Counseling*, 48(4): 159–62.

Small, F (2013) Enhancing the Role of Personal Tutor in Professional Undergraduate Education. *Inspiring Academic Practice*, 1(1): 1–11.

Smith, E (2008) *Personal Tutoring: An Engineering Subject Centre Guide.* Leicester: Higher Education Academy.

Sosabowski, M H, Bratt, A M, Herson, K, Olivier, G W J, Sawers, R, Taylor, S, Zahoui, A and Denyer, S P (2003) Enhancing Quality in the M.Pharm Degree Programme: Optimisation of the Personal Tutor System. *Pharmacy Education*, 3(2): 103–8.

Stenton, A (2017) *Why Personal Tutoring is Essential for Student Success.* [online] Available at: www.heacademy.ac.uk/blog/why-personal-tutoring-essential-student-success (accessed 30 June 2018).

Stephen, D E, O'Connell, P and Hall, M (2008) 'Going the Extra Mile', 'Fire-fighting', or Laissez-faire? Re-evaluating Personal Tutoring Relationships within Mass Higher Education. *Teaching in Higher Education*, 13(4): 449–60.

Stevenson, N (2009) Enhancing the Student Experience by Embedding Personal Tutoring in the Curriculum. *Journal of Hospitality, Leisure, Sport and Tourism Education*, 8(2): 117–22.

Swain, H (2008) *The Personal Tutor.* [online] Available at: www.timeshighereducation.co.uk/news/the-personal-tutor/210049.article (accessed 30 June 2018).

Thomas, L (2002) Student Retention in Higher Education: The Role of Institutional Habitus. *Journal of Education Policy*, 17(4), 423–42.

Thomas, L (2006) Widening Participation and the Increased Need for Personal Tutoring. In Thomas, L and Hixenbaugh, P (eds) *Personal Tutoring in Higher Education* (pp 21–31). Stoke-on-Trent: Trentham Books.

Thomas, L (2012) *Building Student Engagement and Belonging in Higher Education at a Time of Change: Final Report from the What Works? Student Retention and Success Programme.* London: Paul Hamlyn Foundation.

Thomas, L, Hill, M, O'Mahony, J and Yorke, M (2017) *Supporting Student Success: Strategies for Institutional Change. What Works? Student Retention and Success Programme. Final Report.* London: Paul Hamlyn Foundation.

Tinto, V (1987) *Leaving College.* Chicago, IL: University of Chicago Press.

Tinto, V (1993) *Leaving College: Rethinking the Causes and Cures of Student Attrition* (2nd ed). Chicago, IL: University of Chicago Press.

UK Commission For Education and Skills (nd) National Occupational Standards for Personal Tutoring. [online] Available at: nos.ukces.org.uk/Pages/index.aspx (accessed 30 June 2018).

Walker, L (2010) Longitudinal Study of Drop-out and Continuing Students Who Attended the Pre-university Summer School at the University of Glasgow. *International Journal of Lifelong Education*, 13(3): 217–33.

Whittaker, R (2008) *Quality Enhancement Themes: The First Year Experience – Transition to and During the First Year.* Glasgow: Quality Assurance Agency Scotland.

Wilcox, P, Winn, S and Fyvie-Gauld, M (2005) 'It Was Nothing to Do with the University, It Was Just the People': The Role of Social Support in the First-Year Experience of Higher Education. *Studies in Higher Education*, 30(6): 707–22.

Wisker, G, Exley, K, Antoniou, M and Ridley, P (2007) *Working One-to-One with Students: Supervising, Coaching, Mentoring, and Personal Tutoring (Key Guides for Effective Teaching in Higher Education).* Oxon: Routledge.

Wootton, S (2007) *An Inductive Enquiry into Managing Tutorial Provision in Post-Compulsory Education.* PhD. Sheffield Hallam University. [online] Available at: https://search-proquest-com.proxy.library.lincoln.ac.uk/pqdtglobal/docview/1913902798/fulltextPDF/5B739D42F2A846B6PQ/1?accountid=16461 (accessed 30 June 2018).

Yale, A (2017) The Personal Tutor–Student Relationship: Student Expectations and Experiences of Personal Tutoring in Higher Education. *Journal of Further and Higher Education*, 1–12. doi:10.1080/0309877X.2017.1377164

Yorke, M (2001) Formative Assessment and its Relevance to Retention. *Higher Education Research and Development*, 20(2): 115–26.

Yorke, M (2004) Retention, Persistence and Success in On-Campus Higher Education and their Enhancement in Open and Distance Learning. *Open Learning: The Journal of Open, Distance and e-Learning*, 19(1): 19–32.

Yorke, M and Longden, B (2008) *The First Year Experience of Higher Education in the UK* (final ed). York: Higher Education Academy.

Yorke, M and Thomas, L (2003) Improving the Retention of Students from Lower Socio-Economic Groups. *Journal of Higher Education Policy and Management*, 25(1): 63–74.

Zepke, N and Leach, L (2010) Beyond Hard Outcomes: 'Soft' Outcomes and Engagement as Student Success. *Teaching in Higher Education*, 15(6): 661–73.

6 Using solution-focused coaching with students

Chapter aims

This chapter helps you to:

- understand solution-focused coaching and the solution-focused approach;

- consider the key characteristics of using a solution-focused approach in your personal tutoring role;

- explore how solution talk and problem talk questions can impact student success;

- examine the phases within the OSKAR framework in relation to conversations with students.

Introduction

The previous chapters have concentrated on the 'essentials' of the personal tutor role. This chapter and the following ones are aimed at improving your higher-level skills to enable you to develop as an effective personal tutor.

This chapter explores the use of solution-focused coaching techniques and tools and explains how, by employing some or all of these in your day-to-day conversations with students, you can encourage them to aim higher, achieve outcomes faster, explore barriers to learning more positively and, more importantly, help them to find their own solutions. One of the principal features of a solution-focused coaching approach, and one of the reasons why we advocate its use with students through your personal tutor role, is that it can significantly reduce any inferiority students feel about themselves or their current situation. Furthermore, in terms of emotional well-being, experience shows that this approach helps students to think more optimistically, behave more confidently and engage with their goals, which become more self-generated. Not all personal tutoring is coaching but coaching can be an important developmental activity to be conducted as part of the tutor–tutee relationship (Gurbutt and Gurbutt, 2015).

The solution-focused approach grew out of techniques from the world of therapy in America in the 1980s. Solution-focused brief therapy was developed by American social workers Steve De Shazer, Insoo Kim Berg and their team at the Milwaukee Brief Family Therapy Center. Through their practice and research, they discovered that their clients made much greater progress over a shorter period of time when the conversations focused more on the clients' future goals, a positive view of the future, and on their own strengths and competencies. From these early days, the solution-focused approach has grown and is now used successfully in a variety of settings, such as business consulting, hypnotherapy, counselling and coaching within the commercial world. Coaching is becoming increasingly important to student success in the United States and has the potential to deliver real benefit in UK HE by:

- increasing motivation and engagement;
- developing personal or professional competencies;
- aiding retention;
- assisting academic, personal and social success.

(European Coaching and Mentoring Council, 2013; Gurbutt and Gurbutt, 2015; Calcagno et al, 2017; Ralston and Hoffshire, 2017)

What is solution-focused coaching?

There are many definitions of coaching but one of the most widely recognised is: '*coaching is unlocking a person's potential to maximise their own performance. It is helping them to learn rather than teaching them*' (Whitmore, 2002). The solution-focused approach to coaching is, as the title suggests, essentially trying to make greater progress with the student by focusing on where they want to get to and understanding what skills and knowledge they need to get there, rather than spending excessive amounts of time exploring the problem or issue they may be facing.

Solution-focused coaching has links with cognitive behavioural therapy (CBT), which has also led to the development of another strand of coaching called cognitive behavioural coaching (CBC). CBT and CBC are similar, but CBC focuses on achieving personal and professional fulfilment, not an understanding of psychological disturbance, which is a core component of CBT (Neenan, 2009). CBC and solution-focused coaching are also similar; however, CBC is a fusion of cognitive behavioural therapy, rational emotive therapy, solution-focused approaches, goal-setting theory and social cognitive theory (Palmer and Szymanska, 2008). Even though there are similarities between solution-focused coaching and cognitive behavioural therapy, the main difference is that solution-focused coaching primarily focuses on goal achievement rather than healing.

Put simply, there are two different approaches that you can adopt when helping students to solve their problems, as illustrated in Table 6.1. While both can work well, the solution-focused approach enables students to develop self-efficacy, self-reliance and improve independent learning (these are highly desirable outcomes for your personal tutor role and the educational institution).

Table 6.1 *Different approaches to helping students solve their problems (Adapted from Jackson and McKergow, 2007)*

Problem-focus approach	Solution-focus approach
Understand and diagnose the problem.	Recognise what solution or outcome the student would find desirable or is needed.
Know what causes the problem.	Find know-how and resources; in other words, skills or previous experience, which will help the student to work towards the solution or agreed outcome.
Use this information to address and fix the problem.	Taking into account the student's know-how, exploring the solution and agreeing a small action, or actions. Often the problem that the student was facing will either reduce or seem less significant to them and together you may discover a new way to overcome it.

There are a number of factors that can influence the effectiveness of both approaches such as:

- the focus or desired outcome of the conversation;
- the degree of rapport and depth of relationship you have with the student;
- how much time you have for the conversation;
- the level of motivation and emotional intelligence that the student possesses.

Key characteristics of using solution-focused coaching with students

Table 6.2 illustrates some of the key characteristics that will help focus the way you view and use solution-focused coaching in your day-to-day conversations with students and in your personal tutor role.

Table 6.2 *Key characteristics of using solution-focused coaching with students*

Key characteristic	Explanation
Positive change can occur	Solution-focused coaching works on the assumption that positive change can occur with students and that this change can happen quickly.
Clear goals and self-directed action	You should work with the students to define specific goals (Gurbutt and Gurbutt, 2015). The impact of a good coaching conversation doesn't stop when it stops. Set a clear expectation that the students must be self-directed and take the responsibility to implement actions to achieve these goals outside the coaching conversations.

Table 6.2 (Cont.)

Key characteristic	Explanation
Develop solutions and focus on the future; not dwelling on problems within the past or present	Listen to any issues or problems in order to communicate empathy and develop rapport with your students. Quickly move the conversation on to exploring future goals, past successes, and what skills, knowledge and abilities they have.
Students' experience, expertise and resources (Gurbutt and Gurbutt, 2015)	A solution-focused personal tutor is an enabler and facilitator. There is a belief that students are likely to already have the answers and the ability to take themselves forward, and as their personal tutor it is your role to help them notice this. When students feel they have worked something out for themselves, there is a greater chance that they will ask themselves the same questions in the future and coach themselves. The best coaches in some ways become invisible.
Reframe the students' perspective and help them to notice positives	Possibilities include reframing and helping them to notice: • a distant possibility as a near possibility; • a weakness as a strength; • a problem as an opportunity.

Reframing

Reframing students' perspectives isn't always an easy task, particularly if they have a negative belief about themselves or their situation, but experience has shown that it is an effective tool and one that you can hone with practice. The new framing of their perspective needs to be felt, and it usually needs to have an emotional impact and be more emotionally compelling than their old view. Try using the phrase 'Let's look at it another way' and encourage them to reframe their thoughts by exploring the situation through dialogue. Sometimes the student might not be in the right frame of mind to have the view 'reframed'. A receptive mood is usually necessary, otherwise the effort may be wasted.

Reframing can affect students' emotional state, hopefully making them happier, more positive and optimistic. Negative emotions are not always detrimental to their academic progress. However, Huppert (2006) found that particularly in the fields of positive psychology and neuroscience, people who have more positive emotions or are more regularly in a positive mood tend to:

• engage with goal pursuits that are more self-generated and consistent with personal values;

• have a broader focus of attention; in other words they can see the 'bigger picture';

- generate more ideas in problem-solving tasks;
- build enduring coping resources, which leads to resilience;
- evaluate themselves and others more positively.

Helping students to notice

One of the main ways of identifying when students notice something new about themselves or their situation is by noticing a visible change in their facial expressions and/or body language. The best way to enable students to really notice something about themselves is through careful and considered questioning, rather than telling them what they should notice. *Telling* students can sometimes work, but this has limited impact. *Enabling* students to notice crucial aspects of themselves or their situation – in other words raising their self-awareness – is key as this helps to develop more enduring ownership of their situation and self-reliance, which in turn promotes greater self-efficacy.

CASE STUDY

Lee and Steve

The following dialogue is taken from a discussion between Lee, who is studying level 4 Computing, and his personal tutor, Steve.

LEE: *Could I have a chat with you?*

STEVE: *Yes sure, grab a seat.*

LEE: *I'm sorry that I haven't been to all of your classes lately, I've had a few things on.*

STEVE: *Okay, do you want tell me about it?*

LEE: *Well... If I'm honest, I've kind of lost a bit of motivation for the course, which I know isn't what you want to hear. I actually do want to work in computing but I've been doing a lot more hours at my part-time job, which is related to the course, and I've been thinking about whether I should leave and work full-time.*

STEVE: *I've been there when I was at university, so I know quite a bit about what you're thinking about.*

LEE: *Really?*

STEVE: *Yes, I remember when I didn't know whether I should carry on or try and get a job and earn some money. I had a part-time job like you in the evenings, which was good for the money but didn't really help with my uni work. I made the decision to do just enough hours to make sure I had enough money to attend uni and for living the life that I wanted at the time. What I would do is reduce your hours to the point where you can consider how you might be able to structure your part-time work to better fit around your studies. You may be able to work more in the holidays, at weekends or even possibly cut some of your hours. I see this every year from students, it's nothing new. Though the increase in fees may have intensified the financial pressures students face, there are still ways that these can be managed.*

LEE: *Okay.*

STEVE: *You are a capable student and I've seen some examples of really good work at times. In terms of your motivation for the course, do you actually want to continue?*

LEE: *Yes, I think so... as I said, I'd actually love to pursue a career in computing.*

STEVE: *What I suggest you do then is what I did when I thought I didn't want to continue at university. Take a look at the career prospects for the job you are doing now. If you were doing it full time, do you think you would want to be doing that job in three years' time?*

LEE: *That's an easy one to answer, no I don't. Maybe what you've said is right, I might consider speaking to my boss to reduce my hours and try to focus more on my uni work.*

Lee and Steve, take two

(we have omitted the first part of the dialogue to avoid repetition)

STEVE: *You are a capable student and I've seen some examples of really good work at times. In terms of your motivation for the course, do you actually want to continue?*

LEE: *Yes, I think so... as I said I'd actually love to work in computing.*

STEVE: *Okay, suppose you achieve your ideal outcome, what would that look like?*

LEE: *Erm, well, I think it would be me getting my motivation back and doing well on this course, so that I can get into the uni that I want.*

STEVE: *That seems clear. So, if on a scale of one to ten, where ten is you have achieved your ideal outcome and one is where you have not at all and you have no idea how to, where are you now?*

LEE: *I'd say probably about five, I guess.*

STEVE: *Five? That's really good. Okay, when have you overcome a situation like this before?*

LEE: *...Well, now you mention it, I actually had this same issue at school. I totally lost my motivation to revise for my A levels, but I eventually got it back and did quite well in the end.*

STEVE: *Excellent! How did you manage that?*

LEE: *Well, thinking back, I remember I actually did two things. I looked on the internet at what type of jobs I really wanted in the future and looked at the types of courses I could do to get there, which helped. I also did something I don't do very often, I talked to my mum and dad about it. They both work in IT and really enjoy their jobs.*

STEVE: *Okay, that sounds great. So you said you feel you're at five on the scale, what made you be that high up the scale?*

LEE: *...I suppose I don't normally like to give up on something or feel that I'm beaten. I've always been like that in the past, particularly when playing sport, like football.*

STEVE: *Okay, so if there was an expert on these issues here right now, what advice would they give you about tackling this?*

LEE: *Well, I suppose they'd probably say to focus more on my university course as that's what's going to get me to where I want to be in the future and think less about making a few extra quid right now, when I could cope without it.*

STEVE: *Right okay, sounds sensible. So, what are the next small steps that will start to help you achieve that goal, or let's put it another way, what's going to get you up to 5.1 on your scale?*

LEE: *The first thing I need to do is speak to my boss at work and tell him I need to reduce my hours so I can concentrate on my uni work.*

Critical thinking activity 1

In relation to versions one and two, note down your answers to the following questions:

1.   In your view, which of these two conversations would be most useful to the student and why?

2.   What were the differences between them?

3.   What went well?

Discussion

In both examples the focus is on the individual, the task and the context (Gurbutt and Gurbutt, 2015). You may think, quite rightly, that version one shows a highly knowledgeable personal tutor, who clearly has his heart in the right place. At face value, Steve is doing a professional job by providing sensible advice to help Lee. However, Steve is more effective in version two because Lee arrives at the solution by himself, and this makes it more likely that he will believe he has the know-how and resources to achieve it. In reality, the solution has been co-created through solution-focused questioning.

Version two focuses more on identifying Lee's interests and motivations, enabling him to assess the current situation by conducting a self-assessment and reflecting on his own experiences (Ralston and Hoffshire, 2017). This non-directive approach is student centred/driven and acknowledges the importance of students' goals, identified by the National Union of Students as a requirement for outstanding academic support (Broad, 2006; Gurbutt and Gurbutt, 2015; National Union of Students, 2015; Ralston and Hoffshire, 2017). Providing the student with the opportunity to identify a specific and measurable goal, the actions required to achieve it, and the choice to pursue it or not, gives them a feeling of ownership over both process and outcome (Gurbutt and Gurbutt, 2015).

Another important aspect to consider is the length of time you allow for the student to answer your questions. A solution-focused approach is where the personal tutor lets silence 'do the heavy lifting', in other words, allowing for adequate thinking time and avoiding the temptation to jump in with your own answers. Following on from this, you could focus on actively listening to what the student is saying, for example, by noticing the student's resources, skills and know-how.

Solution talk and problem talk

Solution talk is where you focus on discussing:

- what the student wants to achieve or overcome;
- what is already working well for them;
- where else they are making progress;
- what resources and strengths they have;
- who else might be able to help them;
- possible solutions;
- actions the student will take.

One example of solution talk among the many you may have noticed in version two of the case study is where Steve asks Lee, '*Five? That's really good. Okay, when have you overcome a situation like this before?*'

However, problem talk focuses on discussing:

- what is wrong or what issue the student is facing;
- what the student needs to fix;
- who is to blame for the issue;
- who has control over the problem or issue;
- what weaknesses or deficits need to be reduced or overcome;
- whether there is an expert who could help;
- what complications the student might face.

In version one Steve didn't really use much problem talk; however, one thing he did excessively was to present himself as the expert, predominantly telling Lee what to do, instead of helping him to find the solution for himself and promote self-efficacy. Offering advice and guidance as a personal tutor is required on occasion. However, wherever there is an acceptable opportunity to help students find the way forward on their own this is preferable (Gurbutt and Gurbutt, 2015). If you don't coach within your personal tutor role there is a danger that students will see you as the source of all information; coaching actually makes your job easier and your students more self-directed and effective.

When recognising the temporal (time) boundary, we advocate placing greater emphasis on solution talk because it can be a more effective use of the finite time you have. This is not to suggest that the student is unable to explain any issues they are experiencing or what's happening in their lives and how it makes them feel, but it is preferable to spend as much time as possible on solution talk since this is more likely to enable the students to make greater progress and save time.

It is important to consider the impact of the language you use. This can have a big impact on the way that your students feel. You may already use more solution talk when working with students and this is likely to make them feel more optimistic and motivated. Equally, problem talk questions can have a strong impact and be effective in some situations, for example when you are trying to address problematic or disruptive behaviour. Table 6.3 provides some examples of both types of questions.

Table 6.3 *Potential solution talk and problem talk questions*

Solution talk questions	Problem talk questions
How did you know how to do that?	Why did you do that?
What might you do differently?	What should you have done?
What have you done before that worked?	Have you done that before?
What did you do to contribute to the outcome?	Is there anything you did that helped?
What could you do to ensure this happens?	What are the obstacles to you achieving this?
How can you make sure this happens again?	Why can't you do that more often?
What was the best you have ever done at this?	What's the main cause of your difficulty?
What else?	Anything else?

Reproduced with permission, Lincoln (2004)

Table 6.4 Problem talk and solution talk questions

Problem talk questions	Solution talk questions
What's wrong with what you're doing?	What are you aiming to achieve?
Why are you doing so badly?	How will you know you've achieved it?
What's the main cause of your difficulty?	What was the best you have ever done at this?
Whose fault is it?	What went well on that occasion?
What are the other things that make it hard?	What will be the first signs that you are getting better?
Why will it be difficult for you to do any better?	How will other people notice this improvement?

(Jackson and McKergow, 2004)

Critical thinking activity 2

1. Think of one recent standout moment in your personal tutor role where the situation didn't go to plan and which you would have liked to improve or change. With a trusted colleague or mentor, explain the standout moment to them in as much detail as possible.

2. A slightly different set of problem and solution talk questions is provided by Jackson and McKergow (2004) in Table 6.4.

    a. Ask a colleague or mentor to ask you the problem talk questions in Table 6.4 and try to answer them.

    b. Second, ask your colleague or mentor to ask you the solution talk questions from the same table and again try to answer them.

    c. What was different about being asked the first and the second set of questions?

    d. How were your feelings about your standout moment affected by the different question types?

    e. Which of the two types of questions are most likely to help motivate your students to overcome problems or to achieve stretching goals and why?

The OSKAR framework

OSKAR is a framework for structuring solution-focused coaching conversations with students. It is an acronym which stands for the main headings: Outcome, Scaling, Know-how, Affirm and action, Review (see following explanations and Figure 6.1, which contains example questions). It was created by Paul Jackson and Mark McKergow and is explained in their book, *The Solutions Focus: Making Coaching and Change SIMPLE* (2007).

- **Outcome**: this is similar but subtly different to the goal in most coaching models. The outcome is not simply the goal; it is the difference that the coachee (and those around the coachee) want to see as a result of the coaching.

- **Scaling**: this enables you to find out what's working. You can ask students to rate themselves on a scale from one to ten, where the desired outcome is ten.

- **Know-how and resources**: this phase focuses on finding out all about what works or what has worked for a student, rather than what won't work or what is wrong. During the discussion you are able to establish what strategies are already helping the student. A simple but useful question for you to use here is, 'What else?' This will allow you to develop an overview of what is already helping.

- **Affirm and action**: this is where you affirm the student's positive qualities based on what you have heard during the conversation or what you have observed previously. This helps to build the student's self-belief and strengthens the relationship between you and the student (Gurbutt and Gurbutt, 2015; Ralston and Hoffshire, 2017). Your solution-focused coaching should always end in an action. Try to find some small next steps to build on what is already working so that the students can start or make progress towards their outcome. It is often the case with students that either one or a number of small actions is enough for them to start making progress and to build their confidence. Express the small steps by asking what they can do to move themselves from 4 to 4.1 or 5 on the scale.

- **Review**: in the arranged follow-up discussions, try to find out what's working and build on that. Useful phrases to use are 'what's better?' or 'what helped?' Focus predominantly on things that are helping the student to move in the right direction and less on whether previous actions were carried out or what happened.

Each of the sections can be used together to structure a comprehensive coaching conversation or, if needed, they can be used in isolation.

We advocate using a framework because experience has shown that it can be useful to have a logical sequence for structuring coaching conversations with students in order to maintain a clear focus and avoid 'conversational drift'.

There are other frameworks, for example John Whitmore's (2002) GROW (typically a quicker framework to use), CLEAR (Hawkins and Smith, 2006), PRACTICE (Palmer, 2007) and BATHE (Greenstein, 2018), among others, which can be equally effective for structuring solution-focused conversations with students. The key point to remember is to choose whichever framework suits you and your students best.

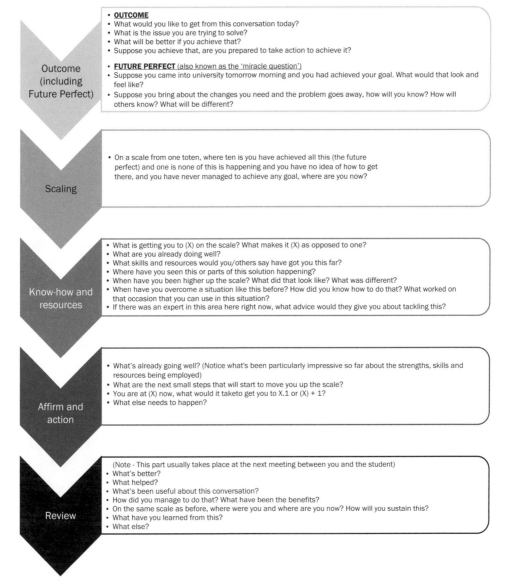

Outcome (including Future Perfect)

- **OUTCOME**
- What would you like to get from this conversation today?
- What is the issue you are trying to solve?
- What will be better if you achieve that?
- Suppose you achieve that, are you prepared to take action to achieve it?

- **FUTURE PERFECT** (also known as the 'miracle question')
- Suppose you came into university tomorrow morning and you had achieved your goal. What would that look and feel like?
- Suppose you bring about the changes you need and the problem goes away, how will you know? How will others know? What will be different?

Scaling

- On a scale from one toten, where ten is you have achieved all this (the future perfect) and one is none of this is happening and you have no idea of how to get there, and you have never managed to achieve any goal, where are you now?

Know-how and resources

- What is getting you to (X) on the scale? What makes it (X) as opposed to one?
- What are you already doing well?
- What skills and resources would you/others say have got you this far?
- Where have you seen this or parts of this solution happening?
- When have you been higher up the scale? What did that look like? What was different?
- When have you overcome a situation like this before? How did you know how to do that? What worked on that occasion that you can use in this situation?
- If there was an expert in this area here right now, what advice would they give you about tackling this?

Affirm and action

- What's already going well? (Notice what's been particularly impressive so far about the strengths, skills and resources being employed)
- What are the next small steps that will start to move you up the scale?
- You are at (X) now, what would it taketo get you to X.1 or (X) + 1?
- What else needs to happen?

Review

- (Note - This part usually takes place at the next meeting between you and the student)
- What's better?
- What helped?
- What's been useful about this conversation?
- How did you manage to do that? What have been the benefits?
- On the same scale as before, where were you and where are you now? How will you sustain this?
- What have you learned from this?
- What else?

Figure 6.1 *The OSKAR framework with some examples of the sort of questions you could use at each stage (reproduced with permission, Lincoln, 2012)*

Scaling

Scaling is a useful aid and can be used in coaching conversations as well as a variety of other situations, but it is particularly effective for conversations on target setting, engagement, motivation and assessing a student's commitment to an action. Allowing students to place a number on how they perceive, for example, their engagement, ensures that they have thought about what has happened in comparison to previous experiences. This self-reflection allows them to focus on their current situation and provides you and them with an agreed and established platform to co-construct desired future improvements.

The use of scaling with numbers isn't always suitable, particularly with issues relating to difficult emotions. If this is the situation, you could try replacing the number scale with polar adjectives, for example, words including and between *strong* and *weak*, *happy* and *sad*, *high* and *low*, *adequate* and *inadequate*, or even the gesture of a *thumbs up* or *down* (or *in-between*). Our experience has shown that asking students to discuss their situation in terms of a scale can really help to open up the conversation.

Using OSKAR in practice

When you are trying to establish, for example, the desired outcome(s) with your students, they may not be immediately obvious and you may need to revisit the idea throughout the conversation. If the nature of the conversation requires you to move forward, backward and around the sections of the OSKAR framework, then this is useful if it helps the student. Furthermore, there is no prescribed time to spend in each section; allowing the conversation to flow naturally is key, bearing in mind the time that you have available.

Don't rush the platform (outcome and future perfect) because this is the foundation for everything that follows and, if possible, should account for approximately 50 per cent of the conversation.

Another thing to consider is the way in which you can support the student to gain a good overview of the situation, to see it more objectively. This can make them see it differently. One way to do this could be to de-personalise the conversation by saying 'how would others know when things are going well?' This may enable them to notice what other people might see.

Critical thinking activity 3

» *Write a fictional dialogue using the OSKAR framework. Use a selection of some or all of the solution-focused tools and questions for a typical personal tutoring situation (you can use real examples). The fictional dialogue should end with a successful way forward for the student. Before starting to write, picture one of your current or previous students for whom the context would apply. Potential examples include the following. A student:*

- – *wants to work towards achieving higher assessment scores to achieve the degree classification that they want;*

- – *explains that they are struggling to meet assignment deadlines. You believe that this is because they are spending too much time focusing on their role as president of the rugby club;*

- – *recognises that they don't attend or engage fully in classes as much as they should but also realises that they need to improve.*

Discussion

Creating fictional dialogues is not easy. It is possible to include typical reactions and responses that you receive from your students as well as your own natural questions and language. This activity can help you to reflect on real-life coaching conversations, and will help you to think through the different ways in which you can structure your solution talk as well as analyse what type of questions you may use in the future. We recommend that, alongside using reflective practice to improve your skills, you continue to write solution-focused dialogues on real issues you are facing, as well as discussing these with trusted colleagues (remember to anonymise the student's name) to jointly develop practice.

Critical thinking activity 4

1. Which tool or aspect of solution-focused coaching or the OSKAR framework do you consider to be the most useful for your own personal tutoring practice and why?

2. In your next five one-to-one conversations with your students, use a solution-focused approach and structure your conversation using the OSKAR framework. After each one, reflect on how it went and write down what was better and what more you would like to improve (read Chapter 7 to explore a number of reflective practice models).

Summary

The tools, techniques and framework within this chapter form part of a toolkit with which you can develop yourself to become an effective personal tutor. They are effective and practical tools that you can use to help remove barriers to learning together with stretching, challenging and motivating your students in the many and varied situations in which you work with them.

The coaching conversations you have with students will not always go well or have the perfect outcome, but practising the tools and techniques from this chapter is key to understanding which you prefer and feel comfortable with, and in which contexts you feel they are and aren't appropriate. You should not get disheartened. Solution-focused coaching can feel difficult and 'clunky'. Undertaking reflective practice (Chapter 7) regularly is important to identify what is and isn't working, as is asking your students for feedback. When feedback is undertaken in a considered way students can offer really insightful and motivational comments.

Learning checklist

Tick off each point when you feel confident you understand it.

☐   *I understand that the primary focus of solution-focused coaching conversations with students is to help co-construct effective solutions or improvements which lead to a greater chance of students developing self-efficacy and taking ownership of their 'next steps'.*

☐ *I appreciate that a solution-focused approach and related questions can help to reduce any inferiority a student may feel about their situation and improve their optimism.*

☐ *I recognise that reframing a student's perspective can affect their emotional state, hopefully making them happier, more positive and optimistic.*

☐ *I can identify the tools of solution-focused coaching and understand that these and the sections of the OSKAR framework can be used in isolation, in groups or as a whole.*

☐ *I recognise that in order to become effective in using these tools I will need to practise and reflect regularly. Also, jointly sharing practice with colleagues will further develop my personal tutoring practice.*

☐ *I recognise that the tools and techniques from this chapter will benefit my students; however, they could also be used to coach my colleagues and even myself.*

Critical reflections

1. To what extent do you feel you are already using a solution-focused approach and similar tools or approaches with your students before reading this chapter?

2. Considering your experiences so far, explain the situations when you feel the solution-focused approach and OSKAR framework would be:

    a. most useful and effective;

    b. less useful and effective.

3. To what extent do you feel that the solution-focused approach fits within the culture, policies and aims of your current institution (if you have taught in more than one institution, use examples to compare and contrast the most recent two).

4. If you find that the tools and techniques from this chapter improve your skills, your performance and your effectiveness as a personal tutor, what could you do to increase their use with the following?

    a. Other staff within your institution.

    b. Other early career academics on your PG Cert in Higher Education.

Personal tutor self-assessment system

See following table.

PERSONAL TUTOR SELF-ASSESSMENT SYSTEM : Chapter 6 Using solution-focused coaching with students

	Minimum standard 1 star	Beginner level 2 star	Intermediate level 3 star	Advanced level 4 star	Expert level 5 star
Individual	I use open and positively phrased questions to encourage my students to define clear goals and think for themselves. I encourage them to think about what experience, expertise and resources they have to achieve their goals.	I regularly practise the use of solution talk style questions (where appropriate) to support my students.	I regularly receive positive feedback on the impact that my students feel my coaching conversations have on their progress.	I use reflective practice regularly to explore and improve my coaching practice. I regularly use the OSKAR framework (or other) to structure my coaching conversations with students.	I measure the impact of my coaching conversations. I share my experiences of the solution-focused approach and OSKAR framework (or other) with my colleagues and am regularly involved in joint practice development activities to explore new ways to support students through coaching conversations.
Institutional	The culture and policies of my institution clearly encourage all staff to take a positive approach towards students and the issues or problems they bring or encounter.	Deans or Heads of School actively support staff to use coaching conversation techniques (where appropriate) with students through discussion, team meetings and appraisals.	My institution regularly delivers or provides opportunities for staff to undertake training in coaching or supportive conversational techniques with students.	Joint practice development opportunities on coaching students are routinely resourced and encouraged by managers to explore current practice and new ways of working.	There is evidence of a positive correlation between the increase and improvement of coaching conversations and the impact on some key performance indicators.

The self-assessment system is available as a free download from the publisher's website and the authors' websites (all listed at the start of the book).

References

Broad, J (2006) Interpretations of Independent Learning in Further Education. *Journal of Further and Higher Education*, 30(2): 119–43.

Calcagno, L, Walker, D and Grey, D J (2017) Building Relationships: A Personal Tutoring Framework to Enhance Student Transition and Attainment. *Student Engagement in Higher Education Journal*, 1(2): 88–99.

European Mentoring and Coaching Council website (United Kingdom version). [online] Available at: www.emccuk.org (accessed 30 June 2018).

Greenstein, E (2018) Academic Tutor or the Accidental Counsellor? Presentation at *UK Advising and Tutoring Annual Conference 2018*, 27–28 March, Derby.

Gurbutt, D J and Gurbutt, R (2015) Empowering Students to Promote Independent Learning: A Project Utilising Coaching Approaches to Support Learning and Personal Development. *Journal of Learning Development in Higher Education*, 8.

Hawkins, S and Smith, N (2006) *Coaching, Mentoring and Organisational Consultancy: Supervision and Development*. Maidenhead: McGraw-Hill Education.

Huppert, F A (2006) Positive Emotions and Cognition: Developmental, Neuroscience and Health Perspectives. In Forgas, J P (ed) *Affect in Social Thinking and Behavior* (pp 235–52). New York: Psychology Press.

Jackson, P and McKergow, M (2007) *The Solutions Focus: Making Coaching and Change SIMPLE* (2nd revised ed). London: Nicholas Brealey International.

Lincoln, S (2004) *Solution-Focused Coaching Training Materials*. Materials from training session.

Lincoln, S (2012) *Solution-Focused Coaching Skills Toolkit*. Materials from training session.

Neenan, M (2009) Using Socratic Questioning in Coaching. *Journal of Rational-Emotive and Cognitive Behavior Therapy*, 27(4): 249–64.

National Union of Students (NUS) (2015) *Academic Support Benchmarking Tool*. [online] Available at: www.nusconnect.org.uk/resources/academic-support-benchmarking-tool/download_attachment (accessed 30 June 2018).

Palmer, S (2007) PRACTICE: A Model Suitable for Coaching, Counselling, Psychotherapy and Stress Management. *The Coaching Psychologist*, 3(2): 71–7.

Palmer, S and Szymanska, K (2008) *Cognitive Behavioural Coaching: An Integrative Approach Handbook of Coaching Psychology: A Guide for Practitioners*. New York: Routledge/Taylor and Francis Group.

Ralston, N C and Hoffshire, M (2017) An Individualized Approach to Student Transition: Developing a Success Coaching Model. In Cintron, R, Samuel, J and Hinson, J (eds) *Accelerated Opportunity Education Models and Practices* (pp 34–50). Hershey, PA: IGI Global.

Whitmore, J (2002) *Coaching for Performance: GROWing People, Performance and Purpose* (3rd ed). London: Nicholas Brealey Publishing.

7 Reflective practice and professional development

Chapter aims

This chapter helps you to:

- identify the difference between reflection and reflective practice;

- understand why reflective practice is important for your personal tutor role;

- consider the benefits of, and potential barriers to, effective reflective practice for your personal tutor role as well as for the institution you work for;

- explore a number of reflective practice models and apply these to typical personal tutoring scenarios;

- understand the professional development opportunities available to you as a personal tutor.

Critical thinking activity 1

» *In preparation for this chapter, it is important to consider the signficance of reflection, reflective practice and professional development, and how this contributes to the approach of the institution you are part of and your beliefs and attitudes as a personal tutor. Copy and complete Figure 7.1, filling in the empty boxes by stating your current approach to reflective practice and professional development. You could include benefits, barriers to carrying it out, relevance or importance to your personal tutor role and the tutoring approach endorsed by your institution. You could also include the professional development opportunities afforded to you as a personal tutor within and outside of your university. Try to make your statements as specific as possible because this will provide you with a reference point and help you in understanding and implementing reflective practice and managing your professional development in the future.*

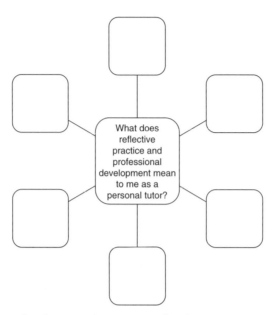

Figure 7.1 *What does reflective practice and professional development mean to me as a personal tutor?*

What do we mean by reflection and reflective practice?

Reflection and reflective practice are important tools to enable professionals to learn from their own experiences. Although they are very similar and complement each other as part of a continuous learning cycle, there are subtle differences between them.

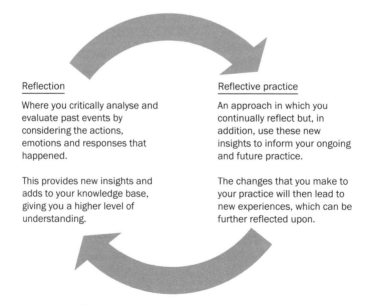

Reflection

Where you critically analyse and evaluate past events by considering the actions, emotions and responses that happened.

This provides new insights and adds to your knowledge base, giving you a higher level of understanding.

Reflective practice

An approach in which you continually reflect but, in addition, use these new insights to inform your ongoing and future practice.

The changes that you make to your practice will then lead to new experiences, which can be further reflected upon.

Figure 7.2 *Reflection and reflective practice*

As mentioned at the start of the book, whether you are a new or an established academic, finding time in the 'whirlwind' of teaching and personal tutoring can be a challenge due to the numerous demands placed on you by your students and the institution you work for. How often have you stopped what you're doing for a *useful* and *significant* period of time and thought about your experiences in an organised way to make sense of them? Valuable thinking or reflection opportunities provide you with the chance to contemplate the aspects of your practice which you would like to change or develop; for example, whether something could work better the next time you try it. Time for reflection should be built into working practices, either on your own or with your mentor. Reflective practice can also help you to understand how personal tutoring contributes to your own development as an academic. With so many institutions focusing on student retention, progression and success, the role of the personal tutor is becoming more central to achieving student-centred strategy. As a consequence, the training and professional development needs of personal tutors is becoming increasingly significant, with a firm focus on developing skills and professional practice networks. Regular reflection can help you to develop tutoring skills, identify areas of interest and support training and professional development needs. Reflection also enables you to work through particular tutoring issues and also helps to recognise patterns of student behaviour, as well as identify themes for discussion with other tutors and colleagues. Finally, reflection on your tutoring role should also inform your overall academic career progression and, in that respect, the tutoring role should be an integral part of the academic performance review process. This is discussed later in the chapter.

Improving your teaching through reflective practice is widely considered as vital for both new and established academics and it is no different when it comes to your personal tutoring role, which is also central to teaching and learning. Fundamentally, reflection involves thinking deeply about an experience in order to understand it and make sense of it. However, reflection alone is not sufficient to stimulate effective learning and improve your personal tutor practice. Even if you regularly reflect on your practice, ten years' experience as a personal tutor may consist of ten years doing the same thing in the same way. The key principle is to regularly act on your reflections, informed by your practice and the perspective of others, which will ensure effective learning and continuous professional development.

Throughout your academic career you are likely to encounter a significant number of theoretical frameworks, definitions and models related to this topic, some of which are explored in the section of this chapter on models of reflective practice. This chapter aims to contextualise reflective practice for your personal tutor role.

Reflective practice and the personal tutor role

A large proportion of your time as a personal tutor involves supporting students individually and this requires a great deal of focus, emotional energy, adaptability, decision-making and, most of all, skill. If you are new to personal tutoring you may consider approaching another academic colleague to act as your mentor. Mentoring by a trusted colleague can help you to critically evaluate your practice and is valuable at any stage of your professional development as a tutor. Mentoring is integral to the reflective process. It helps you discuss skills and specific issues and can also help you to decide how to act upon the advice you are given. Mentoring can help to highlight areas of best practice and can also assist you to evaluate the stage you are at in your tutoring role, as well as explore avenues for further development. Formal academic mentoring schemes may already exist within your institution but mentoring can also take place informally and can usually be set up in consultation with your line manager. Tutoring is a vital part of academic practice and, in line with other teaching and learning activities, tutors must hone the necessary skills and experience to support this activity. To this end, reflecting on and discussing your practice, as well as participating in other professional development activities, will help you to decide how best to invest your time. In terms of your personal tutor role, the following key points highlight what reflective practice is and isn't, as well as the expected benefits and challenges of undertaking this activity regularly.

It is:

✓ a time to think clearly, be honest and consider the facts of your chosen area of reflection;

✓ an activity which can be undertaken individually or with another person (for example a mentor or trusted colleague);

✓ a process which should be undertaken regularly, for example once a week;

✓ a skill which can be learned and honed;

✓ an activity which should be undertaken alongside other professional development activities, such as peer observation, training and work shadowing;

✓ about applying critical analysis to your reflection, such as:

    ○ what actually happened (good and bad);

    ○ what everyone's feelings were at the time;

    ○ what else you could have done or done differently;

    ○ what you might choose to do differently next time.

It is not:

✗ something you need less as your experience as a personal tutor increases;

✗ a waste of your planning and development time;

✗ an easy thing to do, because critically analysing yourself can mean asking tough, probing questions.

The benefits of reflection are as follows.

• It can improve your ability to view events clearly and more objectively.

• It can help you to respond more positively to difficult issues or problems.

- If carried out with a trusted colleague or mentor, it enables you to 'offload' any difficult or emotional issues in a structured, positive and supportive way (sometimes referred to as 'supervision' within other fields).

- It can reduce stress and feelings of anxiety.

- It can reduce feelings of isolation and combat a culture of individualism, particularly when undertaken with a trusted colleague and mentor.

- It can help you to identify your personal strengths and relative limitations and to gain new professional insights.

- It can improve your confidence, professional judgement and practice as a personal tutor.

- It creates a positive, continuous professional development cycle when undertaken regularly.

The challenges of reflection are as follows.

- It can be difficult to find the time to do properly.

- You may lack the experience and/or knowledge to make sense of some issues. This could lead to you following the models more 'mechanically' and not reflecting critically or deeply enough to fully understand the real issue(s). Undertaking reflection with your mentor or an experienced, trusted colleague would help to mitigate this.

- As it requires a critical and honest approach, you could find that you view your areas for improvement as failures, instead of an opportunity to learn and develop. Therefore resilience and a positive attitude is needed.

- You may fear that if you discuss your moments of reflection (such as examples of poor judgement) openly with colleagues, you may be jeopardising or damaging your reputation.

- The educational institution's culture and processes may not actively support you and other personal tutors to be honest and open in your moments of reflection.

Models of reflective practice

Models, sometimes known as frameworks, of reflective practice encourage a structured process to guide your thinking, learning and your application of new knowledge. There are a number of models and theories that you can choose from; however, it is important to recognise that there are various specific models that are used within an HE setting. The model that you choose should help you to reflect constructively on your personal tutoring practice. In this section we will consider a range of models from David Kolb, Graham Gibbs, Chris Johns and Stephen Brookfield. However, there are more models and theories of reflective practice to research and use, such as Dewey (1933), Schön (1983), Atkins and Murphy (1994), Rolfe et al (2001) and Moon (2006). Our experience has shown that it can be useful and appropriate to use one model of reflective practice as a basis, but use questions from other models if they best fit your particular situation. Therefore, it is important to try a number of models and, through trial and error, find which best suits your needs as a personal tutor and even, possibly, create your own personal reflective practice model.

The Experiential Learning Cycle: David Kolb

David Kolb's publications, notably his book *Experiential Learning: Experience as The Source of Learning and Development* (1984) and the development of his Experiential Learning Cycle theory, have been acknowledged as seminal in developing our understanding of human learning behaviour. In essence, the model advocates 'learning from experience' and is typically represented by a four-stage cycle. Kolb viewed learning as an integrated process, with each stage being mutually supportive of, and feeding into, the next. It is possible to enter the cycle at any point and follow through the sequence; however, Kolb believed that 'effective learning' only occurs when you are able to execute all four stages of the model, therefore suggesting that no one stage of the cycle is an effective learning process in isolation.

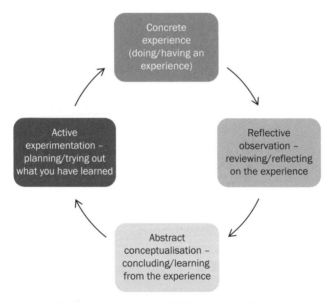

Figure 7.3 *Kolb's Experiential Learning Cycle (1984) – adapted*

Concrete experience

The concrete experience is the 'doing' element which stems from your actual experience of personal tutor practice.

Reflective observation

The reflective observation component of the model derives from your analysis and judgements of events relating to delivery and support activities that you engage in as a personal tutor. You are likely to naturally reflect on your experiences, particularly if you are new to the personal tutor role and possibly less confident in your knowledge and ability. It is very common for practitioners who are new to the personal tutor role to work with a student on a one-to-one basis or in a group tutorial and consider, intuitively, that it did not go very well. This '*common sense reflection*' (a phrase coined by Jennifer Moon, 2004, p 82) is a useful starting point, but how do you really know what was good and bad, and why?

Donald Schön (1983) made the important distinction between the two reflective states: *reflection-in-action* and *reflection-on-action*. Both of these are critical to the personal tutoring role and relate to both the concrete practice and reflective observation elements of Kolb's model. *Reflection-in-action* relates to a setting where your reflection can still benefit the situation rather than deciding how you would act in the future after the moment has passed. This type of reflective tool is extremely helpful in deciding how to act at the time an event occurs. Accordingly, as a tutor, you can decide what might work best for that given situation, drawing on your knowledge and experience. *Reflection-on-action*, however, considers how your practice might develop after the event has passed. Both states are important to the overall development of tutoring practice and can help develop the flexibility to think on your feet.

Essentially, you need to articulate these thoughts or reflections in a clear and systematic way so that you can remember what you thought in order to build on that experience. Examples of ways to capture and crystallise your thoughts could be through keeping a journal of your reflections after one-to-ones and group tutorials or after any significant event at work (see Brookfield's suggestions for reflective journals later in this section). Other useful information which will feed into and add to this holistic reflection might be formal observations of your practice by your mentor, peer observation, appraisals and student feedback.

Abstract conceptualisation

In addition to your reflections on your experience you should be informed by wider reading and educational theory. This may be through reading a book, researching journal articles or HE blogs and websites, attending a training session or speaking to a colleague or mentor who you feel may have sufficient experience in that area. In essence, this section allows you to bring together the theory and analysis from the reflective observation stage, which will allow you to form conclusions about your personal tutoring practice and inform your professional development.

Active experimentation

The conclusions you formed from the abstract conceptualisation stage will form the basis by which you can plan the changes to your practice and turn your reflections into reflective practice. This is where the cycle starts again; active experimentation is where you put into action the desired changes you want in your role as a personal tutor in order to create another concrete experience and thereby create a continuous professional development cycle.

The Reflective Cycle: Graham Gibbs

Graham Gibbs' (1998) Reflective Cycle model provides useful questions to guide your reflections. It encourages a clear description of the situation, analysis and evaluation of feelings, the event, your experience, as well as examining how you might change your practice in the future. As a personal tutor, you will work with students on a one-to-one basis regularly, and an effective way of capturing learning from ad hoc experiences during these one-to-ones and group tutorials is to review completed reflections together to identify any patterns or trends in your practice which may not be immediately obvious. If you choose this model for your reflections, it is advisable to follow the six stages, with each one informing the next. The analysis section is where you will need to use discursive, analytical writing. The other sections require mainly statements of description, statements of value (whether something was challenging or rewarding) and statements of summation or statements of justification (why something was done).

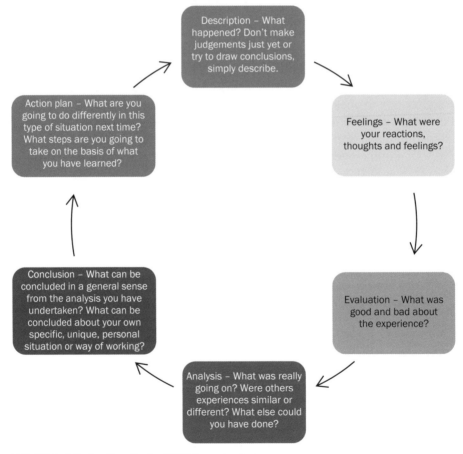

Figure 7.4 *Gibbs' Reflective Cycle (1998) – adapted*

Model of Structured Reflection: Chris Johns

Chris Johns' (1995) model, similar to Gibbs' model, provides useful questions to stimulate and structure your thoughts. This model can be used individually; but the model also supports the idea of undertaking reflective practice with an experienced colleague and refers to this as 'guided reflection'. Talking to your colleagues about what happens when you work with students can sometimes, sadly, become a rare experience. Even though, for the majority of people, reflective practice itself is an intensely personal process, valuable discussions with a colleague or mentor can help shed new light on your experiences as a personal tutor, and even though you may not find a solution, it can be reassuring and sometimes motivating to realise that your experiences are often shared by others.

As discussed in earlier chapters, effective personal tutors develop a high level of rapport with students while maintaining clear professional boundaries, and as a result they tend to find out a lot more about their students than some of their fellow colleagues. Furthermore, it may be that you will find out a lot more about your students through your personal tutoring role, when working with them in one-to-ones, than through your teaching role. The things that you find out can affect your emotions. This is why peer reflective practice is a very useful tool for your personal tutoring role. Another person's point of view removes some of the subjectivity from the reflection, which can be more effective in making sense of, and dealing with, difficult issues.

Even though Johns' model isn't portrayed as cyclical, it is advisable to treat it as such and begin each reflective practice session at the description phase. The questions have not been designed to be asked in a particular order, although there is a progression within the questions. Also, you don't have to use all of the questions in every reflective practice session, and, if appropriate, you can use any question more than once.

Johns' Model of Structured Reflection (1995): adapted

Stage 1: Description

- Write a description of the experience.
- What are the key issues within this description that I need to pay attention to?

Stage 2: Reflection

- What was I trying to achieve?
- Why did I act as I did?
- What are the consequences of my actions for the following:
  - the students;
  - myself;
  - the people I work with?
- How did I feel about this experience when it was happening?

- How did the student/colleague feel about it?

- How do I know how the student/colleague felt about it?

Stage 3: Influencing factors

- What internal factors influenced my decision-making and actions?

- What external factors influenced my decision-making and actions?

- What sources of knowledge influenced or should have influenced my decision-making and actions?

Stage 4: Alternative strategies

- Could I have dealt with the situation better?

- What other choices did I have?

- What would be the consequences of these other choices?

Stage 5: Learning

- How can I make sense of this experience in light of past experience and future practice?

- How do I feel about this experience now?

- Have I taken effective action to support myself and others as a result of this experience?

Four critically reflective lenses: Stephen Brookfield

Even though Stephen Brookfield relates his thinking on reflective practice to the traditional teaching role, some of his suggestions are equally relevant to the personal tutor role, and in places we have adapted them to fit this.

In order to succeed in becoming critically reflective, Brookfield (1995, pp 29–30) asserts that teachers must view themselves through four critically reflective lenses, which are:

1.   Our autobiographies as learners and teachers: using our own unique personal self-reflection and collecting the insights and meanings for teaching.

2.   Our students' eyes: making an assessment of one's self through the students' lens by seeking their input and seeing classrooms and learning from their perspectives.

3.   Our colleagues' experiences: by peer review of teaching from colleagues' experiences, observations and feedback.

4.   Theoretical literature: by frequently referring to the theoretical literature that may provide an alternative, interpretive framework for a situation.

Often academics are required to undertake some of the four aspects of Brookfield's model as part of their PG Cert in Teaching and Learning in Higher Education or Academic Practice and other aspects are likely to be built into the processes of the institution that you work within such as the performance review process. A key aspect, which you may not have been asked to carry out as a personal tutor, is keeping a reflective journal – in Brookfield's terms a 'Teaching Log' (stage one of his model), in our terms a 'personal tutor log'.

Brookfield (1995) argues that it is useful for teachers to keep a weekly record of the events that have impressed themselves most vividly on their consciousness, particularly focusing on events that were positive, stressful or challenging. He argues that one of the principal benefits for teachers of becoming critically reflective is to ground them emotionally, and this is certainly useful within the personal tutor role due to the multitude of issues you can be faced with. In order to make this personal tutor log a feasible task, try filling in the journal weekly for 15 to 20 minutes. Brookfield (1995) recommends some of the following questions and suggests that you should jot down any brief responses that seem appropriate.

- What was (were) the moment(s) this week when I felt most connected, engaged or affirmed as a personal tutor – the moment(s) I said to myself, 'This is what being a personal tutor is really about'?

- What was (were) the moment(s) this week when I felt most disconnected, disengaged or bored as a personal tutor – the moment(s) I said to myself, 'I'm just going through the motions here'?

- What was the situation that caused me the greatest anxiety or distress – the kind of situation that I kept replaying in my mind as I was dropping off to sleep, or that caused me to say to myself, 'I don't want to go through this again for a while'?

- What was the event that most took me by surprise – an event where I saw or did something that shook me up, caught me off guard, knocked me off my stride, gave me a jolt, or made me unexpectedly happy?

- Of everything I did this week in my personal tutor role, what would I do differently if I had the chance to do it again?

- What do I feel proudest of in my personal tutoring activities this week and why?

Despite the fact that our personal tutoring experiences run the risk of being dismissed as '*merely anecdotal*', Brookfield, while conceding that '*all experience is inherently idiosyncratic*', asserts that our autobiographies are '*one of the most important sources of insight into teaching to which we have access*' (1995, p 31).

Regularly updating a personal tutor log is a good way to begin to make reflective practice more of a routine and less of a one-off when the need arises, and it will produce benefits for your ongoing professional development as a personal tutor. As discussed in Chapter 4, your institution may have a dashboard or electronic personal tutor system where you can formally record these reflections in the format of tutor notes or an electronic tutor log. These are usually intended to keep records about tutoring conversations and record specific information about a student's progression. Nevertheless, it is advisable to keep a separate personal tutor log for your own professional development and, indeed, this is good practice. As discussed previously, journaling for personal tutoring is a very important and personal exercise that not only helps you to keep a dated record of details of specific personal tutoring sessions, perhaps in bullet point form, but also helps capture reflections from conversations with students, colleagues and even your mentor. A tutoring log can also help you record notes from any training that you participate in, any reading you complete and other professional development activities that you might undertake for your broader professional development.

Notes which contain details about specific students should be kept confidential by using student numbers rather than names and always ensure that your notes are kept in a secure place.

> ### Critical thinking activity 2
>
> *From your experience of working with students so far, think of one personal tutoring scenario which you feel didn't go to plan and wished the outcome could have been better (for you or the student). Using your preferred reflective practice model, answer the following questions.*
>
> 1. Are there multiple issues for reflection from this single scenario? If so, list them.
> 2. What is the key issue for critical reflection?
> 3. Focusing on the key issue, note down your thoughts for each stage of your reflective practice model and how you could use this new knowledge to make improvements in your practice.

Reflective scenarios

All moments of reflection are different and have varying levels of complexity. Therefore, they require differing levels of analysis and evaluation and also require you to focus on different aspects of your reflective practice model. On occasion, new academics and personal tutors may feel that some aspects require more urgent consideration. Academics new to the reflective process can be tempted to engage with the action plan part of their model more quickly and readily than the other preceding stages. This should be avoided to ensure there is greater consistency between your analysis and course of action. Irrespective of your starting point, you need to engage in the process, recognising that you need to be open, honest and authentic throughout to really benefit while realising that critical reflection will on occasion create uncomfortable professional awareness but ultimately will lead you towards becoming an effective personal tutor.

The following scenario illustrates a potential situation that you could encounter within your personal tutor role. After the explanation of the scenario there is a list of points that contain some further questions and thoughts which could inform the stages of your reflective practice.

Scenario 1: group tutorial

During a group tutorial on the topic of sexuality with a lively class, a small group of students make inappropriate comments regarding sexuality to two other students which you overhear. You firmly address the individuals in question, but the comments between the two groups become more heated and offensive as the class continues. Eventually, arguments break out between different groups. You regain order, but the session is about to finish and the arguments appear to continue in the corridor.

Group tutorial potential reflection considerations

- From your knowledge of the group and in the planning stages for this session, were there any potential issues that you could have pre-empted and taken action to overcome? For example, could you have used a different seating plan?

- Did you establish clear boundaries and discuss expectations before starting the session either at the start of the academic year or within the previous group tutorial?

- Did you reiterate or even need to reiterate the consequences for any poor behaviour within the classroom?

- Were the learning activities and content suitable for this level of students?

- Was the approach to student behaviour fair and appropriate in light of the comments made? Did the approach follow the institution's guidelines and procedures concerning student behaviour and classroom management?

- Should you have kept some or all of the students involved behind afterwards to address the situation?

- What are other colleagues' feelings about these students and this incident?

- Has this type of issue or any other issue happened before between these groups of students?

- What is the overall profile of the students involved? Are there students with particular issues within the group tutorial?

Critical thinking activity 3

Having read the example personal tutoring scenario, consider the following two scenarios within your current educational institution and with your students. Then, imagining that you are the personal tutor in each scenario, answer the following questions.

1. Are there multiple issues for reflection? If so, list all of the potential issues in a similar way to the worked example (see the considerations from the previous scenario).

2. What is the key issue for critical reflection? Is there a distinction to be made here between reflecting, *in-action* and *on-action*?

   Possible reflection considerations are provided in the discussion section that follows the scenarios. However, try to complete the activity before reading these.

Scenario 2

You are supporting Emma, a very academically capable student, through one-to-one meetings. She wants to achieve high marks in her academic assignments so she can graduate with a first. However, after a recent poor exam result her motivation and confidence drops dramatically and she begins to miss many of the SMART targets you had both agreed upon. She regularly comes to see you for advice as her personal tutor and, even though you have many other things to do, you try to find time to help her.

Scenario 3

One of your students, Justin, has apparently been disengaged during class and is falling behind with handing in his coursework. On numerous occasions you have tried to have positive learning conversations with him, but he refuses to talk about these issues, which you find frustrating and, even though you don't want to, you can't help showing it. You eventually get him to talk about the issues, but he just blames everyone else, such as his academic tutors and fellow students.

Discussion

Scenario 2: reflection considerations

- Were the initial SMART targets too ambitious or about right?

- It is important to remember that Emma's academic ability won't have faltered significantly in such a short space of time and to make her aware of this. It is important that you put this particular exam mark in context and help Emma to see this as part of the broader learning and development process.

- Other than the recent poor exam result, were there any other factors that have contributed to the dip in her performance?

- Due to the short space of time that Emma needs to turn things around, what are some small key things that you can discuss with her so that she has the best chance of achieving her aim? If it is a confidence/motivation issue, what are some small steps she can take to regain this? When a student is facing a confidence/motivation issue, finding ways to achieve 'quick wins' is a useful way to create momentum towards a goal and make it feel more achievable. Goal setting with a student can be hugely motivational and help them to quickly realise the benefits of learning from the assessment process by responding appropriately to feedback.

- What do her other tutors say about her past and current performance? When you have identified a way forward with Emma, it would be sensible to reassess the previous SMART targets to see if they are still suitable.

Scenario 3: reflection considerations

- How long has Justin been visibly disengaged in class? Is it a recent issue or more of a long-term pattern?

- What are the *immediate*, *visible* reasons for Justin's poor behaviour and dip in performance? (For example, tired from working too much or staying up or being out too late, issues with fellow students or friends.)

- What do Justin's other tutors say about his engagement and performance in class?

- Are there any additional support needs which Justin may have? Is the institution providing/can the university provide support for this? How can you initiate a referral to some of these central and specialist support services?

- Are there any underlying root causes behind this disengagement? (Are some of these not immediately visible; for example a mental health problem, an unidentified learning difficulty or issues at home.)

- Some personal tutoring situations are frustrating but it is important not to let these frustrations prevent you from supporting the student to improve.

- Disengagement in class, especially when it affects the learning of others isn't acceptable. The university should provide support and procedures for you and your colleagues to address this.

- It is unlikely that you will see an immediate improvement until Justin firstly recognises that he is disengaged and takes ownership of his actions, which should be one of your primary goals.

- In order to support Justin and address this issue you need to explore issues above and below the surface to help him effect real change. Of course, an obvious constraint when trying to do this is time. Start with the immediate and visible reasons to see if this has the desired effect before moving on to other reasons or issues, which may take more time and be harder to identify.

Professional development

While reflective practice forms a key part of the academic professional development process, there are other important activities that you can engage in as a tutor which will not only inform the reflective process but also help you to develop key skills relating to personal tutoring and advising. This section aims to discuss some of these activities and provide you with some key pointers for your consideration.

Peer observation

Peer observation should be seen as a developmental process but is still not common practice in HE personal tutoring. Nevertheless, the feedback from peer observation, particularly if this is done by a trusted mentor, can be really beneficial, especially when used to inform your own development. If you have high expectations of your students, you need to have high expectations of yourself and observation gives you an opportunity to judge how you are progressing. These positive aspects of observation are more likely to happen if your institutional culture embraces a constructive approach to tutoring. It is always possible, however, to set up informal peer observations if no formal scheme exists.

Peer observation is highly effective for the personal tutor role and these also apply to the broader mentor/mentee relationship, as discussed previously. The reasons for this are:

- it is supportive and developmental;

- it provides coaching and mentoring opportunities for you and your peers;

- the giving and receiving of feedback develops the skills you are using with students by enabling you to use them with colleagues too;

- you are likely to have an established and positive relationship with the other person. Among the key benefits of this is good-quality feedback. If there is mutual trust and respect, both sides have permission to offer critical feedback because they want to help one another;

- the support of peers is very important when faced with a variety of challenging student issues;

- the observer (someone in the same role) arguably brings more specific knowledge and understanding;

- it promotes sharing of good practice between people who are performing the same role.

Personal tutor training

Many institutions offer some form of personal tutor training, although the breadth and depth of this differs between organisations. At the time of writing, many institutions are reviewing and considering appropriate training and professional development opportunities for tutors at all levels and these are likely to become more comprehensive over time. The existing training offer for tutors within institutions may take on many forms and is often transactional rather than developmental. We suggest that you take the time to survey your institution to find out what is currently on offer and make enquiries as to how you can inform and support this academic training. It is unlikely, however, that any formal training will prepare you completely for your tutor role so it must be combined with gaining experience of tutoring in action, using a variety of resources and the support mechanisms that we have referred to in this book.

Robust personal tutor training should cover a variety of topics including (but by no means limited to) core values and skills, institutional systems, policies and procedures, setting boundaries, referral processes, reflective practice and record-keeping. It is important that you engage in personal tutoring training as part of your professional development as a tutor. The training in which you participate must be delivered alongside the role that you are performing as a tutor so that you have the opportunity to apply what you have learned in practice. This will not only help you to contextualise and consolidate your learning but also allow you to bring your own insights to the training session(s) that are offered. This is where reflective practice becomes key to your professional development as a tutor and can help you to make sense of the concrete tutoring experience that you are amassing. Training for personal tutors should not happen in isolation and, once training has taken place, this does not signal the end of your development as a tutor. Further opportunities for development can be offered as part of the overall training programme and these can be external as well as internal.

The university environment is in a perpetual state of change with key issues always being brought to the fore such as student mental health and well-being. It is important that you are able to access regular opportunities to reinforce the training that you have been given and find out the latest information about the support that the institution is providing for its students. It is also important that you have the chance to discuss updates and developments, both within the organisation and across the sector, with other tutoring colleagues. Ideally, tutoring refresher training should take place at least once per year and training should be co-ordinated across the institution so that a degree of consistency can be achieved. In addition, training should provide you with the opportunity to discuss challenges with other colleagues in a supportive environment and offer you the chance to work through these challenges with those who have significant tutoring experience. Tutor training is particularly powerful when it is considered alongside the broader development of the personal tutor role including mentoring, tutor networks and more senior tutoring responsibilities. It is important to seek out the training offered by your organisation, if you have not already done so, and to contribute to the ongoing development of the personal tutor training agenda. The feedback that you provide as a tutor will be invaluable and informative to the training process.

Personal tutor networks

Active participation in personal tutor networks is another key aspect of your professional development as a personal tutor. Such networks may exist formally or informally and, indeed, externally as well as internally. In recent years, new national networks for tutors in HE have been established to coincide with the increasing level of importance that tutoring is now being given within institutions. As discussed previously, there are many benefits to attending and participating in tutoring networks: they offer you the opportunity to discuss tutoring practice, work through difficulties and challenges and identify improvements to the tutoring process. It is possible to identify mentors through tutoring networks and to also mentor colleagues who are new to the tutoring process. One particular example of a tutoring network is an action learning set. Some institutions have action learning sets for personal tutoring which are run more formally and offer opportunities to work through more 'thorny' issues. On the other hand, action learning sets can also be set up informally. Action learning sets, like other tutoring networks, can be used for a variety of different purposes but usually have the following objectives for tutors in mind.

- Assist tutors to define the purposes, timescale and results associated with tutoring.

- Assist others by testing and clarifying ideas.

- Ask the questions others will not ask of themselves.

- Provide additional motivation for tutors to take action, individually and collectively.

- Share ideas on resolving difficulties encountered by others.

- Offer information derived from their functional and managerial experience.

- Monitor progress.

- Share "air time" effectively and appropriately.

- Enable tutors to manage themselves and review the effectiveness of that management.

- Take charge of individual and group learning.

- Establish ways of reviewing and improving tutors' learning.

(Adapted from Mumford, 1996)

Tutoring and advising networks

At a national level there are several organisations currently championing the personal tutoring agenda within UK HE, offering those with responsibility for tutoring in universities an opportunity to participate in discussion sessions, webinars, conferences and other developmental activities, such as research. UK Advising and Tutoring (UKAT) is a sector-wide organisation which supports the development of personal tutoring in UK HE, offering an annual conference and other professional development opportunities. UKAT has a website of personal tutoring resources for a fixed membership fee (www.ukat.uk). The Centre for Recording Achievement (CRA) (www.recordingachievement.ac.uk) also hosts a number of annual events and seminars on personal tutoring and some of these are delivered in partnership with SEDA, the Staff and Educational Development Association (www.seda.ac.uk). The CRA and SEDA host an accredited personal tutoring award which supports professional engagement with enhanced practice in personal tutoring via a professional practice portfolio. At international level, UKAT is allied with NACADA, the Global Community for Academic Advising (www.nacada.ksu.edu). This partnership is designed to strengthen the breadth and depth of support for advisors and tutors globally and to champion advising at every level in higher education including advising research.

Summary

Personal tutoring can sometimes take a back seat in comparison to teaching and research. If this is the case, it could well be that your reflections, until now, have not been concerned with personal tutoring. However, the road to becoming an effective personal tutor will consist of many challenging situations and emotive issues, thus making reflective practice in relation to your personal tutoring activities highly important. Reflective practice also informs your continuing professional development as a tutor.

Reflective practice is more than just thinking about what happened, it is an approach of continually reflecting through using a systematic process of collecting, recording and analysing thoughts and observations from yourself as well as trusted colleagues. It enables you to use development time effectively to focus on, or discuss, what has actually happened and consider why. It isn't an easy or quick thing to do. However, by undertaking the process regularly, you will be able to transfer learning from one situation to similar future events and, therefore, you will be less likely to jump to conclusions about situations and you will develop more constructive ideas regarding your personal tutor practice.

To aid your development, we recommend keeping a personal tutor log at the end of each week or after an incident that feels particularly significant with a student (or even a colleague). Furthermore, consider discussing your reflections and potential actions with a trusted colleague and mentor or read up about a particular subject and, as a result, you may try to do something differently or possibly decide that what you were doing was the best way. Writing down and discussing your reflections will also inform your professional development needs as a tutor and help you to decide what opportunities to take advantage of in the future.

Learning checklist

Tick off each point when you feel confident you understand it.

☐ *I understand that reflective practice is an approach through which I should regularly reflect on my practice as a personal tutor and use the resulting insights to inform my ongoing actions and future practice.*

☐ *I understand that reflection and reflective practice can be undertaken either individually or with a trusted colleague, mentor or friend.*

☐ *I know that the choice over which model of reflective practice I use isn't as important as the emphasis I place on being honest in the process as well as identifying what aspects of my personal tutor practice I would change if the incident or issue arose again.*

☐ *I recognise that being critically reflective of my personal tutoring practice is likely to highlight areas for development. I know that I shouldn't view these as my 'failures' but as my opportunities to learn and improve.*

☐ *I recognise that there can be many professional development opportunities available to personal tutors, both within and outside of my organisation.*

☐ *I appreciate that it is useful to review completed reflections together as a set to identify patterns or trends in my practice which may not be immediately obvious from looking at just one reflection.*

☐ *I understand that keeping a personal tutor log is a good way to ensure that I make reflective practice part of my professional development routine.*

Critical reflections

1. From your experience of working as a personal tutor so far:

    a. identify two potential barriers to making reflective practice an ongoing, regular activity;

    b. for each potential barrier, explain one small action you could take to overcome it.

2. Which would you find more effective and why: undertaking reflective practice individually or in dialogue with a trusted person?

3. Identify the key opportunity costs of personal tutors not undertaking reflective practice for the:

    a. individual;

    b. university.

4. Evaluate whether reflective practice is equally important for an experienced practitioner and a newly qualified practitioner.

Personal tutor self-assessment system

See following table.

PERSONAL TUTOR SELF-ASSESSMENT SYSTEM : Chapter 7 Reflective practice and professional development

	Minimum standard 1 star	Beginner level 2 star	Intermediate level 3 star	Advanced level 4 Star	Expert level 5 Star
Individual	I regularly think about what is working well and what could be improved within my personal tutoring practice.	I carry out reflective practice, related to my personal tutor role, as an ongoing, regular activity.	In response to what I am learning from the reflective practice process, I am seeing incremental improvements in my personal tutoring practice.	In response to what I am learning from the reflective practice process, I am seeing incremental improvements in my students' experience and their educational outcomes.	The outcomes of my reflective practice inform joint practice development projects with colleagues.
Institutional	My institution values the professional development of its personal tutors and actively encourages this through providing opportunities to discuss practice and attend training events.	My institution displays its commitment to its personal tutors undertaking effective individual or peer reflective practice through providing adequate time, resources and support for the process. Honest and open dialogue about critical incidents or issues is embraced as positive and developmental.	Deans and Heads of School value the benefits reflective practice can bring to personal tutors and they actively encourage its use within meetings, individual discussions and appraisals.	Peer and individual reflective practice is routinely used by all personal tutors within the institution. There is an active mentoring scheme for personal tutors within the university.	Action research projects and joint practice development opportunities are routinely used by personal tutors as two of the ways to further develop and disseminate the learning from the reflective practice process.

The self-assessment system is available as a free download from the publisher's website and the authors' websites (all listed at the start of the book).

References

Atkins, S and Murphy, K (1994) Reflective Practice. *Nursing Standard*. 8(39): 49–54.

Brookfield, S (1995) *Becoming a Critically Reflective Teacher*. San Francisco: Jossey-Bass.

Dewey, J (1933) *How We Think: A Restatement of the Relation of Reflective Thinking to the Educative Process*. Boston, MA: D.C. Heath.

Fry, H, Ketteridge, S and Marshall, S (2014) *A Handbook for Teaching & Learning in Higher Education: Enhancing Academic Practice*. London: Routledge.

Gibbs, G (1998) *Learning by Doing: A Guide to Teaching and Learning Methods*. Oxford: Further Education Unit, Oxford Polytechnic.

Johns, C (1995) Framing Learning Through Reflection within Carper's Fundamental Ways of Knowing in Nursing. *Journal of Advanced Nursing*, 22 (2): 226–34.

Kolb, D (1984) *Experiential Learning: Experience as the Source of Learning and Development*. Englewood Cliffs, NJ: Prentice Hall.

Moon, J (2004) *A Handbook of Reflective and Experiential Learning. Theory and Practice*. London: Routledge.

Mumford, A (1996) Effective Learners in Action Learning Sets. *Employee Counselling Today*, 8(6): 3–10.

Rolfe, G, Freshwater, D and Jasper, M (2001) *Critical Reflection for Nursing and the Helping Professions*. Basingstoke: Palgrave.

Schön, D (1983) *The Reflective Practitioner. How Professionals Think in Action*. New York: Basic Books.

8 Measuring impact

Chapter aims

This chapter helps you to:

- understand what is meant by 'impact' and 'measuring impact';

- identify ways in which the impact of your personal tutoring core skills, key activities and professional development can be measured at both an individual and institutional level;

- understand what is meant by quantitative and qualitative measures of impact;

- identify reasons for measuring impact, in particular in the context of emerging policy concerning teaching excellence in HE and the Teaching Excellence Framework (TEF);

- critically analyse aspects of measuring impact;

- consider some of the factors that influence the enhancement of student performance – performance in terms of retention, success, attendance, punctuality and student progression – and the relative importance of your personal tutoring core skills and key activities in comparison with these factors.

Introduction

Measuring impact tends to be most commonly talked about by managers and leaders, and is a common feature of the TEF in HE. By showing you the value of measuring impact and how it can be carried out at an individual level, this chapter aims to provide you with clarity about the impact you are having in your personal tutor role. Firstly, however, it's important to consider definitions.

What do we mean by impact and measuring impact?

What do we mean by impact? 'An effect' and 'influence' are likely to be included in most answers. Markless and Streatfield (2006, p 1) use the following definition of impact: '*any effect of the service (or of an event or initiative) on an individual or group*'.

Impact is defined by the Research Excellence Framework (REF) as '*"reach" and "significance" and can encompass the "effect on, change or benefit to the economy, society, culture, public policy or services, health, the environment or quality of life"*' (Research Excellence Framework, nd, cited in The Association of Commonwealth Universities, 2012).

We tend to associate impact with change for the good. However, it can be positive or negative and for that matter can be intended or unintended and direct or indirect (AMOSSHE, 2011, p 9).

Impact is also easy to confuse with other concepts:

> *There is a tendency to confuse impact with customer/student satisfaction. Customer satisfaction focuses on measuring whether or not students **like** or are **happy** with the educational experience and services they receive. Impact, however, is aimed at measuring whether or not the educational experience/service is making any **difference** to what they do and how.*
>
> (AMOSSHE, 2011, p 9)

So, when it comes to impact there is a necessary emphasis on *change*. Therefore, measuring impact needs to be measurement of change, and a comparative element over time is needed.

How we measure impact is also highly important, as you will see in this chapter. It's not a simple process either, and it requires a great deal of thought:

> *Customer satisfaction is relatively easy to measure... Impact, however, is more difficult to measure. Impact is about change, which implies that a situation needs to be evaluated before an action to stimulate change takes place, and after to determine whether indeed change has taken place.*
>
> (AMOSSHE, 2011, p 9)

When assessing and measuring impact it's important to acknowledge how rapidly the HE sector is changing in response to government policy. The TEF, enshrined in the Higher Education and Research Act of 2017, attempts to link the concepts of impact and excellence and relates them specifically to the delivery of teaching and learning. It aims to demonstrate the impact of teaching excellence in HE and use this evidence specifically to raise teaching standards, promote student satisfaction and provide a greater focus on graduate employability to widen participation. TEF ratings (bronze, silver and gold) are awarded, by appointed TEF assessors, according to quantitative impact metrics (such as student retention, student satisfaction and graduate outcomes) alongside a qualitative institutional statement outlining their overall approach to teaching, learning and student success. It must be noted that these metrics, and their weighting, are likely to change significantly as the TEF model develops.

Similarly, the Office for Students (OfS) regulatory framework, which sets out the governance of teaching excellence in HE, is likely to evolve over time.

One of the overall aims of the TEF is to *'place a spotlight on teaching and encourage excellent teaching for all students'*, which was outlined in a Green Paper (Department of Business, Innovation and Skills, 2015, p 18) and followed by a White Paper in 2016 (Department of Business, Innovation and Skills, 2016). This requires impact measures, hence the inclusion of metrics in the overall rating and score. The measurement and impact of teaching *excellence*, in this case, relates to several overall principles: *'excellence must incorporate and reflect the diversity of the sector, disciplines and missions – not all students will achieve their best within the same model of teaching'* (Department of Business, Innovation and Skills, 2015, p 21). While there is no mention specifically of personal tutoring in the Government's Green or White Papers (2015, 2016), the former Higher Education Academy (HEA), now operating as Advance HE, conducted research in 2017 which suggests that proportionally more gold and silver award holders mentioned personalised learning in their institutional statements. Many of these statements reference interventions specifically related to personal tutoring, something especially evident in the institutional statements of those who attained gold awards (Higher Education Academy, 2017, pp iv–v). Therefore, the impact of personal tutoring on teaching and learning, specifically personalised learning, must not be underestimated. As will be discussed later in the chapter, the impact of activities, strategies and processes are difficult to 'prove' given other factors that can influence change.

Self-assessment is a related and relevant term. This chapter is concerned with measuring impact on the student and this directly informs self-assessment. Self-assessment is also closely related to reflective practice, discussed in Chapter 7. Your institution may have mechanisms and reporting requirements in place for you to self-assess your personal tutoring practice alongside other teaching and learning commitments. Commonly these include sections on outcomes for students and factors which may affect their retention and progression (for example, disability, mental health issues, those who are the first in their family to go to university and those from low socio-economic backgrounds). There should be space for you to discuss interventions that have been put in place to support students (both individually and in groups) and this will include a commentary on your personal tutoring approach. This approach can relate to individual and collective tutoring practice and can capture various dimensions of the personal tutoring culture within academic schools or departments.

Despite the use of the word 'self', confusingly, self-assessment can sometimes refer to processes at departmental or institutional level. It often relates to an end-of-year reporting process involving discussion with academics and personal tutors but overseen by Deans and Heads of School. With the introduction of the TEF and annual provider review mechanisms, self-assessment is often incorporated into wider institutional reporting and monitoring on student success, hence the focus on retention, student satisfaction, employability and student outcomes. It can also underpin the academic performance review process which can help to inform professional development needs (as discussed in Chapter 7). This chapter relates to an ongoing process of measuring impact and includes how to do so at an individual level. Reflection (the subject of Chapter 7) may include aspects of measuring individual impact or may be an outcome of it.

The relationship between self-assessment and measuring impact and the subtle differences between them are shown in Figure 8.1.

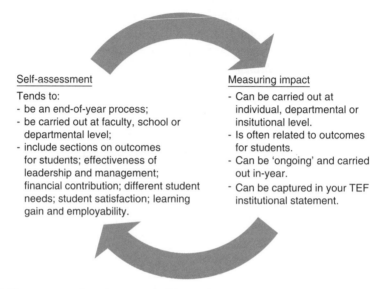

Self-assessment
Tends to:
- be an end-of-year process;
- be carried out at faculty, school or departmental level;
- include sections on outcomes for students; effectiveness of leadership and management; financial contribution; different student needs; student satisfaction; learning gain and employability.

Measuring impact
- Can be carried out at individual, departmental or insitutional level.
- Is often related to outcomes for students.
- Can be 'ongoing' and carried out in-year.
- Can be captured in your TEF institutional statement.

Figure 8.1 *Self-assessment and measuring impact*

What can be measured in relation to personal tutoring and how can it be done?

In the first chapter we suggested that effective personal tutoring included the development of students' intellectual and academic ability, as well as the nurturing of their emotional well-being, through individualised/personalised and holistic support.

Critical thinking activity 1

1. List all the ways in which you think the following can be measured:

    a. intellectual and academic ability;

    b. emotional well-being.

2. What do you notice about the two components and the ways of measuring them?

Discussion

It is likely that it was easier for you to answer question 1a, about how intellectual and academic ability can be measured. Among the answers could be:

- exam and assessment results;

- student retention;

- success rates;

- employability and learning gain.

The second element, emotional wellbeing, is more difficult to measure. In part, this is because you first have to decide what is meant by emotional well-being, and this tends to be subjective in nature. Aspects of emotional well-being often include the following:

- confidence;

- motivation;

- self-esteem;

- resilience;

- satisfaction;

- social integration.

Although it is not appropriate to discuss here the subtle distinctions between these aspects, reflect on what you think they are. It's also worth briefly acknowledging here the complexity of the aspects themselves. Confidence, for example, according to Norman and Hyland (2003, p 6, cited in Dutton et al, 2004) has three elements: '*"cognitive" is a person's knowledge of their abilities; "performance" is their ability to do something; and "emotional" is feeling comfortable about the former two aspects*'.

Emotional well-being is linked to good mental health and resilience, and the measuring of this is helped by knowing more commonly accepted notions of what 'good mental health' looks like. The Mental Health Foundation, for example, defines it as '*the ability to learn; feel, express and manage a range of positive and negative emotions; form and maintain good relationships with others; cope with and manage change and uncertainty*' (Mental Health Foundation, nd, online). Furthermore, institutions have a responsibility to promote good mental health to students, alongside a healthy balance between work, life and study. They should also have an open discussion about the word 'resilience' and what it means in practice. Promoting these key messages to students will have an impact on the way in which they are received and also perceived by staff and students. Recent studies on student resilience in HE, for example, shift the focus away from individual students to instead examine the importance of the student's external environment in helping them to develop resilience and good overall mental health. These environmental factors are multi-faceted and include social networks, learning spaces, peer support facilities, as well as availability of, and access to, co- and extra-curricular activities. Of course, the provision of effective personal tutoring is a very important part of creating an environment that supports and facilitates engagement in student resilience (McIntosh and Shaw, 2017). A report published by the student mental health charity, Student Minds, in 2018, highlighted the importance of good-quality mental health training for academics, many of whom reported that training provided to support students with mental health issues was not adequate, impacting on their levels of confidence in dealing with arising situations (Hughes et al, 2018).

Focusing on the ways in which emotional well-being can be measured should concentrate on students' *perceptions* of how they feel in relation to the aspects previously mentioned, which are:

- confidence;
- motivation;
- self-esteem;
- resilience;
- satisfaction;
- social integration.

The reason for focusing on *perceptions* is because these are subjective topics. For example, if a student rates themselves as nine out of ten for resilience, this does not necessarily mean they *will be* highly resilient if suddenly faced with adversity; rather, it means they *perceive* themselves to be highly resilient.

Methods to measure emotional well-being could include gathering information from:

- results of questionnaires using a graphic rating scale (a system using points on a scale; a common example is zero (strongly disagree) to five (strongly agree)) on these aspects;
- the use of scaling (rating of one to ten) in one-to-one structured conversations with students where they decide where they are on this scale related to these aspects (see Chapter 6 for further guidance);
- feedback within student focus groups.

It's important to remember the point that measuring impact is about change, and thus comparison and timescale are needed (this is discussed in more detail later in the chapter). So, the previous examples could be carried out three times – at the beginning, middle and end of a realistic time range (for example each semester or over an academic year).

Qualitative and quantitative measures

What did you notice about the different ways of measuring the two components of effective personal tutoring (in critical thinking activity 1)? It is noticeable that the measures of intellectual and academic ability tend to be statistical (also referred to as 'quantitative' or 'hard' measures) whereas the measures of emotional well-being tend to be non-statistical ('qualitative' or 'soft' measures). Although there can be statistics involved in the measuring of emotional well-being and resilience (for example results of questionnaires using a graphic rating scale), they are on more subjective topics, and thus the data is arguably 'softer'. Furthermore, the question of how honest students' responses will be (sometimes referred to as 'observational bias') needs to be taken into account. This is another reason why such strategies should concentrate on students' perception of these aspects rather than assuming any absolute 'truths'. However, this doesn't mean there is no merit in measuring factors such as emotional well-being and resilience. Often the number that students give when asked to scale their feelings, for example, is not as important as where the students think they are since it gives a jointly agreed point from which to work. This can open up important dialogue for discussion between students and tutors during the tutorial process. Tutors are then able to help students to explore their perceptions and the information that they draw upon in order to reach these subjective conclusions.

Moreover, the line between 'hard' and 'soft' is not necessarily as distinct as we might imagine.

> They [soft outcomes] *are used to describe gains in confidence and self-esteem, and might also include acquisition of so called soft skills, such as problem solving skills. They are usually seen as intangible and difficult to quantify and therefore different to hard outcomes which are viewed as tangible evidence of success, for instance accreditation or completion of a course of study. In practice, as Ward and Edwards* [2002] *contend, the distinction between hard and soft outcomes is not so clear cut, as even hard outcomes 'are often dealing with degrees of success rather than clearly defined absolutes'.*
>
> (Dutton et al, 2004, p 56)

Intellectual and academic ability and emotional well-being are, arguably, of equal importance to the personal tutor role or, more accurately, they are often strongly linked. In your role as a personal tutor you will be able to see how emotional well-being affects, both positively and negatively, the academic progress of your students.

Research has shown a strong link between learning and emotional well-being as a two-way process. The report quoted previously was produced after research into students' and practitioners' views on the development of confidence – closely connected to emotional well-being – in relation to learning. It states the following in its comprehensive review of literature on the topic: 'Confidence and self-esteem are complex concepts but seeking to understand them in relation to the learning context is important as developing them can bring about enormous benefits for learners' (Dutton et al, 2004, p 15).

Throughout this book we have brought to your attention ways in which you can have a positive effect on students' emotional well-being which will improve their performance. As suggested by the research previously mentioned, improved learning (included within performance), in turn, improves confidence, producing a positive cycle that is beneficial to all.

> The research findings revealed a high degree of consensus of views of the relationship between confidence and learning and the indicators and manifestations of this ... almost all the learners experienced successful learning and their confidence increased. This in turn enhanced their achievements and progression to further learning, but the combination of new skills and knowledge with enhanced confidence and self-esteem brought many broader benefits.
>
> (Dutton et al, 2004, p 31)

Due to external pressures on an institution, for example by the TEF and league tables, the focus of the institution may be more on academic progress than the emotional well-being of its students. However, as shown in previous chapters, there is an increasing interest in the social aspects of student progress, alongside engendering a sense of belonging and connectedness (Thomas, 2017). Moreover, the implications of the above research are that if confidence has a significant effect on both learning and students' lives, the question of whether this should be used as an intended outcome of learning programmes needs raising (Dutton et al, 2004, p 56). Indeed, confidence and resilience are starting to appear more frequently in various graduate attributes frameworks issued by different universities. Both of these are hailed as qualities which institutions expect their graduates to be able to demonstrate. Recent work completed between Australia and the UK on graduate attributes resulted in the new *Citizen Scholar Framework*, which aims to assess the ways in which institutions nurture students to become 'Citizen Scholars'. Embracing change and uncertainty is a key part of citizen scholarship and how students and universities respond to the social mission of HE (Arvanitakis and Hornsby, 2016). Both resilience and confidence are key parts of this framework and, although difficult to measure, are now seen as integral to the overall student learning experience. The reason confidence and emotional well-being are not measurable outcomes of study programmes, in the way that retention and achievement are for example, is likely to be that they are seen as intangible and subjective (Dutton et al, 2004, p 56). However, as such studies and this chapter show, there are ways of capturing and measuring such areas. The Dutton research proposes that developing confidence should be an integral part of teacher training and training for existing tutors (Dutton et al, 2004, p 58).

If the focus is on the academic side and success rates in your institution, then it becomes even more important for you to focus on both aspects of your personal tutor role.

Why measure impact?

Think about the agreed actions resulting from your academic or departmental briefings which have been carried out during the year. If the question 'what was the impact on students?' was asked, what would the response be? What do you think the effect would be if the question was asked of these actions more often or even all the time? These questions highlight the need to keep the students at the centre of the personal tutoring process.

With the focus firmly on metrics and institutional measures of teaching quality, it is worth remembering a maxim from William Bruce Cameron, *'Not everything that can be counted counts. Not everything that counts can be counted* [measured]*'* (Cameron, 1963). Evaluating and measuring impact should always have a specific purpose. Likewise, it is important to accept that certain things are important but are difficult to measure or, indeed, don't need measuring.

We have indicated that exam performance, success rates, employability and learning gain tend to be the main measures of intellectual and academic ability. The filtering of these outcomes by ethnicity, gender or disability, and economic disadvantage give us a picture of whether 'equality gaps' exist and also provide measures of interest and use to the personal tutor.

Measuring the impact of the personal tutor at individual and institutional levels

Critical thinking activity 2

1. List all the ways in which you measure your individual impact.

2. State why you do this for each.

Discussion

1. It is likely you will have come up with some answers that are informal and daily student interactions, for example:

- checking verbally with students how they are getting on;

- checking verbally with students how they are feeling;

- observing students' mood;

- observing students' engagement.

More formal and longer-term examples might include:

- carrying out 'intervention analysis': monitoring attendance and completion of work levels of particular students who have been the subject of specific personal tutoring interactions. This intervention analysis can be carried out during the academic year (monthly) or at the end of the academic year and can analyse trends and changes over time;

- comparing the overall engagement of your students, the ways in which they have integrated socially, their involvement in co- and extra-curricular activities and their levels of well-being, mental health and how their environment helps to improve resilience and confidence. Reflecting on how this has changed because of regular and positive group and one-to-one tutorial sessions;

- analysing how many of your students did not progress as well as they could have the previous year and focus on supporting them through the current academic year through targeted support on progression.

The measures will be a mixture of qualitative ('soft') and quantitative ('hard').

There are many things that you could decide to measure to review the impact of your personal tutoring practice. On the more formal side, it is possible to measure the impact of a number of variables. It's important to take a holistic view of the things that you can measure in order to decide how best to ascertain impact. Some of these impact measures might seem insignificant or 'random' but it may be worth investigating these anyway. It is possible to use the student lifecycle (see Chapter 5) for this analysis and observe the peaks and troughs in the academic year. Every student experiences highs and lows at certain points in the academic year and, broadly speaking, some of these can be anticipated using the student lifecycle approach. For example, many students experience heightened anxiety about starting university and worry about assessments in the middle and at the end of the first term or semester. A number of students struggle over the Christmas and New Year period. A lot of these concerns impact directly on retention and progression. Personal tutoring can play a significant part in normalising student worries and also help to disseminate accurate information, offer advice and provide appropriate support.

It is possible to use your knowledge of the student lifecycle to assess the impact that personal tutoring is having on helping students address their concerns. For example, what is the impact of introducing personal tutoring early on in the induction process? What is the impact of spending five minutes welcoming students and setting the discussion agenda at the beginning of a group tutorial? How does this approach impact on attendance levels? Does tailoring your discussion to the student lifecycle help to engage students during the tutorial and how are you measuring engagement? Are you able to use tutoring to provide accurate information and signpost/refer to other support that could help? If so, how many students are acting on the advice you have given? Does the lifecycle approach open up further avenues for tutorial discussion and impact measures and, if so, what are they?

It's also important to note that you have greater freedom at the individual level. You can look at the impact of variables that you yourself think may have an impact (using both quantitative and qualitative measures). Sharing information about your methods and results with your manager might even result in them being used by others for the wider good of students, peers and the institution.

2.   There are two main reasons for measuring your individual impact:

    o   to check whether what you are doing helps your students (in terms of their learning, progress, motivation and well-being);

    o   to ensure your personal tutoring practice is improving.

At the institutional level, the focus is on key performance indicators (KPIs) and TEF metrics including retention, success, attendance and punctuality, student employability and learning gain, internal progression and, increasingly, destinations of students. At the individual level, the measure that the variable has an impact on, particularly the quantitative measures, will often be the same as one or more of these KPIs and TEF metrics. In the example of adopting the student lifecycle approach and making time to discuss personal tutoring during induction, the impact could be ascertained by measuring attendance. While attendance could be used to measure engagement, it must be noted that all quantitative measures are just proxies for engagement and an analysis of qualitative data may be more useful here. There will be a greater impact institutionally if individual practice (shown to positively affect a KPI like attendance at an individual level) is consistently applied by the institution through awareness-raising, training and joint development of professional practice. Your individual measuring of impact therefore has a strong link to, and influence on, the institutional measuring of impact and also institutional performance.

How you measure impact

Personal tutor impact measures

Remind yourself of the personal tutor core skills and key activities (target setting also included). Concentrate on the following:

- one-to-one conversations with students (including solution-focused coaching techniques);
- group tutorials;
- the tracking and monitoring of students;
- students target and goal setting.

Critical thinking activity 3

1. What are the best ways of measuring the impact of these on students' intellectual and academic progress and emotional well-being?

2. Who will carry out this measuring?

3. What are the success criteria for each and where will the evidence be found?

Discussion

Look at the suggested answers in Table 8.1.

Table 8.1 *Measuring the impact of the personal tutor core skills and key activities*

Personal tutor core skills/key activities	How could impact be measured? (Repeated over a particular timescale)	Who carries out the measuring?	Where will the evidence of impact be found? What are the success criteria? (Comparison within a timescale needed)
One-to-one conversations with students (including solution-focused coaching techniques)	• Peer observation • Quality audit on one-to-one recording • Student satisfaction surveys • Informal discussions with students	• Dean or Head of School • Peers • Personal tutor	• Feedback from peers and manager • Quality audit results and report on elements of effective one-to-ones • Survey results and feedback • Key performance indicators • Retention rates • Success rates • Attendance and punctuality rates • Data on learning gain and employability • Internal progression rates
Group tutorials	• Peer observation • Student satisfaction surveys • Informal discussions with students	• Dean or Head of School • Peers • Students • Personal tutor	• Feedback from peers and Dean or Head of School • Survey results and feedback

The tracking and monitoring of students	• Quality audit on tracking and monitoring recording • At risk meetings with colleagues • Individual 'intervention analysis'	• Dean or Head of School • Personal tutor	• Quality audit results and report on elements of effective tracking and monitoring • Feedback from colleagues in at risk meetings • Key performance indicators (listed previously) with particular attention paid to students at high risk where specific support actions have taken place
Goal and target setting	• Quality audit of recording of processes which include target setting: one-to-ones, tracking and monitoring	• Dean or Head of School	• Quality audit results and report on feedback on the extent to which targets and goals are 'SMART' and 'stretch and challenge' students • Key performance indicators (listed previously) with particular attention to learning gain, employability and progression measures

The list is not exhaustive and other ways of measuring could be included (see also 'informal' measures in the discussion of critical thinking activity 2).

It's important to note that we have listed the principal person responsible for carrying out these actions in the third column, but we could easily have added the personal tutor in each case. You can also complete this impact exercise in collaboration with a trusted colleague or mentor, as discussed in Chapter 7.

In the fourth column we have frequently mentioned quality audit results and reports. This information is usually available on your student records, personal tutor system or institutional dashboard, if one exists. Usually individual tutors are responsible for recording this data to capture tutoring activity, as discussed in Chapter 7. If no electronic system exists in your institution to support this activity, information should usually be recorded in tutor notes which are kept in a safe place. The benefit of institutional systems is that information should be recorded consistently by all tutors across the institution, along with the monitoring of data such as attendance and exam and assessment marks. It is from here that patterns and trends can be identified for reporting purposes. The *results* should inform you whether the action has taken place, for example that the minimum required number of one-to-ones per term have been completed. The *reports* on the relevant activities (for example one-to-ones) should inform you of the quality of the elements of each activity. An audit report should include reporting on the following elements:

* detail;
* knowledge of student;
* use of solution-focused techniques, for example scaling;
* target and goal setting and the extent to which the targets are SMART.

The importance of comparison and timescale

You will notice the mention of timescale and comparison within the titles of the second column (how could impact be measured?) and the fourth column (where will evidence of impact be found and what are the success criteria?). These need to be taken into account in order to measure change and impact. Key performance indicators (KPIs) tend to have this built in as in-year and end-of-year measures. Longer-term trends can be important. For example, if there is a slight decrease in some KPI(s) from one year to the next but the overall trend demonstrates a significant increase since a new support strategy was introduced, there is an indicator of positive rather than negative impact. Viewing the end-of-year figure compared to the previous year in isolation would have suggested the opposite.

When it comes to student satisfaction surveys, the article quoted in the introduction to this chapter stated that they are not measures of impact since measuring whether students *like* or are *happy* with their educational experience (in our case, personal tutoring) is not the same as whether it has made any *difference* (AMOSSHE, 2011). However, this can be addressed in two ways. Firstly, carrying out surveys over a timescale – ideally at the beginning, middle and end of a process – gives you comparative data to measure change. For example, many universities use the results of national student surveys, such as the HEA (now Advance HE) UK Engagement Survey (UKES) to gather student feedback and act upon this before students complete the aforementioned National Student Survey (NSS) in year three of study. Secondly, focusing the questions of the survey on students' perception of their progress in relation to a specific variable rather than what they like or dislike can give you a clearer indication of change in the areas we are interested in: students' progress and emotional well-being, rather than 'satisfaction'. It is important to note that student satisfaction is a key metric for the TEF, using the results of the NSS. The majority of the questions for this survey, and other student satisfaction surveys, are therefore fixed and this provides institutions with benchmark data to ascertain their impact. The focus of the NSS has changed over its lifetime to capture student engagement indicators. This represents a positive move towards assessing the way in which students have engaged with their course and with their institution, rather than a clear focus on satisfaction per se. It is important to note that, at the time of writing, the emphasis on student satisfaction will have a reduced metrics rating in any future TEF exercises.

Using the National Occupational Standards

Historically, student support hasn't been provided with the standards against which to measure quality, and thus to measure impact. It is traditionally associated with the student's emotional well-being and so 'softer' measures have been used. However, the aforementioned National Occupational Standards (NOS) in Personal Tutoring can provide a starting point to consider how to measure the impact of your actions. The National Union of Students (NUS) have also published an *Academic Support Benchmarking Tool*, which considers ten principles of effective academic support. The tool takes each principle in turn and enables institutions, and individuals, to map different levels of support achieved. These levels range from 'first steps', all the way through to 'outstanding' (National Union of Students, 2015).

The NOS give a comprehensive overview of the aspects of the personal tutoring role and are a useful set of benchmarks against which to measure the quality of your role as a personal tutor. They are not an impact measure in themselves but can be used as a way into doing so and for you individually to self-assess your skills (FETN, 2013, p 4). Broadly, if you meet all of the standards, it's more likely you will have a positive impact on your students. We included the 11 standards in Chapter 5 but have reproduced them here to aid the critical thinking activity which follows shortly.

1.   *Manage self, work relationships and work demands.*

2.   *Develop own practice in personal tutoring.*

3.   *Create a safe, supportive and positive learning environment.*

4.   *Explore and identify learners' needs and address barriers to learning.*

5.   *Enable learners to set learning targets and evaluate their progress and achievement.*

6.   *Encourage the development of learner autonomy.*

7. *Enable learners to develop personal and social skills and cultural awareness.*

8. *Enable learners to enhance learning and employability skills.*

9. *Support learners' transition and progression.*

10. *Provide learner access to specialist support services.*

11. *Contribute to improving the quality and impact of personal tutoring and its reputation within own organisation.*

(UK Commission for Education and Skills, nd, online)

Each has its own 'knowledge and understanding' and 'performance criteria' descriptors. Impact measures can be linked to specific aspects of personal tutoring performance by using the performance criteria descriptors as shown in Table 8.2.

Table 8.2 Linking impact measures with a selection of the National Occupational for Personal Tutoring

NOS Standard	NOS performance criteria	Relevant impact measure
LSIPT02 Develop own practice in personal tutoring.	P12 Assess the extent to which own practice is inclusive and promotes equality and diversity.	Retention filtered by gender, ethnicity, learning difficulty and disability to check for any 'equality gaps'.
LSIPT03 Create a safe, supportive and positive learning environment.	P16 Provide tutorial support in an environment where learners feel safe, secure, confident and valued.	Student survey results and feedback on tutorial focusing on students' perception of their safety, security, confidence and how valued they feel as a result of tutorial.
LSIPT04 Explore and identify learners' needs and address barriers to learning.	P26 Communicate regularly with each learner in order to identify at risk indicators.	Individual 'intervention analysis' of attendance and completion of work levels of particular students who have been the subject of specific personal tutoring actions; can be carried out in-year (monthly) or end of year.
LSIPT09 Support learners' transition and progression. (UKCES, nd, online)	P63 Work with learners to identify, where appropriate, goals relating to their career development and suitable and realistic progression options. (UKCES, nd, online).	Internal progression rates for your student groups. Analysis of destination data for your student groups.

Critical thinking activity 4

» *Read the performance criteria from the whole set of standards and choose two criteria from each of the 11 (without repeating those chosen previously) and, as shown in the final column of Table 8.2, give a relevant measure of impact for each criterion.*

Being constructively critical of measuring impact

The adage *'you can't fatten a pig by weighing it'* came from educator Carolyn Chapman in the world of American primary education, referring to the over-testing of children at the expense of actually educating them. In other words, *'we aren't feeding kids' minds when we are assessing them'* (Weuntsel, 2011, online). We can expand this idea to remind us of the dangers of over-measuring. Is too much time and effort spent on measuring so that, ultimately, personal tutoring suffers?

Many academics may also feel that in recent years there has been an imposition of quality criteria (which are more often than not impact measures) on education and training institutions which were originally related to a profit-making commercial context (Gravells and Wallace, 2013). They may point, quite rightly, to the fact that quality outcomes of an educational institution are different to those of a factory for example (Gravells and Wallace, 2013). When discussing higher education institutions, The Association of Commonwealth Universities makes a similar point:

> For universities it is important too, though, that their work – education and research, and what flows from it – is properly understood, so that institutions are not expected to respond with greater yield in the same way as a production line might if given greater input. Before any measures or judgements of impact can be made, the values and goals which underpin educational investments need to be clarified and made explicit.
>
> (The Association of Commonwealth Universities, 2012, online)

In other words, even if more 'input' (for example funding) is given, greater 'yield' (for example positive impact) should not be expected without question. Rather, values and goals need careful thought first.

When it comes to statistical or hard measures it is important to remember the issues beneath this headline data and that any thorough analysis of impact acknowledges these. With attendance rates for example, several factors, alongside personal tutor actions, play a part in contributing to these, both negatively and positively. Again, it is important to be mindful of, and to acknowledge, that it is impossible to measure student engagement per se, and that any associated measures are just proxies for engagement, as already discussed in Chapter 4. This information therefore needs to be contextualised with your own interactions with students and it also needs to be treated with caution or with the necessary caveats. What it does do, however, is indicate a set of trends and actionable insights which provide you with an opportunity for further explanation and discussion with colleagues.

Acknowledging other factors that influence student performance

Critical thinking activity 5

The main key performance indicators relating to the personal tutor role are retention, success, attendance and punctuality, learning gain, employability and internal progression.

1. Choose two of these indicators. For each, with the indicator in the middle, draw a spider diagram showing which factors influence (a close synonym for 'impact') students' performance in this area.

2. Think of two of your students. Estimate what percentage of influence your personal tutor practice has (relative to the other influences) on your chosen key performance indicators for each student and why.

3. Has this influence changed since you first started working with each of them?

Discussion

1. There are multiple factors involved in this exercise. This shouldn't come as a surprise, since, like all people, students have complex needs and interests. Retention rates alone may be affected by a number of things, as shown by the example spider diagram in Figure 8.2.

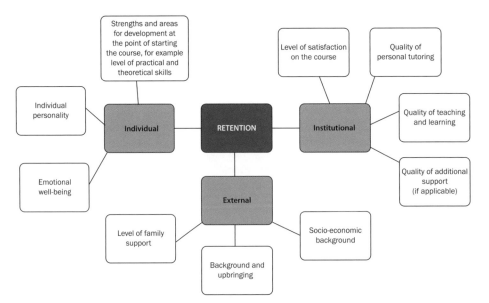

Figure 8.2 *Factors that influence retention of students*

This list is by no means exhaustive. As you can see, our example answer has naturally fallen into three types: *institutional, external* and *individual* factors. You may also notice that the influencing factors are relevant to more than one performance indicator; they are relevant influences on attendance rates, for example. The research and case studies emerging from the *What Works?* and *What Works 2?* reports are also key in understanding impact measures (Thomas, 2012; Thomas et al, 2017) and we recommend that you consult these further for the insight they give on this topic.

2. The estimated percentage varies depending on which student you have in mind. Even considering one student, this is not an exact science due to the complex nature of individuals. However, it is always useful to assess the extent of our influence. If the estimated percentage was low for a particular student, focusing on the significant influences helps you to understand what makes that student 'tick' and you can adapt your strategies accordingly to tap into this, for example by establishing rapport through conversation and showing awareness of their interest or 'passion'. This way your actions are working with, rather than against, other influences.

3. This question is always important to ask since measuring impact is about measuring change and it cannot be done without considering timescale and using comparison within this timescale. Even if your estimated percentage of influence for a student is low, the important consideration is whether it has changed (hopefully increased!) since you first started working with them.

It is important to note that not only is retention a key metric in the TEF, but that institutional factors, rather than external or individual factors, prevail in its measurement. More specifically, all universities report on student non-continuation rates on or after 1 December in their first year of study. This does not take into consideration the various reasons for attrition. It must be noted that there are some factors, including those highlighted in Figure 8.2, which are outside of our direct control, such as a student's socio-economic background. This is why a TEF institutional statement should focus on discussing institutional interventions which mitigate some of the risks associated with supporting students from different backgrounds and with specific support needs. Martinez's (2001, p 3) summary of research shows that students who 'drop out' are not strongly differentiated from students who complete in terms of their personal circumstances, such as personal, family or financial difficulties, their travel costs and ease of journey into university. This is also reflected in the *What Works?* and *What Works 2* reports (Thomas, 2012; Thomas et al, 2017).

Correlation and causation

There is not a straight causal line between your practice and student performance, which means that direct impact is not easy, or even possible, to 'prove'. However, this is no different from anyone else trying to measure the impact of activities, strategies or processes. Markless and Streatfield (2006) explain that the best that can be achieved with any measuring of impact is to find 'strong surrogates' for impact that provide a close approximation.

It is important to remember that *correlation* is not the same as *causation*; in other words there is certainly a correlation (connection) between personal tutor practice and student performance (as embodied in these indicators) but that the former doesn't always have a direct causal relationship with the latter. It is more important to ask to what extent your actions and support have an influence and in what ways this could be increased. By carrying out the measures outlined in this chapter we hope you see that your personal tutor practice initiates students exhibiting improved performance, resilience and emotional well-being, 'strong surrogates' for your impact in this area.

Summary

If measuring impact is approached in the right way, is not overdone and has a clear rationale clarifying its purpose, it should be something which is welcomed rather than feared. Moreover, this should be even more the case when measuring your own impact at an individual level since it engineers ownership of the process and you are often in the best position to measure impact meaningfully.

This chapter has shown you ways in which the impact of your personal tutor core skills and key activities can be measured while at the same time recognising that the complexity of individual students means their progress, both academically and socially/emotionally, can be affected by a number of other factors.

Learning checklist

Tick off each point when you feel confident you understand it.

☐ *I understand what is meant by impact and measuring impact.*

☐ *I can identify ways in which the key elements of intellectual/academic progress and emotional well-being of students can be measured.*

☐ *I understand the differences between quantitative ('hard') information/measures and qualitative ('soft') information/measures.*

☐ *I can identify ways of measuring impact at both an individual and institutional level.*

☐ *I understand the need for a clear rationale for measuring impact.*

☐ *I know how to be constructively critical of measuring impact and acknowledge and analyse factors behind statistical measures.*

☐ *I understand how the National Occupational Standards for Personal Tutoring and NUS Academic Support Benchmarking Tool can be linked to impact measures.*

☐ *I can see the relationship between my practice and student performance, along with the value of assessing the extent of this, while acknowledging that other multiple factors influence student performance.*

Critical reflections

1. To what extent do you think there is a focus on measuring the impact of personal tutor practice on students' performance as follows?

    a. By you, individually.

    b. By your Dean or Head of School, at a team level, in your institution.

    c. By senior managers across your institution.

2. To what extent do you think measuring the impact of personal tutor practice on the emotional well-being of students is carried out in the following?

    a. Across your institution.

    b. On any academic training course you have undertaken.

    If it is not carried out or covered, how could that be changed?

3. To what extent do student-facing staff at your institution perceive measuring impact as having a clear rationale and as meaningful and developmental? What could be done to improve this perception?

Personal tutor self-assessment system

See following table.

PERSONAL TUTOR SELF-ASSESSMENT SYSTEM : Chapter 8 Measuring impact

	Minimum standard 1 star	Beginner level 2 stars	Intermediate level 3 stars	Advanced level 4 stars	Expert level 5 stars
Individual	I am aware of the main ways my personal tutor practice can be measured: retention, success, attendance and punctuality, learning gain, employability and internal progression.	I know the end-of-year figures for the main measures of impact at group level. I consider the different influences on student performance relating to these measures.	I review what the main influences on student performance are at the end of the year and this informs changes in my practice the following year.	I measure my own impact on student performance in a variety of ways in-year and at the end of the year. Quantitative and qualitative data is used to inform my future practice.	I engage in joint practice development activities related to measuring the impact of personal tutor practice.
Institutional	Staff in my institution are aware of the main ways through which the impact of personal tutor practice can be measured.	All staff have knowledge of their end-of-year key impact measures related to their personal tutor practice.	Impact measures of personal tutor practice have a clear rationale which the majority of staff support. Staff carry out individual impact measures on this practice and are supported by Deans or Heads of School in this.	A range of meaningful individual and team-level impact measures of personal tutor practice informs wider institutional practice.	A culture of meaningful impact measuring of personal tutor practice exists which focuses specifically on students' intellectual and academic ability and emotional well-being.

The self-assessment system is available as a free download from the publisher's website and the authors' websites (all listed at the start of the book).

References

AMOSSHE, The Student Services Organisation (2011) *Value and Impact Toolkit. Assessing the Value and Impact of Services that Support Students*. London: AMOSSHE.

Arvanitakis, J and Hornsby, D (2016) *Universities, the Citizen Scholar and the Future of Higher Education*. London: Palgrave Macmillan.

Cameron, W B (1963) *Informal Sociology: A Casual Introduction to Sociological Thinking*. New York: Random House.

Department of Business, Innovation and Skills (2015) Fulfilling Our Potential: Teaching Excellent, Social Mobility and Student Choice. [online] Available at: https://assets.publishing.service.gov.uk/government/uploads/system/uploads/attachment_data/file/474266/BIS-15-623-fulfilling-our-potential-teaching-excellence-social-mobility-and-student-choice-accessible.pdf (accessed 30 June 2018).

Department of Business, Innovation and Skills (2016) Success as a Knowledge Economy: Teaching Excellend, Social Mobility and Student Choice. [online] Available at: www.gov.uk/government/publications/higher-education-success-as-a-knowledge-economy-white-paper (accessed 30 June 2018).

Dutton, Y, Eldred, J, Snowdon, K and Ward, J (2004) *Catching Confidence.* Leicester: NIACE.

Gravells, J and Wallace, S (2013) *The A-Z Guide to Working in Further Education*. Northwich: Critical Publishing.

Higher Education Academy (2017) Evidencing Teaching Excellence: Analysis of the Teaching Excellence Framework (TEF2) Provider Submissions. [online] Available at: www.heacademy.ac.uk/knowledge-hub/evidencing-teaching-excellence (accessed 30 June 2018).

Hughes, G, Panjwani, M, Tulcidas, P and Byrom, N (2018) *Student Mental Health: The Role and Experiences of an Academic*. Oxford: Student Minds. [online] Available at: www.studentminds.org.uk/theroleofanacademic.html (accessed 30 June 2018).

Markless, S and Streatfield, D (2006) *Evaluating the Impact of Information Literacy in Higher Education: Progress and Prospects*. London: Facet Publishing.

Martinez, P (2001) *Improving Student Retention and Achievement: What Do We Know and What Do We Need to Find Out? LSDA report.* London: Learning and Skills Development Agency.

McIntosh, E and Shaw, J (2017) *Student Resilience: Exploring the Positive Case for Resilience. Students Unite.* [online] Available at: www.unite-group.co.uk/sites/default/files/2017-05/student-resilience.pdf (accessed 30 June 2018).

Mental Health Foundation (nd) *What is Good Mental Health?* [online] Available at: www.mentalhealth.org.uk/help-information/an-introduction-to-mental-health/what-is-good-mental-health (accessed 30 June 2018).

The Association of Commonwealth Universities (2012), *Defining, Understanding and Measuring Impact.* [online] Available at: www.acu.ac.uk/membership/acu-insights/acu-insights-2/defining-understanding-and-measuring-impact (accessed 30 June 2018).

The Further Education Tutorial Network (FETN) (2013) *Plenary Presentation: Towards Excellence; National Occupational Standards for Personal Tutoring*. Barnsley: FETN.

Thomas, L (2012) *Building Student Engagement and Belonging in Higher Education at a Time of Change: Final Report from the What Works? Student Retention and Success Programme.* London: Paul Hamlyn Foundation.

Thomas, L, Hill, M, O'Mahony, J and Yorke, M (2017) *Supporting Student Success: Strategies for Institutional Change. What Works? Student Retention and Success Programme. Final Report.* London: Paul Hamlyn Foundation.

UK Commission For Education and Skills (nd) *National Occupational Standards for Personal Tutoring.* Available online: http://nos.ukces.org.uk/Pages/index.aspx (accessed 30 June 2018).

Weuntsel, P (2011) *You Can't Fatten a Pig by Weighing It: Assessment and the Future of Teacher Education.* [online] Available at: www.marquetteeducator.wordpress.com/2011/11/12/you-cant-fatten-a-pig-by-weighing-it-assessment-and-the-future-of-teacher-education (accessed 30 June 2018).

9 What next?

Chapter aims

This chapter helps you to:

- identify your own progress in terms of your personal tutoring professional development, as well as set and prioritise clear improvement actions;

- identify your institution's progress in terms of its approach to personal tutoring and staff development;

- see the 'bigger picture' and think broadly about how you might influence positive organisational change.

Introduction

Following on from reading this book, it's important to identify the next steps in your development as a personal tutor and take some time to set some goals and priorities for the next six, 12 and 18 months. Consider how many of your personal tutoring goals and priorities you will have progressed six months from now. Contemplate how much knowledge you have gained and what you will be putting into practice, as well as what you will have already embedded into your existing practice. What changes will you make? What will you stop doing and what will you start doing? It is a good idea to work with a mentor or a trusted colleague (see Chapters 7 and 8) to help you do this objectively.

As with most academic development activities, setting goals and priorities for personal tutoring should be central to your approach. Nevertheless, there are other factors at play which interface with personal tutor training and development and they can affect how your goals and priorities evolve and change in the medium- to long-term. Some of these things may be outside your sphere of influence but it is important to be aware of them. Effective professional development for personal tutors depends largely on institutional priorities, management buy-in and the relevance of tutoring to your current practice and to students themselves. Nevertheless, it is important to revisit and follow up the key elements of training from time to time. This chapter is intended to provide you with guidelines for retaining the knowledge and understanding that you have gained from reading this book and engaging with some of the activities it suggests, alongside your overall development as a personal tutor. It will provide you with some useful tools to ensure that you are able to reach your goals and priorities and embed some of the principles into your daily practice as a personal tutor.

Why retain the information in this book?

All of the activities you undertake outside your day-to-day teaching, particularly the support you provide for your students through personal tutoring and coaching, have a significant impact on their academic attainment, motivation, confidence and emotional well-being as well as their ability and desire to remain on the course. This directly supports elements related to their programme of study and intended career pathway, such as engagement, enjoyment, stretch and challenge.

Displaying your core values and skills alongside your curriculum delivery will help to ensure that you become a highly versatile and adaptable personal tutor who provides effective, holistic support and learning opportunities for students in the many ways in which you work with them. This alone will help to improve your value to your students and the institution, as well as develop your wider employability skills for your future career. A proactive approach to personal tutoring will also help to tackle issues when they arise rather than working to resolve them after they have been left to become worse. But the learning gained is also key to your institution.

Critical thinking activity 1

»   *If the institution you work within invested in developing effective personal tutoring and coaching practice with students, what possible positive impacts on the following typical key performance indicators would there be?*

- *Retention.*

- *Success.*

- *Attendance and punctuality.*

- *Employability and learning gain.*

- *Internal progression.*

How to retain the information in this book

It is difficult to commit to action unless you feel a strong sense of ownership, empowerment and self-efficacy when it comes to your personal tutoring practice. Without this, the knowledge you have developed from this book and other developmental activities may become too abstract and difficult to translate into tangible actions on the ground. Without dedicated time to devote to translating this new knowledge into practice, it will be difficult to make progress with your intended development actions. Professional development is the responsibility of the individual concerned and to approach it objectively you must appreciate your previous accomplishments and strengths as well as consider your goals and developmental priorities, alongside a commitment to progress.

The importance of self-assessment

The individual self-assessment system found at the end of each chapter has been designed to provide you with a tool to help you understand where you are now and what your next developmental level is so that you are able to plan the best way to get there. The following case study provides an example of a personal tutor called Ruth who works within a large university in the West Midlands.

CASE STUDY

Ruth

Ruth is an academic based in an arts and humanities faculty. She finished her PhD two years ago and, last year, completed a PG Cert in Higher Education. She really enjoys working with students in a teaching capacity, particularly through her personal tutoring role, and she feels passionate about the positive impact that she has on her students' learning. She has a new and supportive Head of School who is open to new ideas and is keen to improve retention and outcomes for students on arts and humanities programmes, the quality of provision as well as the students' experience. Ruth feels valued by her Head of School who recognises her contribution to her personal tutoring role which, she appreciates, is not always reflected in the efforts of other colleagues in the department.

The university that Ruth works at was recently graded silver in the TEF and although the university is quite strong in supporting its students, retention, attainment and employability are three key priority areas for improvement in the coming years. This is particularly the case for the Faculty of Arts and Humanities where the attrition rate is 5 per cent higher than in other faculties and employability is 3 per cent below the current target set for that area in the institutional plan. There have been a number of changes in the senior leadership team and during the recent restructure a number of teaching and support staff have left. Despite these changes, there is a clear spotlight on the Faculty of Arts and Humanities for making a sustained improvement. The university in general has a high proportion of students from low socio-economic backgrounds (63 per cent), a large number of whom have entered university with Business and Technology Education Council (BTEC) qualifications rather than A levels (43 per cent). Many students in the Faculty of Arts and Humanities have additional support needs.

Ruth has recently assessed herself using the individual self-assessment system to understand the level she is working at and to identify actions she can take to improve. The final column of Table 9.1 provides suggested examples of how she could move up to the next level.

The possible actions are only suggestions and the list is not exhaustive. Every person, institution and context is unique and therefore the actions you take to improve need to be appropriate for you and your situation.

Table 9.1 *Ruth's individual self-assessment*

Chapter	Current level (and stars)	Next level to work towards (and stars)	Text from the next level that Ruth wants to work towards	Possible actions (this is not an exhaustive list)
2 Core values of the personal tutor	2 stars (beginner level)	3 stars (intermediate level)	I often reflect upon the impact that the core values have on the performance of my students. The reflections inform my personal development targets.	I will: • choose a suitable reflection model or create my own; • make reflective practice part of my weekly routine; • consider undertaking reflective practice with a trusted colleague; • keep a personal tutor reflection log (see Brookfield, Chapter 7); • speak to my students individually or as a group to obtain feedback on what values they think I show in my work and what impact this might have; • ask a colleague to have a discussion with my students as a group to obtain feedback on the values I project; • ask my students to complete an anonymous online or paper-based questionnaire; • ensure that I make my personal development targets SMART.
2 Core skills of the personal tutor	3 stars (intermediate level)	4 stars (advanced level)	Feedback I receive on my classes, group tutorials and one-to-ones reflect the core skills.	I will: • make a conscious effort to employ the core skills within my lessons, group tutorials and one-to-ones; • include how some of the core skills help my students through a detailed situational analysis; • ask for feedback on specific core skills from my observer; • ask the observer to have a discussion with my students to obtain feedback on my core skills; • develop a resource for the personal tutor resource bank as a result of my feedback.

	1 star (minimum standard)	2 stars (beginner level)	I will:
3 Setting boundaries		I revisit these boundaries in group tutorials. Through one-to-ones and other support meetings, students have a clear idea of these key boundaries.	• (where appropriate) reaffirm the boundaries I discussed at the beginning of the academic year. I feel this would be useful to build into the general discussions I have with my group about their progress and about my high expectations for the rest of the academic year; • discuss with my colleagues or manager the boundary setting in my personal tutor role. For example, if I feel that there isn't an over-reliance of a student on my support then, I take this as a possible sign that my initial boundary setting has been effective.

	3 stars (intermediate level)	4 stars (advanced level)	I will:
4 Key activities: identifying and supporting student populations		Feedback from my students regarding the key activities is consistently very positive. Feedback from colleagues shows they regard them as having a strong impact on student progress and outcomes.	• ask for feedback from my Dean or Head of Department regarding my preparation for, and actions taken following, at risk meetings; • either undertake, or ask someone (for example a trusted colleague) to undertake, an informal quality audit of specific aspects of my tracking and monitoring activities; • ensure that discussion around procedures with colleagues is predominantly focused on the individual needs of the student with awareness of the complex make-up of student populations at my institution; • critically analyse and evaluate on an individual basis, as well as with my department and manager, how these key procedures work to improve my students' attendance, behaviour (in terms of engagement) and completion of work.

Table 9.1 (Cont.)

Chapter	Current level (and stars)	Next level to work towards (and stars)	Text from the next level that Ruth wants to work towards	Possible actions (this is not an exhaustive list)
5 Key activities: effectively supporting all stages of the student lifecycle	4 stars (advanced level)	5 stars (expert level)	I identify and implement methods to measure the impact of individual and group tutorials on my students' progress and outcomes. I reflect and constructively question key activities with managers and others involved to review and improve them regularly. This is a significant factor in improving some key performance indicators.	I will: • adapt the support I provide according to my tutees' progress at any one point along the stages in the student lifecycle; • have individual, informal discussions with my students at set intervals over a period of time to assess whether there needs to be any changes to how I employ the key activities; • undertake peer observation of my ones-to-ones and group tutorials; • plan the support I provide to my tutees as part of an effective curriculum of personal tutoring.
6 Using solution-focused coaching with students	1 star (minimum standard)	2 stars (beginner level)	I regularly practise the use of solution talk style questions (where appropriate) to support my students.	I will: • trial the use of solution talk questions with students either in one-to-ones or, if appropriate, in the classroom and/or corridor situations; • experiment individually using solution talk with one group of my students and not with others over a period of time (I may choose to use problem talk with the other group as a clear means of contrast). Through discussion with my students at the end of the action research, I will endeavour to find out how they felt about these approaches and conversations in relation to their intellectual and academic performance and emotional well-being. Before doing this, I will consider the ethical issues of forcing solution talk on one group who may not want or need it and depriving another group of students who may need it. I will examine some of the points and issues raised in the BERA (British Education Research Association) ethical guidelines (BERA, 2018).

7 Reflective practice	4 stars (advanced level)	5 stars (expert level)	The outcomes of my reflective practice inform joint practice development projects with colleagues.	I will: • organise joint practice development sessions with colleagues (within and across departments) to explore the benefits that reflective practice can bring to personal tutoring practice. If I am able to make these sessions a useful and regular event, I will broaden the scope to cover other areas of practice; • facilitate a training session on reflective practice on a staff training day; • enquire if any colleagues are willing to undertake reflective practice sessions together; • explain how reflective practice has helped me to improve my personal practice when discussed in team meetings.
8 Measuring impact	2 stars (beginner level)	3 stars (intermediate level)	I review what the main influences on student performance are at the end of the year and this informs changes in my practice the following year.	I will: • undertake a review of what I feel have been the main influences on my students' performance while also comparing this against changes in the key performance indicators for the academic year. My judgements are likely to be drawn from areas such as my general observations and experiences, discussions with colleagues and managers on how they feel the academic year has gone and what progress students have made, student surveys, mentoring (peer and formal) and course reviews, at-risk information and institutional measures; • evaluate and decide what the key changes I would like to make from the review are and ensure these are considered in my planning (for example session plans, schemes of work, new techniques and approaches) for the next academic year.
9 What next?	2 stars (beginner level)	3 stars (intermediate level)	I use the individual self-assessment system regularly and, for all of the aspects where I am not yet expert level, I have SMART targets to guide my development.	I will: • keep a reflective personal tutor log to inform the SMART target reviews; • always set a review date (for example at the end of each term or semester) for when I will reassess myself against all of the sections of the individual self-assessment system.

Critical thinking activity 2

1. Using Ruth's context as a guide, write your own current context. You may choose to include, but not be limited to, areas such as:

    a. your strengths and areas for development;

    b. your personal tutor values;

    c. your future career goals;

    d. key strengths or 'drivers' of positive change within your department and the institution;

    e. areas for development or aspects that might hold back positive change within the department and the institution;

    f. current feedback from student surveys and HEA (now Advance HE) fellowship assessments;

    g. key performance indicators such as retention, success, attendance and punctuality, learning gain and employability and internal progression;

    h. student experience feedback.

2. Undertake the individual self-assessment system at the end of each chapter to understand:

    a. what level you are currently working at for each chapter theme;

    b. what your cumulative score and overall level is.

3. For each level identified within question 2a, write down one realistic action that you can take to move up one level. You may wish to do this with a trusted colleague or mentor.

4. Using the headings below, list all of the actions you want to take to improve (from question 3) and order them with the highest priority being number one and the lowest priority being the highest number. Ensure you include a date for completion or to review each. Priority should be influenced by factors such as the impact on the students' intellectual and academic progress or emotional well-being, targets from your mentor, appraisal, or even departmental or institutional priorities.

Number	Action	Date by when you will have achieved this or when you will review the progress

The bigger picture

The most effective personal tutors (and teachers) tend to be not only excellent practitioners, both within lectures and seminars and working with students in a variety of settings, but they are also the ones who ask the most questions and are curious about how what they do at an individual level impacts students and learning more broadly within their institution. This is not to say that the best practitioners aim for academic promotion, but that they are individuals motivated to excel in their role and consistently seek out opportunities for new learning. This can be through seeking new ways to have a positive impact on learning and students, whether that be at an individual, class, departmental or institutional level.

This section of the book provides you with an opportunity to think more broadly about your personal tutor role and even how you might influence other colleagues and effect positive organisational change. Leadership of teaching and learning is a key part of the UK Professional Standards Framework and, therefore, HEA (now Advance HE) fellowship particularly at Senior and Principal Fellow levels. Think about the phrase 'universities don't change but people do'. Universities are made up of people, you can move them and put structures, job titles, responsibilities, quality checks, reporting and communication lines in place to try to improve performance, but, ultimately, *people* are the most important factor in achieving success.

Developing high-performing people and a high-performance culture in education is not an easy goal to achieve.

Institutional self-assessment

Similar to the individual personal tutor self-assessment system, the institutional template has been designed to provide a forward-thinking personal tutor, existing or aspiring manager or leader (with a remit for personal tutoring development) with a tool to understand where their institution is now and what the next level is so that they are able to plan the best way to get there. The following case study and with Table 9.2 provide an example template which can be applied to most institutional contexts.

AN INSTITUTIONAL CASE STUDY

A post-1992 university in the south of the UK has recently been awarded silver in the first TEF exercise. The university metrics on retention, student satisfaction and employability are still at bronze level but the support systems put in place for students at the institution contributed to its silver TEF award status. Over the last academic year there have been a number of improvements in teaching, learning and assessment, retention and employability. Nevertheless, student attendance and attainment require additional focus, alongside support for students with disabilities, students from different ethnicities and those from low socio-economic backgrounds. There is a strong senior and middle management team, who are participative in their approach and open to new ideas of working. Staff morale is good and most are agreed that improvements can be made via enhancements to the existing tutorial system. The university is located in an area of economic regeneration with a high number of students from the surrounding locality. The institution is a low-tariff one and many students have additional support needs.

The university has recently assessed itself using the institutional self-assessment system to understand the level it is working at and to identify actions for improvement. The final column in Table 9.2 suggests how it can provide enhancements to its existing approach. The actions have been written from the perspective of a senior manager of, or leader in, the institution.

Table 9.2 *University institutional self-assessment*

Chapter	Current level (and stars)	Next level to work towards (and stars)	Text from the next level that the institution wants to work towards	Possible actions (this is not an exhaustive list)
2 Core values of the personal tutor	3 star (intermediate)	4 star (advanced level)	All staff have a clear understanding of the core values and the importance of embedding them into their day-to-day work.	I will ensure that: • senior managers talk to staff informally and visit team meetings for feedback on how we are meeting the core values and where we still need to do further work; • I will explain the benefit of institutions having shared core values in order to attempt to create an institution that feels it has an identity and that staff, students and stakeholders are happy to be a part of; • the core values form part of the content of all staff recruitment and selection processes; • we visually display the core values in appropriate places within the institution; • curricular and non-curricular operational planning work, such as course reviews, departmental self-assessment reports and quality improvement plans identify which core value is being displayed through actions.

Table 9.2 (Cont.)

Chapter	Current level (and stars)	Next level to work towards (and stars)	Text from the next level that the institution wants to work towards	Possible actions (this is not an exhaustive list)
2 Core skills of the personal tutor	3 stars (intermediate level)	4 stars (advanced level)	The core skills are consistently and routinely improved through varied strategies. Staff are encouraged to implement ways of assessing how effective the core skills are at improving student outcomes.	I will ensure that: • core skills are part of the feedback asked for in student surveys which will directly feed into the strategy for learning; • a clear and consistent skills analysis is carried out with personal tutors, which feeds into departmental and overall institutional analysis. This information will inform professional development priorities and influence budget allocation; • personal tutors are asked about which specific skills they feel they would like to develop further and support is offered where possible; • quality processes are viewed as developmental and that these recognise the effective core skills displayed as well as appropriately challenge staff to improve where required. The institution will provide support where needed. • peer and/or developmental mentoring processes include ways in which feedback on the core skills used with students are discussed; • sufficient resources are allocated to joint practice development and training opportunities with a focus on the value that the core skills bring to students' intellectual and academic progress and emotional well-being.

	4 stars (advanced level)	5 stars (expert level)	
3 Setting boundaries		A range of different types of boundaries are set by departments or support functions which are informed by students themselves. As a result of this and other factors, students take responsibility and are independent.	I will ensure that: • information from student surveys is shared clearly with personal tutors in order to inform boundary setting; • boundary setting and recognition for the purpose of student independence and staff welfare form part of the content of all staff recruitment and selection processes; • boundary setting informs mentoring feedback, both in terms of student independence and staff welfare; • a culture of positive boundary setting and recognition exists within the institution, not only in classroom practice but in meetings at all levels. The latter will be ensured by clear 'rules' and purposes to all meetings which all managers responsible for chairing meetings will have as an expectation.

	1 star (minimum standard)	2 stars (beginner level)	
4 Key activities: identifying and supporting student populations		The strategy for supporting specific student populations is effectively communicated to all new staff and updates for existing staff are frequent. Where dashboard analytics systems are used there is basic uniformity in their application to record student interactions.	I will ensure that: • dashboard-based analytics are in use across the institution and analysis of the data they produce informs programme and department-level planning; • the institution's student support strategy (including for specific populations) is systematically reviewed against relevant data on key performance indicators; • a rigorous self-assessment system for student support is in place at departmental level leading to quality improvement plans with SMART outcomes; • dashboard and analytics systems are incorporated into staff training and development to promote continuity of practice.

Table 9.2 (Cont.)

Chapter	Current level (and stars)	Next level to work towards (and stars)	Text from the next level that the institution wants to work towards	Possible actions (this is not an exhaustive list)
5 Key activities: effectively supporting all stages of the student lifecycle	4 stars (advanced level)	5 stars (expert level)	The key activities are regularly reviewed involving all relevant student-facing staff and a selection of students. As a result, staff feel invested in them. There is a highly consistent approach to the key activities across my institution.	I will ensure that: • there is a clear strategy for managing the progression of all individuals through the student lifecycle and this is reflected in the key activities; • a strong emphasis is placed on the importance of embedding the key activities as a core part of the student academic experience; • there is clear communication to students about the key activities and how they fit in with central support services in a useable and handy format; • students are consulted for their views on the activities and these will be taken into account when shaping how they are developed in future.
6 Using solution-focused coaching with students	1 star (minimum standard)	2 stars (beginner level)	Deans or Heads of School actively support staff to use coaching conversation techniques (where appropriate) with students through discussion, team meetings and appraisals.	I will ensure that: • managers include coaching techniques as a regular item on their team meeting agendas; • personal tutors are encouraged to gather student feedback on their use of coaching techniques and for this to inform appraisal; • coaching conversational techniques are used, where appropriate, in managerial meetings at all levels within the institution so that managers embody this approach and can support staff in its use.

7 Reflective practice	1 star (minimum standard)	2 stars (beginner level) My institution displays its commitment to its personal tutors undertaking effective individual or peer reflective practice through providing adequate time, resources and support for the process. Honest and open dialogue about critical incidents or issues is embraced as positive and developmental.	I will ensure that: • time and support is provided for personal tutors to undertake reflective practice; • training, which explores reflective practice, is offered throughout the year or on staff training days; • Deans or Head of School, where possible and appropriate, try to encourage reflective practice to take place in pairs either within the department or with other staff from other departments; • there is a person within the institution who has considerable knowledge and experience of various aspects of reflective practice and he or she is encouraged to discuss this with staff proactively or answer questions reactively, if needed; • where appropriate, Deans or Head of School speak to the personal tutors about what progress they feel they are making as a result of their reflective practice.
8 Measuring impact	3 star (intermediate level)	4 star (advanced level) A range of meaningful individual and team-level impact measures of personal tutor practice informs wider institutional practice.	I will ensure that: • I encourage a culture of 'experimenting' ethically and responsibly with different variables in order to positively impact student performance; • measuring impact is regularly discussed within teams along with innovative ways of doing so.

Table 9.2 (Cont.)

Chapter	Current level (and stars)	Next level to work towards (and stars)	Text from the next level that the institution wants to work towards	Possible actions (this is not an exhaustive list)
				• there are small 'action research' teams where willing academics and personal tutors work collaboratively to examine a variable(s) or technique(s) that they feel may influence student performance; • a range of impact measures are included in departmental self-assessment reports and quality improvement plans; • senior managers collate significant departmental impact measures and use this to inform institutional practice.
9 What next?	3 star (intermediate)	4 star (advanced level)	My institution is making progress against the institutional self-assessment chapter themes. My institution critically analyses the institutional self-assessment system and has adapted it to make it better and, where appropriate, more applicable to its context.	I will ensure that: • the institutional self-assessment system is reviewed and adapted to meet the aims and context of our institution, taking into account the views of as many student-facing staff as possible; • on a yearly basis we review and critically analyse all of the self-assessment tools we use within our institution to ensure that the content and process is still useful and relevant.

The possible actions are suggestions for enhancement and the list is not exhaustive. Every person, institution and context is unique and therefore the actions you take to improve need to be appropriate for your institution.

Critical thinking activity 3

Depending on your current role and experience, you may need to speak to a manager or someone on the senior leadership team to be able to fully complete questions 1 and 2. This will be valuable experience, particularly to understand these aspects more fully.

1. Using the above Institutional Case Study as a guide, describe your own current context, referring to yourself as an existing or aspiring senior manager or leader for the educational institution you work within. You may choose to include, but not be limited to, areas such as:

    a. key institutional aims;

    b. key strengths or 'drivers' of positive change within departments and the institution;

    c. areas for development or aspects that might hold back positive change within departments and the institution;

    d. the perceived culture from an institution-wide perspective;

    e. typical student profile;

    f. current student feedback.

2. Undertake the institutional self-assessment system to understand:

    a. what level your institution is currently working at for each chapter theme;

    b. what your cumulative score and overall level is.

3. For each level identified within question 2a, write down one realistic action that can be taken to move up one level.

It is important to bear in mind when reading this table that we have written the actions while drawing on leadership and managerial experience. If you have not had this experience, you may find that the actions you come up with are less comprehensive. This is not a concern; the important point is to start thinking more broadly about your personal tutor role and the 'bigger picture', and to start identifying relevant actions.

Summary

The self-assessment systems that you have used are intended as a helpful guide for how you and your institution might continually improve. It is important to be constructively critical of them and adapt or improve them to make them even more relevant to you and your institution.

At the beginning of this book, you placed yourself on a scale of one to ten in terms of your knowledge and practice as a personal tutor. On the same scale as before, where are you now and why?

We hope you feel clear and positive about the next steps that you can take to develop effective practice and that this is the beginning or continuation of the increasingly positive impact you will have on your students and the institution you work within.

Learning checklist

Tick off each point when you feel confident you understand it.

☐ *I understand that in order for the learning from the book to become embedded, I need to take ownership and set myself small incremental actions which I will take to improve my personal tutoring practice.*

☐ *I appreciate that all students, staff, departments and institutions are different and that any decisions made should be relevant and appropriate for each particular context.*

☐ *I recognise the value of seeing the bigger picture because this will help me to, firstly, recognise why some decisions are made and, secondly, be able to fully understand how I can influence the institution more broadly.*

☐ *I understand that critically analysing the self-assessment systems and adapting them to be even more relevant and useful not only shows that I think critically about my personal tutoring practice but that I am willing to take ownership of my own development and attempt to influence the development of my institution.*

Critical reflections

1. In relation to all of the learning from the book, identify and explain which aspect you feel:

    a. most proud of in terms of your own personal tutoring practice and why;

    b. you would like to develop first and why;

    c. the institution you work within should be most proud of in terms of its own personal tutoring practice and why;

    d. the institution you work within should consider developing first and why.

2. In relation to 'bigger picture' decisions that affect students, staff and the institution more broadly, explain what you feel the three key critical success factors are which will ensure that a new idea, policy or procedure has the greatest chance of being effective.

3. To what extent do you think that, in order for an institution to become most effective, it is all about developing the culture and people?

4. If you skim read this book to identify the key messages from all of the chapters, what would you identify as the top five recommendations in order to make your personal tutoring practice most effective?

Personal tutor self-assessment system

See following table.

PERSONAL TUTOR SELF-ASSESSMENT SYSTEM : Chapter 9 What next?

	Minimum standard\n1 star	Beginner level\n2 stars	Intermediate level\n3 stars	Advanced level\n4 stars	Expert level\n5 stars
Individual	I feel a strong sense of ownership of my professional development and ultimately view it as my responsibility.	I reflect and think holistically about all aspects of my personal tutoring practice.\n\nMy ultimate goal is to achieve expert level in all chapter themes.	I use the individual self-assessment system regularly and, for all of the aspects where I am not yet at expert level, I have SMART targets to guide my development.	I am making progress against the individual self-assessment chapter themes.\n\nI critically analyse the individual self-assessment system and have adapted it to make it better and, where appropriate, more applicable to my context.	I have achieved expert level for all of the chapter themes within the individual self-assessment system.\n\nI am now investigating ways in which I can develop my personal tutoring practice, and that of my colleagues, further.
Institutional	Generally, the personal tutors in my institution feel consulted and supported with regard to their professional development. One of our aims is to help staff take ownership of their professional development.	The majority of our personal tutors are making progress against the individual self-assessment criteria.\n\nOur ultimate goal is to achieve expert level in all chapter themes.	My institution uses the institutional self-assessment system regularly, and for all of the aspects where we are not yet at expert level we have SMART targets to guide our development.	My institution is making progress against the institutional self-assessment chapter themes.\n\nMy institution critically analyses the institutional self-assessment system and has adapted it to make it better and, where appropriate, more applicable to its context.	My institution has achieved expert level for all of the chapter themes within the institutional self-assessment system.\n\nWe are now investigating ways in which we can sustain this level, as well as continue to develop our staff, systems and processes further.

The self-assessment system is available as a free download from the publisher's website and the authors' websites (all listed at the start of the book).

References

BLR (nd) *Reinforcing Your Employee Training – Are You Sure Your Training Program is Effective?* [online] Available at: www.blr.com/trainingtips/training-program-reinforcement (accessed 30 June 2018).

British Educational Research Association (BERA) (2018) *Ethical Guidelines for Educational Research* (2nd ed). London: BERA. [online] Available at: www.bera.ac.uk/researchers-resources/publications/ethicalguidelines-for-educational-research-2018 (accessed 30 June 2018).

Department for Education (2018) *Securing Student Success: Risk-Based Regulation for Teaching Excellence, Social Mobility and Informed Choice in Higher Education – Government Consultation Response.* London: Department for Education. [online] Available at: https://assets.publishing.service.gov.uk/government/uploads/system/uploads/attachment_data/file/683616/Regulatory_Framework_DfE_government_response.pdf (accessed 30 June 2018).

Morgan, M (2012) *Improving the Student Experience: The Practical Guide for Universities and Colleges.* London: Routledge.

Thomas, L (2012) *Building Student Engagement and Belonging in Higher Education at a Time of Change: Final Report from the What Works? Student Retention and Success Programme.* London: Paul Hamlyn Foundation.

Thomas, L, Hill, M, O'Mahony, J and Yorke, M (2017) *Supporting Student Success: Strategies for Institutional Change. What Works? Student Retention and Success Programme.* Final Report. London: Paul Hamlyn Foundation.

Index

Note: Page numbers in **bold** and *italics* denote tables and figures, respectively